Presentation
SECRETS

Presentation
SECRETS

DO WHAT YOU NEVER THOUGHT POSSIBLE WITH YOUR PRESENTATIONS

Alexei Kapterev

WILEY

John Wiley & Sons, Inc.

ACQUISITIONS EDITOR: Mary James
SENIOR PROJECT EDITOR: Kevin Kent
TECHNICAL EDITOR: Mike Stevens
SENIOR PRODUCTION EDITOR: Debra Banninger
COPY EDITOR: Kezia Endsley
EDITORIAL MANAGER: Mary Beth Wakefield
FREELANCER EDITORIAL MANAGER: Rosemarie Graham
ASSOCIATE DIRECTOR OF MARKETING: David Mayhew
MARKETING MANAGER: Ashley Zurcher
BUSINESS MANAGER: Amy Knies
PRODUCTION MANAGER: Tim Tate
VICE PRESIDENT AND EXECUTIVE GROUP PUBLISHER: Richard Swadley
VICE PRESIDENT AND EXECUTIVE PUBLISHER: Neil Edde
ASSOCIATE PUBLISHER: Jim Minatel
PROJECT COORDINATOR, COVER: Katie Crocker
COMPOSITOR: Craig Woods, Happenstance Type-O-Rama
PROOFREADER: James Saturino, Word One
INDEXER: Robert Swanson
COVER IMAGE: © Chad Baker / Lifesize / Getty Images
COVER DESIGNER: Ryan Sneed

Presentation Secrets: Do What You Never Thought Possible with Your Presentations

Published by
John Wiley & Sons, Inc.
10475 Crosspoint Boulevard
Indianapolis, IN 46256
www.wiley.com

Copyright © 2011 by Alexei Kapterev

Published by John Wiley & Sons, Inc., Indianapolis, Indiana

Published simultaneously in Canada

ISBN: 978-1-118-03496-5

ISBN: 978-1-118-17045-8 (ebk)

ISBN: 978-1-118-17047-2 (ebk)

ISBN: 978-1-118-17046-5 (ebk)

Manufactured in the United States of America

10 9 8 7 6 5 4 3 2 1

For general information on our other products and services please contact our Customer Care Department within the United States at (877) 762-2974, outside the United States at (317) 572-3993 or fax (317) 572-4002.

Wiley also publishes its books in a variety of electronic formats and by print-on-demand. Not all content that is available in standard print versions of this book may appear or be packaged in all book formats. If you have purchased a version of this book that did not include media that is referenced by or accompanies a standard print version, you may request this media by visiting http://booksupport.wiley.com. For more information about Wiley products, visit us at www.wiley.com.

Library of Congress Control Number: 2011934628

To my mom and dad

About the Author

Alexei Kapterev is one of the world's leading experts on presentations. Having had many years of experience with international and Russian consulting firms, he decided to focus exclusively on presentations in 2007. That same year he published a presentation titled "Death by Powerpoint," which saw more than one million views, all with no advertising or promotion. Kapterev currently has a private consulting practice in Moscow. As permanent lecturer, he teaches at the Graduate School of Business Administration (Moscow State University) and as guest lecturer at the Moscow School of Management Skolkovo. He is also working in cooperation with Mercator, Russia's premier studio producing corporate presentations, films, and business graphics. One of his presentation scripts was awarded the finalist award at the New York Festivals competition.

About the Technical Editor

Mike Stevens, as creative director for several Silicon Valley advertising agencies, has won numerous awards over the years for creative excellence in communication and has honed his own presenting skills in highly competitive situations as an agency owner. He is also a talented writer and editor, whose credits include the high-tech thriller *Fortuna* (as author) and Nancy Duarte's highly acclaimed book on presentations *Resonate* (as editor).

Stevens is a Phi Beta Kappa graduate of the University of California at Berkeley with a B. A. in English and is fluent in several European languages.

Acknowledgments

I would like to thank:

Garr Reynolds and Hugh MacLeod for inspiration;

Andrey Skvortsov for many invaluable experiences;

Nancy Duarte for great advice during the early stages of the process;

Mary James (Acquisitions Editor at Wiley) for convincing me to write this book;

Kevin Kent (Senior Project Manager at Wiley) for his tactfulness and patience;

All the viewers of "Death by Powerpoint" at SlideShare.net and elsewhere for support and encouragement.

—Alexei Kapterev

Contents at a Glance

Read This First   **xiii**

Chapter 1 ▶ What Is Presentation?   **1**

PART I ▶ **STORY**   **23**

Chapter 2 ▶ The Story's Focus   **25**

Chapter 3 ▶ The Story's Contrast   **51**

Chapter 4 ▶ The Story's Unity   **75**

PART II ▶ **SLIDES**   **103**

Chapter 5 ▶ The Slides' Focus   **105**

Chapter 6 ▶ The Slides' Contrast   **133**

Chapter 7 ▶ The Slides' Unity   **163**

PART III ▶ **DELIVERY**   **197**

Chapter 8 ▶ Focus in Delivery   **199**

Chapter 9 ▶ Contrast in Delivery   **221**

Chapter 10 ▶ Unity in Delivery   **243**

Chapter 11 ▶ Where to Go Next   **265**

Index ▶ **279**

Contents

Read This First   xiii

Chapter 1 ▶ **What Is Presentation?** 1

    What Are Presentations?   2

    Story   4

    Slides   7

    Delivery   13

    The Three Principles of Presenting   14

    Summary   22

PART I ▶ **STORY**   23

Chapter 2 ▶ **The Story's Focus** 25

    Not All Stories Are Created Equal   26

    Focusing on One Idea   26

    Setting the Goal   27

    The Customer Isn't Always Right   35

    Gathering the Material   39

    Inventing the Truth   47

    Can You Sell Without Lying?   47

    Summary   48

Chapter 3 ▶ **The Story's Contrast** 51

    Problems and Solutions   52

    Hero and Villain   63

    Summary   73

Chapter 4 ▶ The Story's Unity **75**

Making Your Story Unified 76

Case Study: The Story of Tomato Sauce 80

The Problem of Balance 82

Case Study: A Company Introduction 99

Summary 101

PART II ▶ SLIDES **103**

Chapter 5 ▶ The Slides' Focus **105**

Producing Your Slides 106

Zen and Vajrayana 107

Designing Zen Slides 113

Summary 131

Chapter 6 ▶ The Slides' Contrast **133**

Energizing Lifeless Diagrams 134

Using Comparisons 136

Data Visualization 144

Lies, Damned Lies, and Statistics 155

A Word on Animation 159

Where to Go Next?—Visualization Resources 161

Summary 162

Chapter 7 ▶ The Slides' Unity **163**

Avoiding Ugly Slides 164

Slide Design for Non-Designers 165

Working with Pictures 188

United World in a Slide Deck 191

Summary 195

PART III ▶ DELIVERY **197**

Chapter 8 ▶ Focus in Delivery **199**

What Should You Focus on During Delivery? 200

Clarity 202

Pace	205
Voice	207
Engaging with Your Audience	208
Making Eye Contact	212
Addressing Any Questions	218
Using Humor (or Not?)	218
Summary	220
Chapter 9 ▶ Contrast in Delivery	**221**
The Opposite of Monotony	222
Being Perfect Versus Being Passionate	223
Don't Avoid Confrontation	226
Learning from Other People	232
Summary	241
Chapter 10 ▶ Unity in Delivery	**243**
Going with the Flow	244
The Pros and Cons of Improvisation	247
Relaxing Control	251
Summary	263
Chapter 11 ▶ Where to Go Next	**265**
Presentation Checklist	266
Taking Further Steps	269
General Presentation Resources	269
Storytelling Resources	270
Slide Resources	273
Delivery Resources	275
Presentations Transform	277
Index	279

Read This First

I have been specializing in presentations for the last 5 years, but before I was approached by Wiley, I had no ambition to write a book. It never felt like the right time, never felt like I had enough to say on the subject of presentations to justify the whole book. But when I made a decision to write, a magical thing happened. All the questions that I was postponing answering for years started coming back to me. The questions that I wasn't obliged to answer before now returned all at the same time: nagging me, bothering me, demanding to be answered. It wasn't a totally pleasant experience; after all, there were good reasons why I wasn't answering those questions before. Those questions were tough:

- ▶ How do I make a script that is dramatic but not pretentious?
- ▶ How do I make slides that are simple yet project credibility?
- ▶ How do I become spontaneous and react to the audience during a live presentation despite hours of planning and painstaking rehearsals?

And, of course, there were many, many more. I spent months answering those questions, and I am proud to have answered many of them. In terms of progress in my chosen profession this book is the absolute best thing that ever happened to me. My only hope now is that *Presentation Secrets* will be as useful for you as it was for me.

WHO THIS BOOK IS FOR

This book is intended for those of you who disagree that contemporary slide presentations are the necessary evil. For those who believe that preparing and delivering presentations is something one might actually enjoy. For people who want more from their presentations: more fun, more adventure, more challenge, and more results. For people ready to explore, ready to stop being just "presenters" and become scriptwriters, graphic designers, and improv artists—at least so some extent.

It doesn't matter whether you present in business, educational, political, or scientific contexts. Nuances do exist, of course, and I address them in the book. However, for the most part I write under assumption that your audience is simply human. Humans have common psychological and physiological traits that don't depend much on their chosen field. We all like stories, our capacities for processing raw facts are limited, and we mostly trust people who look authentic. These needs aren't easy to meet, but armed with advice from this book, if you at least attempt to meet these needs, you might well succeed.

Beginners will find the "Focus" chapters (Chapters 2, 5, and 8) to be most useful. Those chapters provide the foundation for all the work that you will be doing, whether you are working with your structure and slides or delivering your presentation live. The "Contrast" chapters (Chapters 3, 6, and 9) offer more advanced tips, and the "Unity" chapters (Chapters 4, 7, and 10) also invite into the discussion those of you who are experienced in the art of presentations.

WHAT THIS BOOK COVERS

This book covers three major topics concerned with presentations: structure, slides, and delivery.

In the first part (Part I) you will learn the basics of storytelling, how the narrative part of your presentation should be constructed. I will walk you through the process of establishing your story's goal and finding the best hero your audience can associate with. You will establish the controlling conflict by trying to answer the question, "Who is fighting whom for what?" You will also create a sequence to lead the audience from established status quo through the conflict to the resolution and new balance.

Part II has to do with slides, which serve four major goals: to remind, to impress, to explain, and to prove. By answering the question "What's the purpose of this slide?" you will learn to choose the proper slide type and the proper visual concept. I will briefly mention various ways of visualizing data and common pitfalls to avoid. The last chapter of Part II is dedicated to aesthetic design, which I believe is becoming increasingly important as the new language of communication.

In the last part of the book (Part III) you will learn about the most important things to focus on during a live presentation. I will also touch on more strategic, time-consuming but ultimately rewarding ways of improving your public speaking skills. Finally, I will share my thoughts on the subject of speaker's authenticity, perhaps the hottest topic in today's presentation discourse.

Overall, this book is organized as a 3×3 matrix, one axis being "Structure, Slides, and Delivery" and the other "Focus, Contrast, and Unity." The latter are the core principles that I follow in my own approach; you will find the detailed descriptions for them in Chapter 1.

WHAT YOU NEED TO USE THIS BOOK

You need at least some experience with preparing and delivering presentations. Even a couple of attempts to get your point across with slides will be enough. If you have never delivered any presentation in your life, you will have a hard time understanding what all the fuss is about.

Also, I don't offer much technical advice about Microsoft PowerPoint or any other application in this book. I assume that you are already familiar enough with some slide editing software. If need to improve your skills here, I suggest you read other titles from John Wiley & Sons. (*PowerPoint 2010 For Dummies*, for example, is an excellent book.) However, this information is important only for Part II of the book, which deals with slides. Other parts of the book that deal with structure or delivery are much more technologically independent.

FEATURES AND ICONS USED IN THIS BOOK

The following features and icons are used in this book to help draw your attention to some of the most important or useful information in the book, some of the most valuable tips, insights, and advice that can help you unlock the secrets of presentation.

▶ Watch for margin notes like this one that highlight some key piece of information or that discuss some poorly documented or hard to find technique or approach.

SIDEBARS

Sidebars like this one feature additional information about topics related to the nearby text.

TIP The Tip icon indicates a helpful trick or technique.

NOTE The Note icon points out or expands on items of importance or interest.

CROSSREF The Cross-Reference icon points to chapters where additional information can be found.

WARNING The Warning icon warns you about possible negative side effects or precautions you should take before making a change.

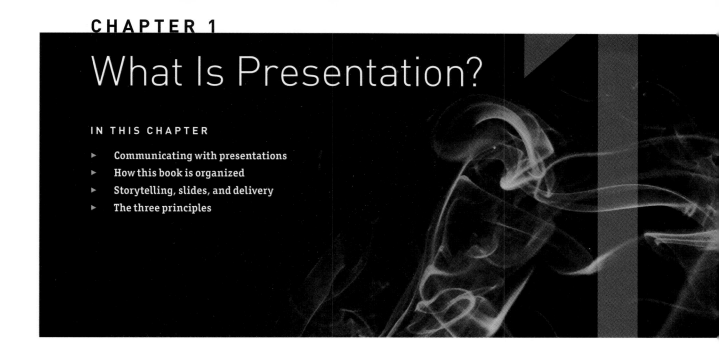

CHAPTER 1

What Is Presentation?

IN THIS CHAPTER

▶ Communicating with presentations
▶ How this book is organized
▶ Storytelling, slides, and delivery
▶ The three principles

In late 2003, I was working for a consulting company as an analyst.

The firm specialized in policy advising. Our clients were Russian ministries, senators, regulators, and formerly state-run, now privatized, companies. My job was to write reports to support decision-making processes. I had almost no contact with the clients, and frankly, I didn't suffer much because of that. I was quite happy just writing. But then came "the day." One of the firm's partners (to whom I am now very grateful) decided that it was time for me to see the big world. I had to present one of my recent reports before the firm's client.

> **NOTE** I tried to transform my report into a presentation in a PowerPoint deck. It was a bullet-point, teleprompter-style nightmare, which is becoming rare nowadays. I remember my boss telling me to use more pictures. In 2004, "pictures" came mostly from a clip-art gallery, which came by default with Microsoft Office. Also, I had zero design skills and my taste wasn't exactly ideal. So, yes, there were a few pictures, but frankly, it would have been much better without them.

I spoke for about 30 minutes and it all went very well, or at least I thought so. Unfortunately, it turned out that the client didn't quite share my view. He didn't understand why the report was prepared, what the findings were, and why we wasted so much time and money. My bosses had to improvise another presentation on the spot, one which, happily, did the job. The client calmed down but asked that they never delegate any presentations to me again. I was so frustrated that I promised myself to master the skill in the next few months.

This is how it all started. Two years later, the client (albeit a different one) asked for me to present whenever possible. Four years later, I'd read Jim Collins's book *Good to Great* and decided to do for a living what I found I could do best—give presentations. Next year, I published a presentation called "Death by PowerPoint," which to my utter surprise went viral, having been viewed by more that one million people as of now. It was the greatest reassurance that the path that I've chosen is the right one. I'm currently teaching presentations at one of Russia's best business schools, doing corporate workshops, practicing as a consultant, and occasionally working with Mercator, Russia's leading producer of corporate films, business presentations, and infographics.

WHAT ARE PRESENTATIONS?

We live in a world in which nobody knows how to do anything. What I mean is that capitalism is based on the idea of division of labor and the labor is divided as never before. With division of labor as great as ever, we have to connect via words, symbols, and electronic code. We have to connect via phone conversations, written reports, e-mails and instant messaging, blogs, micro-blogs, and via just plain water cooler conversations—and presentations, yes, via presentations. We have to speak publicly more now than ever.

Presentations are an extremely complex and expensive form of human communication. The interaction is relatively short but the combined time of all the people involved costs a lot. The only explanation as to why people continue to give presentations despite their complexity and cost is that they are also sometimes tremendously impactful. Also, sometimes, there's a lot at stake. People give presentations before commencing expensive projects and after finishing them. It makes sense to conduct extensive preparations in these cases, and there's almost no limit on how deep and wide you can go. You can rehearse, you can rearrange your slides, and you can research for new arguments in support of your point. So, whenever I am asked to "help with a presentation," my first question is inevitably, "What is the presentation in this case?" Answers differ vastly.

People frequently think that presentations are about delivery, about acting skills, and about how you say what you have to say. In the end, these aspects are what we see and hear, but are only the tip of the iceberg. People also think that presentations are mostly about slides. This is what I am asked to do a lot: make slides. The word "slides" has become synonymous with the word "presentations" in some organizations. People spend lots of time designing the right slides, making them so they can work with or without the actual presenter.

▶ Moreover, with more presentations being e-mailed rather than presented, this part is quickly becoming less important.

Apart from slides, there's another part that has to do with structure and argumentation, which is whole different domain. It has to do with what you say rather than how you say it. This part requires storytelling, script- and speechwriting skills, and a deep knowledge of the content. Can any single person possibly become an expert in all these fields? Can you become a present-day Renaissance person: a scriptwriter, a graphics designer, and a master of verbal and nonverbal delivery?

The short answer is "yes," but let me make a confession first. My education is in finance. As you are probably aware, finance is one of the most tedious professions on Earth. It's really not far from accounting. I spent three years working as a financial controller for Citibank. At some point, I even considered a career in one of the "Big Four" auditing firms. Before my involvement with presentations, I never seriously thought of myself as a "creative type." I was never good at oral communications; my only serious strength was writing. I wasn't even a good storyteller, as my reports didn't require any storytelling skills (or so I thought at the time). As I mentioned, I never studied graphics design in any systematic manner. I wasn't a good actor. So, yes, it is possible to become good at something as complex as presentations. It is possible even without any existing skills and without dedicating your whole life to it. After all, I didn't quit my job to learn how to give presentations. The first thing you need is motivation. I studied because of my initial failure; you might study because of your initial success. The second thing you need is a plan. The purpose of this book is to give you the plan.

Three more points about this book:

1. Figure 1-1 is a slide from my presentations training workshop. It's what I show people when I want to explain what presentations are. Coincidently, this is also how this book is organized. It is split into three major parts. Part I is about story structure, Part II is about slides, and Part III is about delivery. Also, I have three broad principles that I use in my work. In each part there are three chapters and each chapter will follow one broad topic, thus producing a nice three-by-three matrix. In this chapter, I give you a brief introduction to the three parts and three principles.

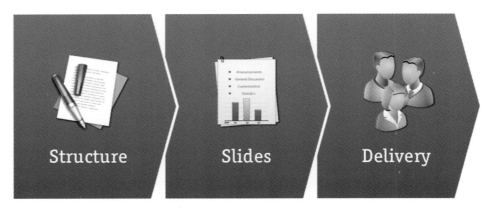

FIGURE 1-1: How this book is organized.

2. This book comes with illustrations, and I designed almost all of them by myself with no external help. I briefly considered hiring a professional graphics designer but realized that it would not be fair. If I say that everybody can learn to design slides by applying some principles and practicing, I should at least be able to do it myself. So I did. I am not a professional designer but at least they are authentic (which I believe is exceptionally important).

3. This book mostly relies on my five years of deliberate practice in the art of presentations. This is not a scientific book. I love science, and I care a great deal about empirical evidence. Unfortunately, however, some of the topics I discuss here are grossly under-researched. Sometimes, I have no other choice but to jump to conclusions, which just seem logical to me and are based on nothing but experience.

So, that's it for the introduction. Shall we get started?

STORY

Everyone who studies public speaking sooner or later gets to Aristotle's *Rhetoric*. It is hardly a joyful read, so I'll just give you one concept from it. Aristotle says that there are three modes of persuasion: *logos*, *pathos,* and *ethos*. Logos is an appeal to the rational, pathos is an appeal to the emotional, and ethos is an appeal to the personality, which are the qualities of the speaker. That was in the 4th century B.C. Unfortunately, in the centuries that followed, scholars of rhetoric perfected logos and ethos and rejected pathos. You can see their attempts to appeal to pathos in the *New Oxford American Dictionary,* which gives the second definition for the word "rhetoric" as "language designed to have a persuasive or impressive effect on its audience, but often regarded as lacking in sincerity or meaningful content." Well, pathetic.

I think I know precisely what led to this. It seems that scholars of rhetoric deal with pathos because they think they have to, not because they truly want to. Public speakers always put themselves in opposition to poets. In their eyes they were decision makers and the seekers of truth, while poets were lowly entertainers. But canons of public speaking always included entertainment. Hence, the classical Roman *docere, movere, delectare* (educate, motivate, entertain), but only because the public demanded entertainment. Speakers would love to just inform and motivate, but, unfortunately, this isn't an option. So, they struggle with it, poor chaps. Even today I meet speakers (mostly scientists) who believe that an appeal to reason is inherently ethical and persuasive, whereas an appeal to emotions is deceptive and unworthy of a real educator. They are doing it only because they can't avoid it.

By contrast, poets—and I use this word in its broad Greek sense meaning also artists, dramatists, and writers—always loved entertaining. This was their job. Aristotle himself admits, "It was naturally the poets who first set the movement going." It seems that in the past couple of centuries, our civilization has made truly dramatic progress in storytelling. We started to tell more and better stories. Better yet, we learned how stories should be constructed.

I won't be covering logos much in this book. This isn't because I hate logos (I love it); it's because this field is pretty much covered already. For those of you interested in pure logos, I recommend an excellent book called *The Minto Pyramid Principle: Logic in Writing, Thinking, & Problem Solving* by Barbara Minto. Problems with logos are well known. Such presentations look very reasonable and even persuasive but aren't very motivating. People nod their heads and then mind their own business. Nelson Mandela said, "Don't address their brains. Address their hearts." However beautiful this phrase is, I don't fully agree with it. I don't think we should avoid addressing the brains. As scientists, businesspeople, and activists, we have to deal with facts and logic. Storytellers love to contrast stories with statistics by saying that stories are a much more persuasive and effective means of communication, but really, there's no clear evidence for that. They are more entertaining—that's obvious—but that does not necessarily make them more effective from a practical standpoint. But secondly and most importantly, there isn't much difference between storytelling and fact telling anyway. Storytelling is and always was the essence of business presentations. Storytelling is nothing but putting facts in a sequence and making connections.

Funny as it may sound, storytelling should not be confused with telling stories. Telling an anecdote is just an attempt to illustrate your concept, to provide an example or counterexample, to make your audience more engaged. This might be a useful tool but that's not what Part I of this book is about. I don't just suggest you use stories within your presentation, I suggest you adopt the story structure for the whole presentation.

NOTE There's an ongoing dispute about the relative persuasiveness of stories versus causal evidence and statistics, with no clear winner. Some empirical studies have concluded that stories indeed elicit significantly fewer objections than statistical evidence, supposedly by going around the conscious mind (Slater, 1990; Slater & Rouner, 1996, 1997). Some studies have concluded that anecdotal evidence is more persuasive than statistics, and other studies have concluded otherwise. Meta-analysis by Allen and Preiss in 1997 found a small but statistically significant advantage of statistics over storytelling. But again, these people are using statistics to prove that statistics are more persuasive. I think it is safe to say that the jury is still out on this one.

▶ Stories aren't just facts; stories are facts with souls.

Yes, storytelling is a popular, even hip, subject. We are a storytelling species, and as far as I'm aware, there's nobody else in this game on this planet. Stories as a form of communication existed well before writing and they were optimized for oral transmission of facts. Stories engage emotions to make facts more memorable. Your long-term memory and your emotions come from the same part of the brain: the limbic system of our paleomammalian brain. Stimulating emotions improves recall of facts; this is a well-established scientific fact.

Stories don't have to be in opposition to logic, either. You can't have a story without logic. The plot has to develop according to certain rules; you can't just introduce random stuff whenever you please. Stories are the logic of life. Stories are meant to explain events; they form the chain of cause and effect. Of course, this explanation might be just an illusion, but you cannot have an explanation without a sequence, right? Any sequence of events is a proto-story. You just need to structure it properly and add some spice. So, I don't think you need to contrast storytelling with statistics or causal explanations. You need to contrast structured fact-telling with unstructured fact-telling.

▶ Stories unite multiple disjointed facts and concepts into one solid experience.

In any case, most presentations consist of facts or logical arguments put into a sequence. The problem is that this sequence often makes no sense. It is dull. It is difficult to follow. It gives no answer to the question "So what?" We are forced to follow the train of thought without understanding where it is leading us and why. Presenters tend to put a lot of dots on the board without really connecting them. It's no surprise that with structure like this, they have trouble following their own train of thought. They forget what to say next. How can you forget what to say next in a story? Stories are convenient to tell, pleasant to listen to, and easy to remember.

It is true that a purely factual story is usually not as entertaining as a made-up one. The good news is that a factual story is much easier to create. You don't need to make up facts. The facts are already there. All you need to do is select the right facts and put them in a sequence. If this seems like cherry-picking to you, you are right. You have to engage in cherry-picking. Your time is always limited, and you have to speak about some topics and leave some others out. But storytelling isn't about leaving inconvenient facts out of the story. Rather, it's about integrating them. Inconvenient facts have a surprising effect, and surprise is one of the cornerstone elements of a well-crafted narrative. So, no, storytelling isn't about picking "the right" facts; it's about making what seem like the "wrong" facts work together. It's about making meaning out of chaos. And this is what Part I of this book is about.

SLIDES

In 1979, Hewlett-Packard introduced the first program for editing presentation slides. It was called BRUNO. It didn't become a big hit (or, in fact, any hit at all) and was soon discontinued. However, the idea of a visual slide editor endured. The demand was great, but software limitations at the time were severe. Only eight years later, when a small startup called Forethought, Inc., produced a piece of software called PowerPoint 1.0, did presentation software become a major hit. Microsoft bought the company, and PowerPoint soon became part of its Office suite. Ten years later, PowerPoint was everywhere. It became ubiquitous in boardrooms, conference rooms, classrooms, ballrooms, and even churches. As with any early mass-production attempt, the quality was quite poor, and the environment suffered. In 2001, Angela Garber, a journalist writing for *Small Business Computing*, coined the phrase "Death by PowerPoint." The world had enough. "Why can't you turn off the projector and just speak like a person?" people would ask, and every other book on delivery skills was trying to address this problem.

Let me make a confession: Despite all the bad rep, I love slides. I think they are fantastic. I have loved them all my life, even when I didn't know they existed. In school my favorite class was biology, where we had a gigantic tree of species painted all over the wall. I loved visual aids, and I loved filmstrips. Tinkering with slides is what I do to procrastinate. I don't agree with the notion "you are the star, not the slides." I like showing the slides to the audience. I love that look on people's faces when they see a great slide. It took me a while to figure out how to make them properly and I am proud to share with you some of my insights.

To me, there are two reasons you should leave your projector on:

▶ For one thing, we might simply forget what to say next, which might be because we didn't bother to make our structure memorable enough to begin with, but never mind that for now. PowerPoint might have created many problems, but it solved at least one: The fear of forgetting what to say is gone. In Ancient Greece or Rome, speakers didn't use notes (mostly because there was no paper) and *memoria*, the art of memorizing, was one of the five core skills that speakers needed. Thanks to PowerPoint, we no longer need to memorize anything, and we can speak without notes. I don't know about you but I hate memorizing things. I think this change has fundamentally revolutionized public speaking.

The downside, of course, is that slides became notes. We started using the slide projector as a teleprompter (and when I say "we," I am proudly including myself). Figure 1-2 shows one of the first presentations I ever prepared (in 2004). This was a 20 minute–long talk, with nine slides and just two diagrams. Then, I discovered *Presentation Zen: Simple Ideas on Presentation Design and Delivery* by Garr Reynolds and *Beyond Bullet Points: Using Microsoft Office PowerPoint 2007 to Create Presentations That Inform, Motivate, and Inspire* by Cliff Atkinson. They explained to me what the slides are for; slides are visual aids, not prompters. This changed everything for me. Figure 1-3 is an excerpt from my presentation circa 2006. As you see, there's much less text and many more pictures. The design is still horrible, though.

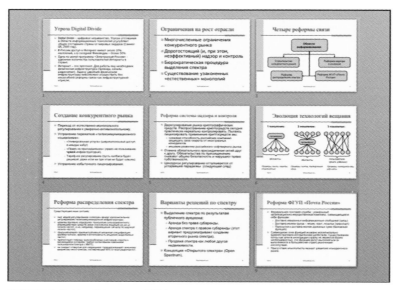

FIGURE 1-2: My slides from 2004.

▶ The second reason to leave our projectors on is a widely known phenomenon called the *pictorial superiority effect*. Simply put, it means that under most circumstances, people are much better at reading and remembering pictures than words.

NOTE   In one widely cited study by Weiss and McGrath (1992), people were able to recall in 72 hours just 10 percent of what they heard but 20 percent of what they saw—twice as much. What's even more stunning, they were able to recall 65 percent of the information when it was presented in both visual and auditory form. So, by turning off your projector, you are doing your audience a great disservice. Don't do it; just make sure your slides are worth viewing.

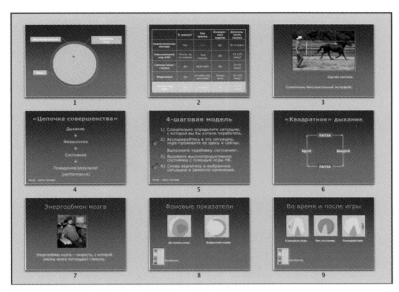

FIGURE 1-3: My slides from 2006—getting better.

Our capacity for processing concrete images is much greater than our capacity for processing abstract knowledge. Danish science writer Tor Norretranders, in his book *The User Illusion: Cutting Consciousness Down to Size,* quotes neurophysiological research measuring the bandwidth of various human senses. The results are summarized in Figure 1-4. Notice that the second diagram is in kilobits per second, which is 1,024 times faster than bits per second" shown in the first diagram. Not only is our processing mostly unconscious, but the unconscious bandwidth for vision is 100 times more powerful than for hearing.

There's an old English saying, "A picture is worth a thousand words" and a corresponding Russian saying, "It's better to see once than to hear a hundred times." Visual aids take advantage of all this bandwidth, but, of course, only if you use pictures rather than text. If you use text projected on a screen, because processing of text is mostly conscious, you are still engaging the conscious mind; the advantage here is much less dramatic.

So leave the projector on. It helps. Still, despite the progress with slides made over the past 10 years, there are many more unanswered questions. Most of them have to do with illustration and design. Slides aren't like anything we've ever encountered before. They are not reports; they are much more condensed, focused, and concise. They are not spreadsheets; they aren't made for analysis. The reader should be able to grasp the meaning of the slide in several seconds. They are not like printed materials; they are not made for careful reading. They should grab your attention and quickly influence you. They should inform, explain, or persuade.

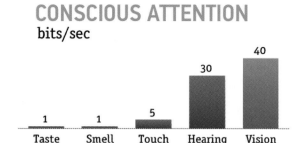

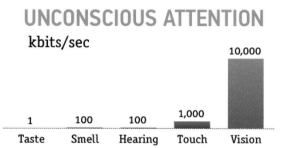

FIGURE 1-4: Conscious and unconscious bandwidth.

In order to design slides, you have to use information architecture. You have to understand how to visualize and illustrate and know how to make it all look aesthetically pleasing. This requires a lot of investment of time and effort on your part. Is it worth it? The answer largely depends on the nature of your job, that is, how much do you need to communicate and how important it is. Overall I think yes, it is well worth it. Let me give you three reasons to invest your time in design—or rather, three rebuttals to the excuses I always hear for not investing.

1. **"It's all very subjective."** I hear this a lot. No, it isn't. Of course, it isn't a precise science, but it's not wild stabs in the dark, either. There are certain rules and principles one can follow, and there are well-established tools one can use that almost guarantee better results. Companies that invest in design do dramatically better than companies that don't. Why would it be different for individuals?

   In 2004, the British Design Council, one of the world's oldest design associations with 60 years of history, released the Design Index Report. The report analyzed the impact of investments in design on the company's stock performance. The authors separated what they call "design-led" companies like Easyjet or Reuters, known for their massive investments in design, from the rest of the market. It was no surprise that those companies produced much better performance for their investors and, I'm quoting from the report, "not just for a few weeks or months but consistently over a solid decade." The difference between the Design Index and the British Index FTSE 100, which includes the country's 100 largest companies, was a full 200 percent. In the last 10 years, the price of Microsoft's stock went down by 27 percent while the stock of Apple rose by 2,880 percent. Okay, Apple did start quite low and not all of it can be attributed to design, but almost 3,000 percent difference? Isn't design *the* secret to success?

2. **"Yeah, but I'm not a designer. Let the designer do this job."** This is known as "the division of labor argument." Although I do agree that specialization is key in any field, the problem is that design is not just "any field." Over the past 20 years, design has emerged as an interdisciplinary language. We now communicate in design. In the 10th century you had to be able to talk and to follow established civility protocols to function successfully as a member of society. People who were able to write had an advantage. By the 20th century you had to be able to write; that was the standard requirement. At this point, in developed nations, there are very few jobs you can get if you cannot write, and those you can get aren't particularly safe or well paid. Everybody knows how to write, so it is no longer a competitive advantage. My point is that design is the new writing, much like writing was the new talking once.

The problem with leaving design to the designers is that they mostly don't care about your content. All they can do is make it pretty, but not more meaningful. And being meaningful is what communication is all about. Of course, there are good designers who actually study the subject before designing anything, but they are really expensive. For most of your presentations, you won't be having access to those kinds of designers. The argument for why you are the best designer for your slides is summarized in Figure 1-5.

▶ If you want your ideas to have that competitive advantage, if you really want to sell your ideas to your audience, you have to learn something about design and apply it to improving your slides.

A designer, who...

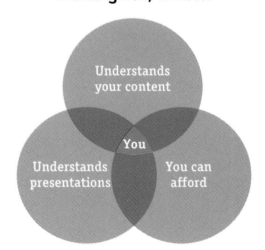

FIGURE 1-5: An ideal presentation designer is you.

It certainly makes sense to hire a professional designer or even a specialized presentation design firm if you need a sales deck that every salesperson will be using or if you are about to go for an IPO. But for most of your routine, everyday presentations, you will be the one doing it. Also, what if you have to change something in your presentation prepared by the pros? You're stuck if you don't know how. In *An Inconvenient Truth*, a documentary following Al Gore's presentation about climate change, we can see Gore himself tinkering with his slides. Even Al Gore does it.

3. **"Who cares, these are just slides."** Every salesman knows that polished shoes help selling. You may not work in a business where people wear formal shoes, but I think you still get what I mean. So, salespeople polish their shoes. As far as I'm concerned, slides are much more important than shoes. Why don't they get the same polish? "But I'm not a salesperson." Yes, you are! We are all in the business of selling. We sell ideas to our bosses, to our colleagues, to our employees, to our students, and to our peers. Of the slides shown in Figure 1-6, which one do you think has a better chance of selling anything?

FIGURE 1-6: Which one sells better?

The left slide is from a random presentation I pulled off the U.S. Department of Education's website. Sad, isn't it? The right slide was "designed" by me in about two minutes. I didn't change the content and even tried to preserve the original colors. I replaced the font with a somewhat more readable one and removed the busy background. Suddenly, it looks much more respectable and more dignified, and is definitely easier to read.

If the presenter doesn't care, people sense that. Some people care about the content but don't care about the look, and I think this is wrong. Beatrice Warde, an American typographer, wrote once, "People who love ideas must have a love of words, and that means, given a chance, they will take a vivid interest in the clothes which words wear."

What she meant by "clothes which words wear" was typography, but I think this quote applies to a much broader field of design, too. If you love your content, you have to care about the form. If you care about your audience, you have to care about your slides. I don't see how you can avoid it. Part II of this book will help.

DELIVERY

Delivery is the final and most challenging part of a presentation. Not the most difficult or the most important—that award goes to storytelling—but the most challenging, the most frightening. I never heard of slide preparation fright or storytelling fright, but stage fright is common. The reason delivery is so frightening is because it's live and it's final. You cannot undo it; once it's done, it's done.

NERVES VERSUS STAGE FRIGHT

I never had stage fright. This isn't to suggest that I was always good onstage, but I don't remember being scared. In my childhood, I was the lead singer in a children's band and coming onstage was a relatively mundane experience for me. I was nervous but never frightened. Later, I came onstage as a dancer, singer, martial arts practitioner, business trainer, business school lecturer, personal development coach, comedian, and actor. I was still getting nervous (but never to the point of being paralyzed), and I think it is pretty much normal to feel this way. Anxiety never quite goes away, and it's always worse when the role or the place is new to me.

If you have serious stage fright, one that really prevents you from speaking, I suggest you seek professional help. Scientific branches of psychotherapy (like cognitive behavioral therapy, CBT) have made some truly dramatic progress over the past 20 years. But if all you have is general anxiety, just live with it. Trust me, nobody will notice.

There are basically two ways to deal with your fear: the first is to prepare and the second is to learn to improvise. And this is what Part III of the book is about—preparation and improvisation in public speaking. I think there are two versions of public speaking, there was 1.0, and now there is 2.0. The first approach was to be very formal and regulated. Books on public speaking 1.0 overwhelm you with advice on all things proper: proper dress, proper speech, proper timing, proper posture, and so on. Public speaking 2.0 is much more relaxed and much more demanding at the same time. You cannot get away with simply following the rules anymore. You have to put in your soul. You cannot just do the prepared talk and leave. You must have a conversation with your audience and react to their feedback, both verbal and nonverbal.

Public speaking 1.0 was built around the idea of control. Controlling time, controlling emotions, and controlling the audience. Public speaking 2.0 (or should I say presenting?) is built around the idea of losing control. Of course, in order to lose control, you first have to have it. You can't lose something you never had in the first place.

Public speaking is a lot like martial arts in this sense, or, in fact, like any activity that requires complex coordination of the mind and body. When a student first comes to a martial arts school, they know how to fight intuitively. If somebody attacks them, they react, sometimes quite effectively. However, when their teacher starts telling them what to do, they soon become disoriented in the sea of new information. After a while, they master formal exercises that may look cool but aren't really very close to an actual fight. The next stage is when you stop doing attacks, blocks, or holds that you know, and focus on the one thing you can focus on (which is your opponent) and just let your body do the rest of the job. It's the same in public speaking. If you want to do well with your public speaking, you have to let your body do the job.

You cannot plan your speech pretty much like you cannot plan your fight. I once read in Brian Tracy's book on public speaking (1.0) called *Speak to Win: How to Present with Power in Any Situation*, "The very best talk of all is when the talk you planned, the talk you gave, and the talk you wish you had given all turn out to be the same." Let me tell you: no, it's not. First of all, it never happens that way. Never, ever. But second, if the talk you planned is exactly the same as the one you gave, it's because you knew beforehand everything your audience knows, which is unlikely to the point of being impossible, or you missed an opportunity to learn something from your audience. If everything goes as planned, if nothing unexpected is happening, you will soon be dying of boredom and so, by the way, will your audience. If the talk you gave is the same as the one you wanted to give—that means you either reached your life's ideal (which, again, is highly unlikely) or you stopped developing. My very best talks of all were the ones where I came prepared and my plan *almost* worked, which means that while following the plan, I encountered new and entirely unexpected problems, solved them creatively on the spot, and came out victorious. This is public speaking 2.0.

I'm not suggesting that Brian Tracy or any other remarkable speaker of the past stopped at the formal stage. But they taught what they'd been asked to teach, which was the formalities. These formalities aren't enough anymore. This is why the last chapter of Part III is devoted entirely to the most difficult and daring topic: stage improvisation.

THE THREE PRINCIPLES OF PRESENTING

This book is built around three principles that I follow in my work. I think having principles is important. Principles are not rules; they are much broader and less intrusive. Although you don't always have to follow these principles, you do need to think twice before going against them. On the downside, they are much less concrete. You have to figure out how to apply them in any given situation. English writer Somerset Maugham said once that there are three rules for writing novels, but unfortunately, nobody knows what they are. It's the same with presentations. I would love to give you three rules for presenting, but I don't know what they are. So I am giving you three principles with lots of examples. You have to figure out the rest yourself. The principles are *thesis*, *antithesis,* and *synthesis*—or, as I call them for the purposes of my work, *focus*, *contrast,* and *unity* (see Figure 1-7).

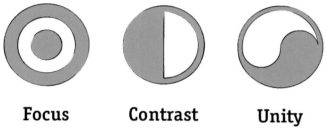

Focus   Contrast   Unity

FIGURE 1-7: The three principles of presenting.

> **NOTE** These principles are fairly universal and not unique to presentations in any way. I did not invent them; I had heard of them well before I started studying presentations, but I only really understood them through my work. They've been around for a couple of centuries after being brought to prominence by the German author Heinrich Moritz Chalybäus in his account of the philosophy of Georg Hegel. It turns out, however, that Hegel used these terms only once and attributed them to Immanuel Kant. The names for the principles were probably suggested by another German philosopher, Fichte. It's a complicated story. My subsequent investigation led me to believe that the ancient Hindus developed these principles 5,000 years ago. In other words, they've been around for quite a while.

The principles are, of course, somewhat arbitrary. There are probably other useful principles out there; these are simply the ones that I can keep in my short-term memory and apply successfully. As I said, I did not invent them. They crystallized after I noticed that I keep repeating mostly the same words during my workshops. As Jim Collins said in *Good to Great*, "it doesn't so much matter what your values are, it really matters that you have them." So, I have them. Let me tell you what they are so you can have them, too.

Focus

The principle of focus states that every story, slide, or performance has the key focal point to attract attention. In any successful communication, this point is defined very early and the rest of the content is organized "around" this point. In a story, this is usually the hero. On a slide, this is usually the focal point, the brightest, the biggest, or the most emotional element (like a human face) of the composition that attracts the eye. In a live performance, this is most likely to be the speaker's persona, the answer to the question, "Who is presenting?"

Why do you need a focus? Simply put, because you cannot say everything you know and the audience can't remember everything you say (see Figure 1-8). The audience has its cognitive limits; that's why you have to prioritize and thus make certain elements of your communication more important and others less important.

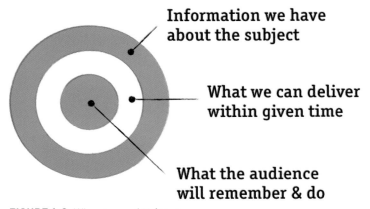

FIGURE 1-8: Why you need to focus.

How limiting are those limits? In 1957, George A. Miller, a Harvard psychologist, published an article that became not only one of the most cited papers in the history of psychological research but the subject of a popular urban legend as well. You've probably heard of it. It was titled "The Magical Number Seven, Plus or Minus Two: Some Limits on our Capacity for Processing Information." It gave birth to one of the older PowerPoint "rules," which is seven bullets per slide and seven words per bullet. When I first heard of it, I found this rule way too strict. No more than seven words per bullet? How on Earth am I supposed to express myself?

NOTE   Miller's original paper is available online at `http://goo.gl/NOTCp`.

It turned out I was right in resisting the "rule," but for entirely the wrong reasons. First of all, the original research obviously had nothing to do with PowerPoint or presentations; it was conducted well before PowerPoint came to existence. Second, Miller was researching a short-term memory limit in terms of "chunks" of information, but nobody really knew at the time what exactly constituted a "chunk." In his original experiments, he presented students with letters, words, or numbers and asked how many they could recall after the presentation. Most of the subjects were able to recall five digits without any mistakes; more than five digits often constituted a problem (see Figure 1-9).

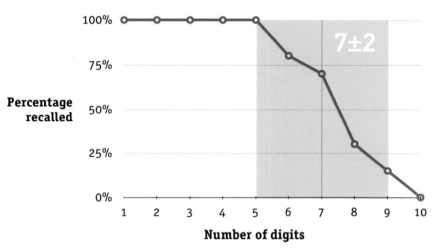

RECALL OF DIGITS

FIGURE 1-9: Miller's digit-recall diagram.

However, it later turned out that digits aren't the same as words or concepts. Subsequent experiments by Murdock (1962) and others came to different figures for the working memory limit: between three and five chunks. Building on this research, Nelson Cowan, professor of psychology of the University of Missouri, suggested that the limit for an average adult is about four chunks, which is where the scientific consensus currently stays. In 2002, Klaus Oberauer proposed an extension to this model by adding even more narrow focus embedded in the four-element focus, which holds just one chunk at a time. What he means is that we can actively pay attention to just one thing at a time. But we can switch our attention to any of the other three things (no more!) that we simultaneously keep in our short-term memory.

NOTE   In late 2010, Apple announced an update to its iOS, its operating system for mobile devices. It was described as having "100+ new features and innovations." However, the landing page for the new iOS did not list all those 100+ features. Instead, it showcased just four of them, presumably the most important for the users: multitasking, folders, AirPrint, and AirPlay. Apple's marketers understood that our attention is limited and that you can't show everything you have.

▶ So this is the focus principle: build your communication around one central message and accompany it with three to four supporting messages.

When I design a storyline for a presentation, I try to have one core message and no more than four major parts. When I design the slide, I always ask myself, "Where is the center of this slide?" I formulate the key message and try to put it in the header in the largest font. Although I am not the biggest fan of bullets, when I have bullets, I try to have three, maximum four, bullets. This also applies to pictures on the same slide. And when I press the Next button on my remote during a presentation, I try to make sure that I expose the audience to no more than one message at a time. If I have a complex diagram, I present it either in small chunks or give the audience time to digest it before I start talking again. You might think that this is the same mindless, robotic application of the 7±2 rule, except now it's the 4±1 rule. Well, I have to say that you might be right except that this one actually works. Can I do 5? 6? 10? Of course, I can. I will think twice, though.

Contrast

▶ The principle of contrast states that ideas are understandable only in contrast with other ideas.

As the old saying goes, "who has never tasted bitter, knows not what is sweet." The problem with most business presentations is that they consist of facts and only facts. The facts don't have any inherent meaning of their own. They only make sense in relation to other facts. You need to compare things. Your audience needs to understand the proportions. They need to see the background. They need to see change. They need to see opposition. If you saw *Jurassic Park,* you might remember that a T-Rex can only see things when they move. In a way, we are all like this: We pay attention only when we see things changing and becoming different.

There was a joke about an English gentleman who was marooned by pirates and who built three huts on his island. One was his home, the second was his club, and the third was the club that he ignored. It's funny because it's true. We need that club that isn't our home. And we need that second club, too. Without the second club, the first club doesn't look all that attractive. This might seem irrational, but this is how things are.

> **NOTE** Dan Ariely, a behavioral economist at MIT, gives the following example in his book *Predictably Irrational: The Hidden Forces That Shape Our Decisions.* Suppose you are looking for a house and your estate agent offers you three houses, one of which is contemporary and two that are colonial in style. They all cost about the same but one of the colonials has a certain disadvantage. According to Ariely (who actually conducted this experiment), in the end, people are much likely to choose the colonial without the disadvantage, even over the contemporary house, because it is easy to compare, and they feel like they understand something about it. They feel like this one won the competition.

Sports in which two teams cooperate aren't particularly popular. There is no TV show or commercial movie without a conflict, a drama, a struggle. Every religion defines things in terms of black and white: saints and sinners, heaven and hell, samsara and nirvana. A conflict grabs people's attention. Conflicts have unpredictable outcomes; they are inherently interesting to follow. But there isn't much conflict in a typical business presentation. That is why the audience falls asleep. Presenters tell only positive aspects of things. They shy away from conflict and controversy. Or they stage a weak conflict where one side is the clear winner right from the beginning. They make things predictable, and predictability is boring. The great physicist Niels Bohr once declared that a great truth is a statement whose opposite is also a great truth. We need to learn to stage fair fights. Of course, there's a risk of not winning, but that's the whole idea (see Figure 1-10).

The same applies to slides. Side-by-side comparisons are always interesting to watch. Charts that show change are the best proof. Diagrams that have "the reds" fighting "the grays" will never be boring. On the aesthetic level, you need contrast, too. You need to separate headers from the rest of the text. You need to separate important data from the supplementary. You need to separate text from the background. There is a fine distinction in design between a good conflict (usually called contrast) and bad conflict (usually called conflict). You'll need to understand this contrast, too.

In delivery, contrast is as important as anywhere else. Most presenters have a certain pace and style. After several minutes, the audience adapts to this style, and the presenter stops being new and, therefore, interesting. Especially with longer presentations, you absolutely need to be different. And that is the contrast principle: remember to provide an antithesis to your thesis. There is a dark side (sometimes literally) in anything, and the audience needs to see it to remain engaged.

Unity

This is the most difficult principle to explain. In a story, there are certain parts that produce a psychologically satisfying experience. If you lead your audience through the right points, they feel like they got something that goes beyond the journey itself, something transcendent, something transformative. The path that great presentations travel looks like the S-curve, which seems to be a universal model of change (see Figure 1-11).

▶ The principle of unity states that once properly aligned, conflicting parts create a whole that is greater than the sum of its parts.

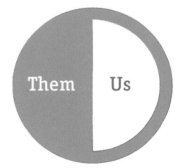

FIGURE 1-10: Contrast.

FIGURE 1-11: The unity S-curve.

We travel through difficulties (contrast) toward a greater goal (focus). This experience is memorable. Once people hear a well-crafted story, they remember it very close to how you told it. They cannot forget the beginning or the end—maybe something in the middle. They can replace the end if they don't like it, but they can't forget it. The story now lives beyond you.

Which of the two shopping lists shown in Figure 1-12 do you think is easier to memorize? When I ask this question at my seminars, about 30 percent of the audience get it, mostly those who cook. Items on the second list make up a recipe (for pancakes). Items on the first list are just random stuff one buys at the supermarket. There's no unifying pattern. Any of the hundreds more items at the supermarket could be there on that list. Conversely, the second list is closed. If you forget one item on the list for pancakes, you can fill in the blank. In essence, there is just one item on this list, not six. This is what unity does; it compresses information without losing anything.

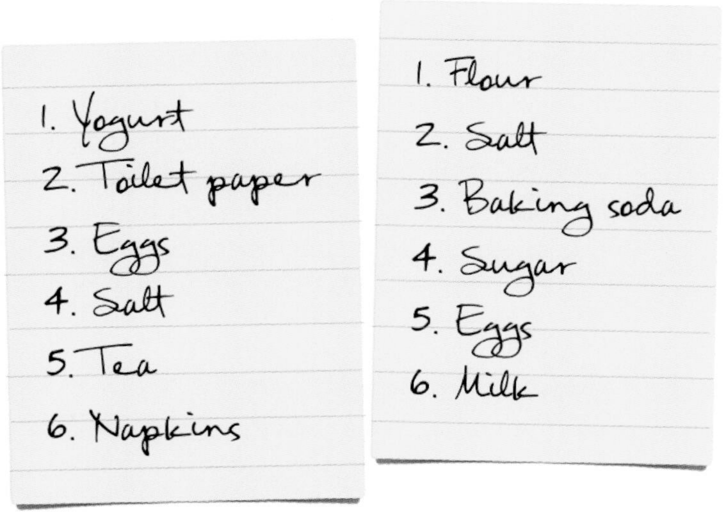

FIGURE 1-12: Which list is more memorable?

It takes a lot of time to produce the second list. All the ingredients are carefully matched. If you mess up just one of the ingredients, the whole deal will be off. Items on the first list are replaceable and nobody would notice if you deleted one of them. What makes the second list work is the connection. This makes things whole, believable, and authentic.

> **NOTE** Take *The Lord of the Rings* by J. R. R. Tolkien as an example. It is authentic not because it's factually true. It's not. It is authentic because of Tolkien's fanatical devotion to details. Tolkien managed to create a united, consistent world with potential for many stories. Tolkien chose to tell just a couple of those stories and many more remained untold. This is why the trilogy produced an unprecedented amount of fan art. Once the rules of the game are balanced, many more people jump on the bandwagon.

It's the same with slides. Elements of your slide should come together to produce a unified whole. If your slide background imitates wood, your bullets should imitate nails. This is consistency. If this is too artsy for you, don't make a wooden background in the first place. It is also not just about adding stuff. It's about deleting stuff, too. Anything that doesn't fit should be mercilessly removed. Extra lines, unnecessary elements, all the scaffolding you used for the purposes of design, need to be cleaned up.

It is also the same with delivery. When you are onstage, there is only one thing that is important. And it's not what you say. It is who you are. You are a character, and this is your role. You have your personal history. You have your story to tell, and you are telling it. Nobody else can tell that story as good as you. When people retell your story later, your character is traveling with it. They are inseparable. Of course, that is if you are an authentic character. You are not an actor; you cannot just become anybody. This isn't about pretending. You must be yourself, but slightly different: prepped for the stage, for the dialogue, and for action.

> ▶ Strange as it may seem, despite all this care and attention to details, excellent presentations are never perfect. The art of leaving imperfections in your work is subtle but deeply touching.

NOTE In terms of presentations, TED is perhaps the best conference in the world. If you haven't seen it, go look at **www.ted.com** and experience it yourself. They put most of their speeches online, and they are very good with almost no exceptions. The time limit there is just 18 minutes, so it won't take you much time to watch a couple of presentations. It's a great place to learn. Al Gore, Malcolm Gladwell, Seth Godin—all the best speakers are there. Check it out.

Sir Ken Robinson, a British educational expert, presenting at TED in 2010, spoke about how education is destroying people's authenticity by dislocating them from their natural talents. Human talents are tremendously diverse, he says, but instead of cultivating those talents individually, we've adopted a "fast food model of education." Of course, it's much cheaper that way, but the results are sub-par. A lot of books and workshops on presentations adopt precisely the same approach by giving out lots of advice on "proper," standardized behavior onstage. I would argue that is not what many of us need. We need to learn to be ourselves.

Being yourself onstage is really difficult. People are complex creatures, with many different character traits. If your presentation is just 20 minutes (or even 18 if you are at TED), you have to choose which side to show. Showing just one side violates the contrast principle, showing too many sides violates the focus principle. You have to select the traits that go well together. Ken Robinson, whose 2006 TED talk has been watched more than 8.5 million times as of this writing, switches between being dead serious and being hysterically funny. Jill Bolte Taylor (also more than 8 million views) looks like a very nice woman until she brings onstage an actual human brain, which is creepy! Psychologist Barry Schwartz (2 million views) looks quite comfortable in his T-shirt, shorts, and sneakers, something you should consider twice before wearing at a high-profile conference even if you're not presenting.

So, unity is about establishing constraints, sometimes completely arbitrarily, and following them to ridiculous lengths. It is about being consistent yet imperfect. It is about being human. And this is what the last part of this book is about.

SUMMARY

Table 1-1 gives a brief starting summary for the book. It works nicely as a checklist. When I say briefly, I really mean it. You might want to write your own questions here. I will be covering much more than three questions in each chapter. Some questions may not be clear yet, but keep in mind that this is just the beginning.

TABLE 1-1: A Summary of Presentation Secrets Key Questions

	FOCUS	CONTRAST	UNITY
Storytelling	What's the goal? What's the point? What are the 3–4 supporting points?	What's the problem? What's the problem for the audience? Who is fighting whom for what?	Does the story follow the S-curve? What's the overall, united theme? Can I delete anything?
Slides	What's the goal of the slide? What's the focal point on the slide? Do those two match?	What am I comparing? Is the focal point really different from the secondary, background information?	Which style does the slide follow? Does the font match the background? Can I delete anything?
Delivery	Am I being clear? Am I making eye contact with the audience? Am I reacting to their feedback?	Who am I fighting? What's my inner conflict? Am I really challenging the audience?	Who is my character? What are my error-handling routines? Am I going with the flow?

PART I
STORY

CHAPTER 2   **The Story's Focus**
CHAPTER 3   **The Story's Contrast**
CHAPTER 4   **The Story's Unity**

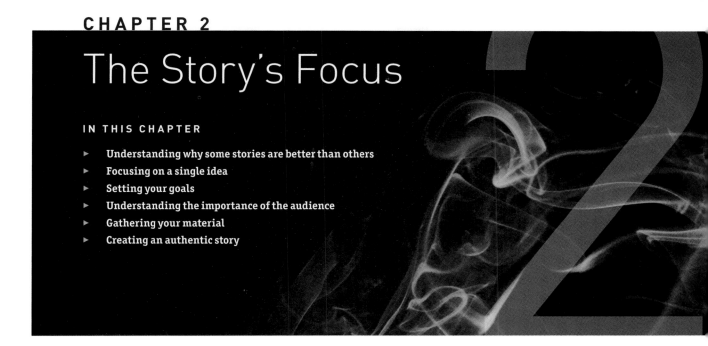

CHAPTER 2

The Story's Focus

IN THIS CHAPTER

▶ Understanding why some stories are better than others
▶ Focusing on a single idea
▶ Setting your goals
▶ Understanding the importance of the audience
▶ Gathering your material
▶ Creating an authentic story

This chapter discusses the basics of storytelling: setting your story's goals and organizing the initial material. This step is very obvious—which is probably the reason why it is so frequently neglected by both novice and experienced presenters alike. Your goal is to try to find the intersection between things that you want to say and things the audience needs to hear. This chapter helps you start gathering and arranging the thoughts and facts—the building blocks for your story.

NOT ALL STORIES ARE CREATED EQUAL

Not all stories are created equal; some stories are better than others. "Better" can mean at least two things. Some stories are more popular. They spread better than others, sometimes very rapidly, like wildfire. Urban legends are like this. They stick. (Chip and Dan Heath explored this concept in great detail in their highly successful 2007 book *Made to Stick*.) But after a period of time they might fade away just as quickly as they spread—or mutate beyond recognition. Some stories stick in a different way: they just don't die. They aren't hugely popular, but somehow they are always around. They become history. Myths and other great classical art fit this category. Both types of stories can be considered successful and therefore "good." Depending on your sensibilities, you might prefer one to another. I believe both are worthwhile goals.

But most stories just disappear, almost instantaneously and without any fanfare. TV broadcasts, news articles, blog posts, conversations between friends—the moment people stop talking about them they are dead and forgotten. Nobody ever remembers these stories or acts according to the idea or the bottom line of the story. Why is that? Well, the simple answer is that people don't act according to the moral of the story because the storyteller never bothered to formulate the moral of the story in the first place. I am not saying that you always need to do this explicitly, like in a fable. This looks pompous and unnecessary. But if you want to show something, you have to formulate it for yourself first. Very few people do this.

Two questions regarding a good story might arise at this moment:

▶ What do you need to create a good story? Do you need just an idea or is there something else?

▶ Should you explicitly include the moral? In a PowerPoint presentation?

The answer to the second question is yes.

But let me address the first question first.

▶ *In fact, I am going to argue that the moral of the story is the single most important aspect of a business presentation.*

FOCUSING ON ONE IDEA

Most books on storytelling—this one is no exception (because making a presentation is ultimately storytelling)—begin with the same advice. You need one idea for your story, so decide on it early. As screenwriter Peter Dunne in *Emotional Structure* puts it, "[W]riters have to make choices. The first choice is to choose one, and only one, idea to develop into a screenplay." Likewise, presenters have to make two decisions: to make a presentation and to decide on the one idea to develop. You might say "Hey, the topic of my presentation is so complex there's no way I can distill it down into one idea; my presentation is not a fairy tale." It doesn't matter whether or not your presentation is complex; you still need one idea to organize it around. I would even argue that if your topic is complex you absolutely need one idea. It will give you focus and direction and help the audience stay oriented. Otherwise, your presentation is in real danger of becoming the convoluted mess that most presentations are.

If your focus is wrong, you can always shift it.

Are you afraid that if you start with one idea you'll end up having a simplistic presentation? If so, consider Johann Sebastian Bach. All his great fugues of incredible complexity, all his violin concertos and fantasies, representing the apex of baroque music with multiple voices and mind-blowing embellishments, were developed from one simple theme. Sometimes you need to be a trained musician to hear this theme; sometimes—like in *Toccata and Fugue in D Minor* and in most fugues—they are clearly audible from the beginning. But there is always was just one clear starting point; one idea.

You may think coming up with a central idea is hard; experience tells me that's not the case. Ideas are cheap. The hard part is "one." For most people it is psychologically difficult to settle on just one idea. When they start thinking about the presentation they think, "What am I going to say?" which is never just one thing. If that's the case, if you find yourself asking that, go one step back. It's not "What am I going to say?" you should ask, but rather "What do I want to happen as a result?" It's not about the means, it's about the ends.

SETTING THE GOAL

The second question I ask in my typical consulting session is "What is the goal of this presentation?"

The right goal motivates you and is worthy and achievable. So, what's the goal? The answer I typically get is "I want to tell them that. . ." or "I want to inform them about. . ." Beep! Wrong answer!

Even experienced executives fall into this trap. You may have guessed by now that the correct answer should connect the audience and the presenter, as shown in Figure 2-1. The correct answer should sound something like "I want them to give me their business card" or "I want them to believe that my plan is going to work." A good goal is phrased as an answer to "What do I want them to do?" or sometimes "What do I want them to remember?"

I learned this principle very early in my consulting career; really, this is one of the first and most obvious principles you learn in consulting. When I started working with presentations, I was shocked to discover how quickly people tend to forget about it. We all know setting goals is important, yet we either skip this step entirely or just fill the blanks in a checklist without really thinking.

▶ All great presentations can be distilled into one idea, and it's not always the same idea the author started with. The process of creating the presentation can transform the idea. So prepare for change, but start with an initial idea.

▶ I cannot overemphasize the importance of this question. There is nothing more important than setting the right goal.

THE GOAL CONNECTS!

FIGURE 2-1: The goal connects the audience and the presenter.

When I say we, I include myself in this category. I can't even count how many times I caught myself skipping the goal-setting part. What's even worse, I didn't realize the mistake until after the presentation, and I am a presentation consultant! I wholeheartedly believe that having the right goal is the key to success, but even I tend to slack here. Why!?

If Goal-Setting Is Important, Why Do People Skip It?

The first reason is that people are afraid of failure and you simply cannot fail if all you want is to inform people. The possibility that your presentation will be interrupted by a tsunami or Martian invasion is relatively low. If no *force majeure* occurs, you will make it. You will inform your audience; they will be informed. So you have nothing to fear. This is much easier than having a challenging goal; something you might actually screw up.

Another aspect is, of course, measurability. There are many ways to quantify the results, and it's particularly easy in webcasts, arguably the fastest-growing segment when it comes to presentations. If you quantify your results, you are definitely facing your fear of failure.

I can't even estimate the number of books written about tackling one's fear of failure. Personally, I am not very fond of jumping into the abyss. I am the "pick battles small enough to win but big enough to matter" kinda guy. I am not asking you to do the impossible. But "informing people"? Come on! You can do better that this. Just raise the bar a bit; it is set too low.

▶ In the process you become aware that the bar exists. To me, this is the most important part.

Secondly, precisely because goal setting is obvious, it is often overlooked. This is why thinking outside the box is so damn hard—you always need to consider the box. The box is easily forgotten because it's very stable and it's always there. People never say "the glass fell down and broke because of the force of gravity." No, we tend to blame a live human being for that. Their behavior changes and is clearly visible. It takes a genius like Newton to identify the gravity and blame it for that one.

It is the same with presentations. It's easy to blame somebody's trembling voice and closed posture. "Oh, he's not confident enough. He needs more confidence!" Those are easy to spot. Asking yourself what the presenter is trying to accomplish requires conscious effort. This is work, and, let's face it, we don't like work. Not unless we choose it.

THE IMPORTANCE OF ASKING (AND ANSWERING) THE OBVIOUS QUESTIONS

I chose to ask other people obvious questions as a way to earn my living. Did you? Probably not. Do you choose to ask yourself obvious questions? If not, maybe you should. In his 2005 Stanford commencement speech, Steve Jobs, CEO of Apple, mentioned that every morning he looks in the mirror and asks himself, "If today were the last day of my life, would I want to do what I am about to do today?"

This is one of those obvious questions most people never ask themselves. I think one should have a list of those questions. I do. I think success and happiness in life depend on answering these questions honestly.

So, what is the goal of your presentation?

Recall and Impact

Again, the question to ask is this: What do you want from your audience? Write an answer in one clear sentence. This will be your first draft. I know it's hard. If you have multiple goals, write them all down and then choose the most important one or find a way to consolidate them in one sentence. Having multiple goals is a bad idea because:

▶ Sometimes they conflict and you end up accomplishing neither.

▶ Even if they don't conflict, there's always a risk of spreading the jam too thin.

So, just one goal, agreed?

Okay, next question. Is the goal about the audience's thinking or actions? When people scientifically measure the impact of a presentation (believe it or not some people actually do this), they mostly measure two things: recall and impact:

▶ **Recall** is whether people remember what they've been told.

▶ **Impact** is whether they act upon what they've been told.

These are different things. Moreover, these two measures may very well be in conflict.

For instance, text that's written in a fancy font that requires effort to read might be more memorable than something written in plain and unimaginative font, like Arial. You are more likely to remember a visually interesting logo than a visually dull one, right? However, when it comes to tasks, there's research suggesting that people associate the ease of reading the task with the actual task itself. So, if a slide encouraging people to complete a task is visually complex, the audience may be more likely to remember the slide, but less likely to complete the task.

In one experiment[1], two groups of students were presented with instructions for an exercise. One group received the instructions in an easy-to-read font (Arial), and the second group in a difficult-to-read font (Brush Script). After reading, each group was asked to estimate how difficult they thought the exercise would be and how much time it would take. Readers in the first group assumed that the exercise would take on average 8.2 minutes to complete, whereas readers in the second group thought that it would take nearly twice as long, 15.1 minutes. The first group also thought that the exercise would flow quite naturally, and the second feared that it would be a drag.

Although recall and impact are not quite the same, they do intersect, as illustrated in Figure 2-2.

Sometimes people remember what they've been told but don't act upon it. Sometimes they act yet don't quite remember why. You can have both, but you need to plan for it. Give your audience the reasons to act, as you want them to act—and nothing else.

Consider this great Chinese proverb "Tell me and I'll forget; show me and I may remember; involve me and I'll understand."

Do you want your audience to understand your presentation and act on it? I bet you do. Then don't just inform them. Involve them. Go for impact.

Sometimes—especially in the context of education—people are trained for recall. They have tests to fill out later, formulas to memorize, and so on. With Wikipedia and wireless Internet everywhere, this goal of recall is becoming increasingly obsolete. Go for impact.

▶ *If certain information in your presentation doesn't contribute to the action you want from your audience, you should ask yourself if you really need this information in your speech.*

[1] Song, H., and Schwarz, N. (2008). "If it's hard to read, it's hard to do: Processing fluency affects effort prediction and motivation." *Psychological Science*, 19(10): 986-988.

THE SWEET SPOT

FIGURE 2-2: Recall and impact are not the same.

John Kennedy said that the only reason to give a speech is to change the world. Part of his point here is definitely one of valuing impacting your audience over merely informing them. If you have an audience that will listen to you for 5, 10, 15, or 45 minutes, be sure to use this time wisely. Go for impact and involvement.

Values Are States of Motivation

Believe it or not, I've spent a great deal of my time trying to inform people and hoping that new information would change their actions. For some of them it did, but for most, it didn't. Involve your audience. Give meaning to your presentation. Give them the real goal, the goal they are likely to achieve. Granted, some people want to "just inform" because of their deep respect for the audience. They think that their audience consists of mature and intelligent people who can connect the dots themselves. They don't want people to act on emotions without proper thought. They don't want people to do the right thing for wrong reasons. I appreciate that. That is why I believe you absolutely need to give the information to support the actions. But still, go for actions. I also believe that you should connect actions to the higher level of thinking, to the level of values. I think that your presentation should have a theme beyond its contents, if possible.

As Simon Sinek, the author of the book *Start with Why* (watch his presentation at www.TED.com; it's brilliant!), says you need to understand and discuss, "not just what to do, but *why* do it." And by "why" he doesn't mean purely logical reasons, but also and mostly emotional. It's not only "why," but also "in the name of what." One example is energy-saving products that also have political implications. What's your idea or product about on a larger scale? Is it about saving lives or making them easier? Both are worthwhile aspirations.

DON'T INFORM—INVOLVE!

I grew up in the Soviet Union and like the rest of the students at school I was a member of the Pioneer organization, a movement loosely modeled after Scouts. As you might expect, quite unlike Scouts, the movement was heavily politicized and once a week on Mondays we had extra 15 minutes of study, an obligatory "political information session." Some unlucky student was appointed to inform the rest of the class about the latest political developments in the world. The struggle of international proletariat against the forces of imperialism, you know. It was a nightmare.

It was a nightmare not because we didn't believe in the communist ideology. As a matter of fact, we did and quite passionately so because if there was one thing the socialist state did well, it was indoctrinating children. The problem was that the "political information" had no real purpose; it served no real goal. We had no idea what we were supposed to do with all this information. There was no space for questions and we didn't discuss anything. We "just informed" each other.

So each and every week on Mondays for several years we had to get up and come to class 15 minutes early. For no reason. For nothing. I don't know if you remember, but 15 minutes seems like a lot when you're a little kid, especially early in the morning. We hated it. Please don't inflict this on *your* audience. Please don't "just inform" other people. Excite them, involve them, impact them, and engage them, but don't just inform them with empty information.

If you want to know more about the role of values in business, read Jim Collins' bestselling book *From Good to Great*. One of the core ideas of the book is that companies that consistently outperform market have one thing in common: they all have a strong corporate culture based on a set of values. They don't just "do business"; rather, they are doing business and promoting their values, which are the source of their market resilience. These are great companies. It is the same with presentations. If you want to go from good to great, you have to think about values.

Promoting these values might not be necessary in your routine "status update" presentation you make for your bosses. But for a conference speech, for a larger audience I think this is an absolute must. Don't just inform them and don't just ask them to do something for you. Motivate them; inspire them. Show them a vision to aspire to.

NOTE A vision is the ideal world based on your values. You can't have one and not the other. If you know your values you'll have no problem coming up with a vision. If you have a vision you will distill values from it. So, I use those two terms interchangeably.

Consider this definition of values: "Values are different states of intentionality that when activated guide behavior and create meaning." The credit for this brilliant definition goes to Scott Bristol of www.LJMap.com, who, as I understand it, compiled it from works of Benjamin Libet and Viktor Frankl, both famous psychologists. So, values are internal emotional states. They answer the question "why?" and the answer is "because it feels right." They are complex feelings of intentionality and motivation. When we practice our values, we perceive our life as full of purpose and meaning. It makes us happy.

NOTE The problem with mere logic (that is logic without connection to vision or values) is that people will agree and won't do anything afterwards. If you want people to do something, you need to induce an appropriate state of motivation. You can't induce the state by simply repeating "excellence, excellence" or "cooperation, cooperation;" it doesn't work. On the other hand, stories work well. If your story has a theme, you can connect with your audience. Not only you are asking them to do something that makes logical sense, but you also are connecting this task to a higher purpose they are likely to subscribe to. You are not just asking them to do something, you are making them better people in their own eyes. Isn't it great? They will be grateful to you for that.

Every Great Presentation Is About Vision

If you examine any great presentation, you will find that it is really about vision. Go search "great presentation" on Google. Better yet, check out http://tinyurl.com/top10pres. It's a list compiled by a personal acquaintance of mine, Frank Roche of www.KnowHR.com. Watch the presentations shown there. You will find that every one of them is about vision. Every single one of them. This is what makes them great. They are connecting people's actions to a higher purpose. Ten is too much for this book, so I will review the first five, and you will do the rest, deal? You have to watch them, but they are freely available on the Internet.

1. Steve Jobs' presentation of Macintosh in 1984. Steve comes on stage and presents the first "computer for the rest of us," a computer for small business owners and creative professionals. What is the presentation about? Computers? No. Well, I mean yes, but not just about computers. It's about democratization of technology. His vision is a world where technology is not only accessible to large corporations, but also to common folk—and not

those "home computers" suitable for games only. Computers for business, for creating content. Almost 25 years later, we can say that Steve's vision is largely realized.

2. Dick Hardt's *Identity 2.0*. This is a charismatic CEO of a small company delivering a humorous presentation with what seems to be one million slides. This one's difficult; his greatness is mostly in the form and not in the content. It's about having a non-boring technical presentation. The ideas he presents didn't spread but the presentation style did.

3. Guy Kawasaki's *Art of the Start*. This rather long talk has several recurring themes. On the surface, it's about starting a business, but really it's about having guts in whatever you do and not letting bozos get in your way.

4. Dr. Martin Luther King, Jr.'s *I Have a Dream*. This is probably the most obvious example of a person having a moral vision that came true to a very large extent.

5. Lawrence Lessig's *Free Culture*. This one can be summarized in four sentences: "Creativity and innovation always build on the past. The past always tries to control creativity. Free societies enable the future by limiting the past. Ours is a less and less free society." He calls to limit copyrights, but really it is about freedom of expression.

Okay, I will do another one because Dr. Martin Luther King, Jr., was too obvious. Let's look at Malcolm Gladwell's 2005 presentation at SXSW. The presentation is about snap judgments and first impressions. Gladwell tells multiple stories about people making good and bad judgments in different environments.

Just before the end he tells a story of an African-American named Amadou Diallo who was shot 41 times by the New York City police—by mistake. He then suggests concrete steps to reduce the amount of similar police errors. The presentation ends with a call to examine our environments where we have to make snap judgments and to eliminate those where our judgments tend to be erroneous. By doing this, he suggests we might end up with a better world.

Can you continue the list by yourself? There are still four presentations left and there are another 10 in the reader's choice list. Watch them. They are all about the values. All of them.

▶ Never try to play with the values that don't appeal to you even abstractly, just for the sake of marketing. It's a bad idea; people will see your bluff.

One final point about values/vision—don't create a vision because you need it for your presentation. Have a vision because you mean it. If you are not sure about your vision or the vision for your presentation, start writing it down or saying it out loud and see if it resonates with you on the inside.

This is one of those exercises that people seldom do because it feels so superficial. I once heard a 2-hour long presentation in which a trainer was speaking about a mysterious exercise that completely transformed his life, made him substantially richer, and much happier. In the end, it turned out the exercise was simply to describe his perfect day. The little secret was that he did the exercise for four hours and really got to the core of what he wanted. When people first write their visions, they mostly want to finish them as soon as possible. But persistence is key.

> ### WARNING—PEOPLE DON'T WANT TO BE LECTURED
>
> Samuel Goldwyn, the late founder of Metro-Goldwyn-Mayer, famously said once: "If you want to send a message, try Western Union." He was addressing, of course, the directors and screenwriters trying to propagate their vision at the expense of box office. From a presentation standpoint, it is crucial to understand two points about his comments:
>
> ▶ The audience is not interested in you telling them your vision: they want a good story. Good story contains vision, but that's like soup containing spices. You don't eat the soup for the spices. You can't eat spices alone.
>
> ▶ You cannot communicate values by just naming them. They are way too abstract. Tell stories and let people figure them out.
>
> Remember you don't want your audience to merely *recall* your vision or values. You want to impact them with your vision and values so that they might act.

THE CUSTOMER ISN'T ALWAYS RIGHT

You have no doubt heard the expression that the customer is always right, right? Yet we all also know of situations where we don't agree with this phrase, where the customer is clearly not right. For example, if the customers are abusive, negligent, or just plain drunk, they are not right. Go to the www.clientsfromhell.net website if you want more examples. One of the recurring themes of this site is "I did everything as the client said and they are still not happy." It is too simplistic to say that clients or customers are always right. Oftentimes they sound pretty confident while in reality they have little clue what they really want.

In terms of giving presentations, we've embraced the attitude of "the customer is always right" to combat the "what do I want to say" attitude we have. We force a focus on the audience, leading to a "what do they want to hear" attitude instead. But giving clients solely what they want isn't a good idea now, and it never was! Consider these quotes from the early 20th century:

▶ **Henry Ford, entrepreneur:** "If I had asked people what they wanted, they would have said faster horses."

▶ **Samuel Rothafel, impresario for many of the great New York movie palaces:** "Giving the people what they want is fundamentally and disastrously wrong. The people don't know what they want . . . [Give] them something better."

When Ford and Rothafel said those words, the idea that the customer isn't always right was a novel thought. But by now it seems relatively obvious, and there are numerous examples supporting the idea that the customer isn't always right. Why do we think still think that the audience is "always right"? Why do we try to please them at all costs, often sacrificing our own vision?

▶ Give the audience something they might not even know they need, something they haven't considered.

Sometimes it's a good idea to start your presentation with what the audience wants but end it by showing how what they want might be limited or short-sighted. In other words, don't just give them something they want.

Treating the audience as though they are always right, as though you are the one who has to avoid stepping on their toes, doesn't quite achieve the results you want. More likely it can make you come off as servile and craven. You lose authenticity because you are afraid so say what you think and believe. You come off as apologetic. Don't be a servant to your audience. If they don't like you, you'll find another audience. Having your own opinion, being authentic in your presentation, is far more important that trying to please your audience. Not every audience is going to be receptive to your message, and trying to please everyone is futile. Focusing includes not only choosing the right message, but also the right audience.

You are the one in the spotlight, and that means for the length of your presentation you are in charge. Trying to please the audience is sometimes less risky than putting your own thoughts and values out there to be judged. But by pandering to your audience you lose yourself and your point. By pandering to the audience you might affirm them, but you will never impact them. Sure, the audience may like you (or at least the image you are projecting) if you say things that are pleasing to them, that they want to hear. But by trying to please the audience, you can make only a good presentation, never a great one, never an impactful one.

George Handel, a popular 17th century composer (whose music I am listening to as I'm writing this) once received warm appreciation for providing entertainment for his audience, to which he replied: "I should be sorry if I only entertained them; I wish to make them better." Don't just make the audience feel good. Make them better.

Impudence Is the Second Happiness

There's a Russian saying, "Impudence is the second happiness." I never quite got what that meant. I thought it was about people having impudence to cut a long waiting line, to have a seat when everybody else has to stand. You know those people. They're arrogant, they're loud, they're overly competitive, and they don't respect others.

But then I got it. Several years ago, I was looking at a slide deck of a prospective client. They had just prepared slides for their upcoming board meeting. They wanted my feedback, and I didn't like those slides the least bit. There was no visible structure, they were overloaded, and were badly designed. And yet my prospects just made a great effort in putting those slides together and probably expected to hear something good. "Well . . ." I said. And then I gave them my "your slides stink" look. "They are bad, aren't they?" said the client. I was relieved. I was happy. I didn't have to lie, and I won the contract.

Criticizing a client's product/process/situation requires impudence. I don't suggest you say anything like this unless you really mean it; not unless you have a couple of good heartfelt arguments to support your point of view. But if you do, go ahead and say it. This is where your presentation becomes interesting. Essentially, there is no point in saying something everybody agrees with. It will be a truism. If you want to say something, just say it. Go straight to the controversial part.

I'm not suggesting you should be arrogant and abusive to be interesting. Lots of people do try to attract attention this way. The difference between good impudence and bad impudence is that good impudence is constructive and creative. It adds value. It is done in good faith. Sir Ken Robinson, an author and a spokesperson on a topic of creativity, defines creativity as "having original ideas that have value." Having original ideas requires impudence; all original ideas are controversial by definition.

> ▶ Don't shy away from controversy, embrace it! It can create tension and stir attention. If there's nothing controversial in your presentation, it will be boring, guaranteed.

SHOULD THE AUDIENCE LIKE YOU?

As a speaker, you have to understand that the audience doesn't have to like you all the time. This is not necessary for you to change them. Literature and cinema are full of characters who are difficult to sympathize with. Consider the main hero of Dostoevsky's *Crime and Punishment.* He is quite unsympathetic. He kills an old lady for her money. One of the main heroes of *The Silence of the Lambs* is unsympathetic. He eats people for lunch. And yet they are still able to evoke our empathy (which is different from sympathy), and by living through their stories, we are changed.

So don't worry whether the audience likes you or not. Don't sweat too much about what they want. What they want is of secondary importance. If you have a message to spread, the one that's truly yours, go ahead and spread it. This is your only chance to get passionate and, ultimately, to have impact.

What Do You Want Your Audience To Do?

You now have a choice. What goal for engaging your audience do you want to aim for? These different goals are like nesting *matryoshka* dolls, as shown in Figure 2-3.

WHAT DO I WANT THEM TO...

FIGURE 2-3: The nested hierarchy of goals.

- ▶ **Hear your message:** You can simply choose to have the audience hear your message right now, in the moment, and be entertained or engaged by it.

- ▶ **Remember your message:** You can choose to just inform your audience. You can choose to be memorable.

- ▶ **Do something:** You can choose to motivate your audience to act. For that, they have to remember something of your speech. If they don't remember a thing you said, chances are they won't do anything.

- ▶ **Improve themselves:** The ultimate goal is to change the audience, to make them better people. People do not become better just by listening or remembering stuff; they become better by making choices and acting on them. It is not the act itself that changes people. It's the choice that does.

So go ahead and chose any two:

- ▶ "I want them to hear X and to remember it."

- ▶ "I want them to remember X and do Y."

- ▶ "I want them to do Y because of Z."

I'd love it if you'd go for the ultimate goal.

GATHERING THE MATERIAL

When you have your goals set you can finally get to PowerPoint, right? Lots of people begin building their presentation at this point. Don't. The problem with slideware is that you get to the very small details like font size or diagram setup too soon, and thus you lose the big picture. After about 30 minutes of struggling with colors, you don't remember what you want to say.

Don't start in a word processor either. A word processor ultimately forces you to think linearly and you need to think hierarchically first. I know this sounds cryptic, so let me explain.

Stories are linear. They have a nice flow, a sequence of events, one after another. Slides or a cinema tape (which is essentially the same thing) is a good metaphor for the story: one thing after another and another. That's how the audience sees the story, but that's not how the author (or presenter) sees it. For the author, the story is a hierarchy! Have a look at the Figure 2-4.

The audience doesn't need to see the hierarchy. Even though some presentation software exposes the underneath hierarchy (most famously, perhaps, `www.Prezi.com`), I don't see the reason for this. It confuses people and makes them think about the presentation's structure rather than living through the presentation (which is your goal).

▶ Don't ever start building your presentation in PowerPoint or any slide-oriented software for that matter. You'll too quickly become caught up in the minutia of your slides.

▶ As far as presentations are concerned, design and delivery are fundamentally different things and need to be separate.

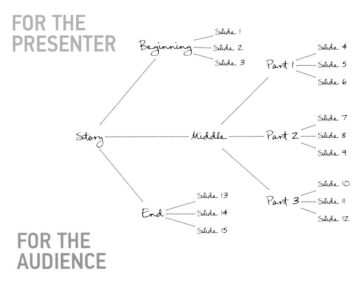

FIGURE 2-4: Presenter and audience: two different views.

Your presentation has big and important messages and also small and less important messages supporting the bigger ones. Trust me; you don't know which ones are which unless you look at them all at the same time. If you start in slideware, you will mess them up. I had the most stunning example of this while working with one of the Russia's largest industrial conglomerates on a strategy presentation for a business unit. When I came in the group of managers had already been working for quite a while; they'd produced an enormous amount of materials including more than 30 densely packed slides. It was Wednesday evening and they had to present before the board on Friday.

I looked at their slides first thing. They were a mess. So we started building a story from scratch. I gave them some theory about storytelling and then asked them what were the most important things they wanted to say. As they were speaking, I was writing their messages down on sticky notes. So we ended up with a wall like in Figure 2-5.

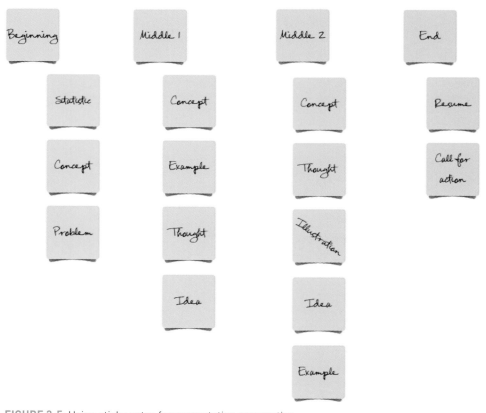

FIGURE 2-5: Using sticky notes for presentation preparation.

> **NOTE** Sticky notes are a fantastic tool. If you have a large table, a wall, or a whiteboard, try using sticky notes. They are very easy to manipulate and work especially well when you have to prepare a presentation in a group. I've used them numerous times with great success. They're very democratic in that everybody can write a sticky note. Also, everyone can suggest a new place for their thought in the general scheme simply by placing their note somewhere else without asking for anyone's permission. I love it.

We created a classic story sequence (more on this in Chapter 4) and then went back to the previously designed slides to see whether we could use any of them. Most were unusable or had to be radically simplified. Then we reached the slide shown in Figure 2-6.

The group said "Oh, this is our most important slide! This is our strategy! It says that we are currently a magenta triangle, concerned mostly with production. We have poor marketing and engineering. And the green triangle is what we want to be: to outsource our production (because we are losing money there), to improve on marketing, and essentially we want to become an engineering company."

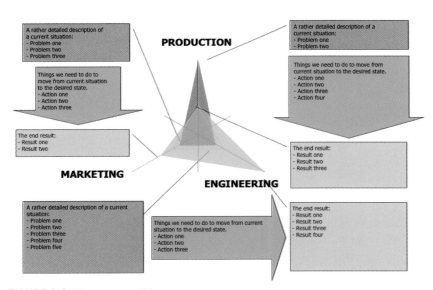

FIGURE 2-6: The strategy slide.

Then they looked at the presentation structure we've just designed and said: "Oh, darn. We have a piece on production and a piece on marketing, but we've completely forgotten about engineering. We didn't prepare any materials on that subject. We put it on this slide, and then it just slipped away. We don't know how that happened. We now have just one day left and we've just discovered that we are missing the most important piece. Well, at least we know."

This is what I mean by slipping into details and losing sight of the big picture. Slideware does that to people, so don't start in PowerPoint. Start in a program that is designed to deal with hierarchies visually, as the next section discusses.

Visual Thinking Tools

When working solo or with a single client I use computer software designed for visual thinking rather than sticky notes. Personally I find it much more clean and convenient. Unlike handwritten notes, you can copy and paste. You can use three types of software: outliners, mind mapping applications, and concept mapping (graph) editors.

WORKING WITH OUTLINERS

An outliner is software that allows you to create headings in multiple levels. Below the headings you can write your text, which can be collapsed or expanded at your convenience. A similar approach is widely used in file managers like Windows Explorer or the Finder on the Mac. The output from outliners tends to look like Figure 2-7.

This is the simplest software for editing hierarchies. It is also the most readily available. Microsoft Word and PowerPoint both have outliner modes. However, neither was designed to be used primarily as an outliner, and they lose out to products more focused in this domain. Other outliners you can use:

▶ **KeyNoteNF for Windows:** This is freeware; I used this one when I was on Windows.

▶ **Noteliner for Windows:** This is a freeware note editor. It has a solid outlining system, is very small in size, doesn't require installation or any additional libraries, and is extremely easy to use. You can even run it from a thumb drive.

TYPES OF DOGS
Outline

1. Hunting dogs
   1.1. Gun dogs
      1.1.1. Pointers
      1.1.2. Retrievers
      1.1.3. Setters
      1.1.4. Spaniels
      1.1.5. Water dogs
   1.2. Hounds
      1.2.1. …
   1.3. …
2. Herding dogs
3. Sled dogs
4. …

FIGURE 2-7: Using an outliner you can create headings in multiple levels.

- ▶ **OneNote for Windows:** Part of Microsoft Office. OneNote's most overlooked feature is its outlining capability. Each note you create there actually becomes part of an outline.
- ▶ **OmniOutliner for Mac:** Commercial software; was shipped with Mac OS X 10.4 "Tiger" for free so you might have it if you are a long-time Mac user.
- ▶ **Thinklinkr.com:** A web-based, collaboration-friendly program.

The problem with outliners is that they are children of the printer era. They create pages in portrait orientation for top-down reading, which isn't an optimal usage of a screen space. Another problem with the top-down approach is that you get a sequence even if you don't want one—and for now you don't.

WORKING WITH MIND MAPPING APPLICATIONS

Mind mapping applications do not have the outliner's limitations. They are optimized for landscape, and you can arrange topics without imposing any sequential order on them. The learning curve is steeper and the retail prices of commercial products are higher, but trust me—they are well worth the money. In the end, they allow you to build tree-like structures with most ease. A typical mind map looks like Figure 2-8.

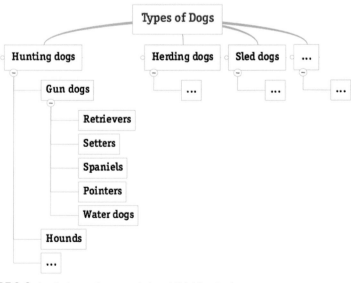

FIGURE 2-8: A mind map is a great visual thinking tool.

Consider these mind mapping software products:

- ▶ **MindManager, both Windows and Mac:** Expensive but really good. It is beautifully designed; it has the familiar ribbon interface on Windows and is minimalistic on a Mac. It is integrated with Microsoft Office and SharePoint. It has numerous useful plugins and add-ons like Gantt charts and an iPhone client. It even has a presentation mode (on Windows only).

- ▶ **FreeMind, both Windows and Mac:** Compared to MindManager, it looks somewhat amateurish. But it's free and the basic functionality is there. Again, as with other free software, there's a catch. This one requires downloading a Java runtime environment if you don't have one already installed.

- ▶ **MindMeister:** A web-based, collaboration-friendly program. It has both a free and paid version, and supports FreeMind and MindManager file formats.

WORKING WITH CONCEPT MAPPING EDITORS

Yet another type of software is the concept mapping editors. Concept mapping is a technique that was invented by Dr. Joseph Novak of Cornell University in the 70s and is currently used very widely, especially in network diagramming and business process mapping.

Compared to mind mapping, concept mapping is much more free form. You can have multiple hubs and clusters, unlike mind maps, which allow only one conceptual center, the trunk of your tree. See Figure 2-9 for a look at a concept map.

Concept maps give you much more freedom, which is good especially if you need to really think and formulate some new idea for your presentation. Do keep in mind, however, they require much more conscious effort to create effectively. I know people who use these tools for presentation structure design; to me they are more suitable for general knowledge management. But if you have an extremely complicated scientific or engineering topic and your presentation is more than an hour long, you might find them useful. Some concept mapping editors you might consider are:

- ▶ **The Personal Brain, both Windows and Mac:** Free and paid versions are offered.

- ▶ **yEd:** Free and very sophisticated graph editor; I'm slightly ashamed to recommend it for this small aspect of its functionality.

- ▶ **IHMC CmapTools:** A free, collaboration-friendly program.

▶ *For me, nothing beats the speed and spontaneity of the mind map. I suggest you go for a mind mapper.*

It's Time for a Brain Dump

Now, with your goals clearly stated, you can proceed to a brain dump. This is where you answer the question, "What do I want to tell them?" I assume you're a creating a business, engineering, or scientific presentation, so you don't have freedom to say just anything. There are facts and your opinions about facts; that's pretty much it. Answer "What do I want to tell them?" in the most honest way possible. The order of things doesn't matter at this point. Ideas might have gotten a bit tangled inside your head—no problem. You'll get them untangled as you work along.

RELATED CONCEPTS
Concept map

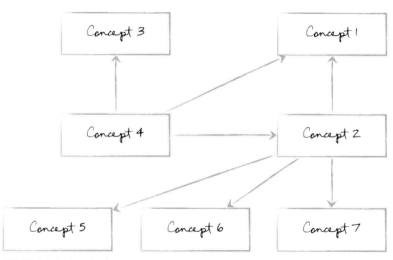

FIGURE 2-9: A typical concept map.

All the rules that apply to brainstorming apply here. Write everything down; it doesn't matter whether you think it's important or not. You can start from the middle, from the end, from anywhere.

Don't write complete sentences; don't get sucked into lengthy descriptions. Write short, bullet-point-style reminders. Move. In my consulting sessions, I typically allow for the client to speak for an hour or two, all the while writing things down.

The key questions are these:

► What do I need to say?

► What do I want to say?

► What do they want to hear?

► What do they need to hear?

► If any thoughts, even stupid, unrelated ones, cross your mind, get them on the table. If you get stuck, write down whatever you're thinking: worries, concerns, and so on. This really helps you to brainstorm. You can eliminate unimportant stuff later.

Hierarchy Is Your Friend

The next step is to impose some sort of order on your thoughts, some sort of classification. I suggest you go for hierarchy, by arranging thoughts in levels—above, below, or at the same level in relation to each other. You need to build a tree-like structure. This, by no means, is the final presentation structure. The only reason to arrange things at this point is to know where to find them when you need them. If your presentation is short (say, you have less than 10 thoughts), you may as well leave them as they are. But most of the time you will be better off by creating a hierarchy. Figure 2-10 shows an actual mind map from a presentation I created.

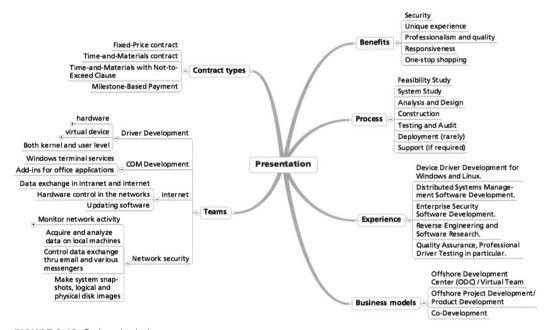

FIGURE 2-10: Ordered mind map.

This mind map is not a presentation structure yet. It's just raw material. Think of it as of serviceman arranging tools in his kit prior to working, or a builder arranging materials before starting the actual construction. A stack of bricks is not a building. But the building will be easier to build if your bricks lie in a nice stack and not in a pile. Chapter 3 helps you to construct a story out of those building blocks.

INVENTING THE TRUTH

By the end of the process I've discussed in this chapter so far you should have two things:

- ▶ Your goal.
- ▶ A huge amount of points to make.

You will be creating a story from these raw materials in the next two chapters, including an emotional structure, an envelope, and packaging for the facts. Now, before you begin, I want to get one thing absolutely clear. I know some people hate packaging. They think it's wasteful and it also hides lies, in that it presents the product in its best way rather than objectively. Some people might think that it's immoral to tell stories because of that. This doesn't worry me at all. What worries me is that some people get into storytelling because they think that it will help to sell bad products. It won't.

If you want to create a fictitious story, this book is not for you. The bad news is that books about fictional stories are not for you either. Peter Dunne, a scriptwriter whom I quoted earlier and will be quoting again, said, "The story is the journey for truth."

Even if you are free to say whatever you want, you still have to tell the truth. I sometimes do workshops titled "Self-presentation" where I teach people to construct stories from their own biographies. Some students come to the workshop to create marketing "legends" for themselves. Some come to attempt to understand who they really are. The latter ones get much better results as far as marketing is concerned.

Authentic stories don't require much practice to tell. When somebody tells true stories about his or her weaknesses and failures—but also about successes, even minor ones—they work. They create empathy, they transform people, they create action. When people tell a fictional story about themselves, we don't trust it. It requires a lot of really good acting for us to believe.

In the end, the only thing you can be accused of is cherry-picking; that is, picking only facts that fit well. But for a story to work you have to pick not only sweet cherries but also rotten ones. This is what a story is, a journey from rotten to sweet (or sometimes vice versa).

▶ Storytelling (and presenting) is not about inventing facts; it's about arranging facts in a sequence so they are meaningful.

CAN YOU SELL WITHOUT LYING?

A friend of mine wrote in her secret blog recently: "The CEO of our company told me that I have to learn to lie if I want to do business. Apparently I don't." Can you do business without lying? 100 years ago the answer was more obvious than now. Now people strive for authenticity. "We are tired of living in a bubble of fake bullsh*t," as game designer Jesse Schell put it. Even in sales! The problem with truth-telling is, of course, that it hurts, either the one who tells, or the one

▶ When I interview people I ask obvious and dumb questions to get at the dark side of a situation. You need the dark side for your story. No story can work without the dark side. So if you omitted the dark side in your brain dump, go one step back.

who listens, or both. Sometimes the truth isn't nice. But if we've learned something from 100 years of marketing it's that there are many ways to tell the truth.

Another friend of mine once recommended a three-hour long black-and-white Polish film from the 60s based on a 19th century Polish book. It was shot by a supposedly famous Polish film director Wojciech Jerzy Has. Ever heard of him? Neither had I. "Watch it, it's a cool movie," said my friend in a calm and unemotional voice. This was his presentation of the film. How do you estimate my chances of watching the film? You're right; they were close to zero. But then he told me the story of the film.

It turns out that the film, called *The Saragossa Manuscript,* was well received in the 1960s and won some minor festival awards. A shortened version even ran in the United States! But then—as it happens to most movies—it was forgotten almost entirely and the original tape was so badly damaged the film was considered lost. However, a couple of fans, people who saw the film in the 60s, came to rescue. The film was restored to its uncut glory in the 90s by Jerry Garcia (of Grateful Dead), Martin Scorsese, and Francis Ford Coppola, who financed the restoration. It also turned out that Luis Buñuel, David Lynch, Lars von Trier, and Harvey Keitel have at various times described *The Saragossa Manuscript* as their favorite film and a source of inspiration. Now it wasn't just an old Polish film. It was a recovered treasure.

My friend's pitch was perfect: he didn't skip the unattractive "Polish black-and-white" part. Instead he used it to create a fascinating mystery. I sat for 3 hours mesmerized. It was a great movie. Everything my friend told me was true. It was in fact a 3-hour-long black-and-white Polish movie from the 60s. In Polish! (Okay, there were English subtitles.)

It had almost every imaginable surface trait of a boring film. But hey, it also had a great story. An extra bonus was that the movie itself was about storytelling. It tells many stories in a sequence so in the end you start noticing patterns. So, there are many, many ways to tell the truth. Now, go get the movie, and I'll see you in the next chapter.

SUMMARY

The key points to remember from this chapter are as follows:

- ▶ **Start with a goal.** The story, the emotional structure of your presentation, needs a clear goal. Without one clear goal, it will be a mess. Ideally, the goal lies on the intersection of what you want the audience to do and what they need to do for their own sake and benefit.

- ▶ **Have a vision, too.** Having a vision is key to a great presentation. Not only do you need to tell people what you want from them, but you also need to tell them why they should care.

By bringing values into the game, you are improving motivation and making them better people in their own eyes. That said, there's nothing more pathetic than a naked vision that's not supported by a good story.

▶ **They don't know what they want.** Telling the audience only what they want to hear and how they want to hear it sounds servile or suspiciously manipulative. Treat your audience with respect and dignity. If you don't have your agenda, you're going to be boring. Have your agenda, but don't force it.

▶ **Don't start with slides.** After setting the goals, gather your thoughts together. Don't start in PowerPoint, start in a mind mapping application or with a pack of sticky notes. Write down everything that's on your mind as far as your goal is concerned. Next, impose an order and arrange your thoughts in a hierarchy. Don't skip the dark side, the unpleasant facts. You will need them for your story.

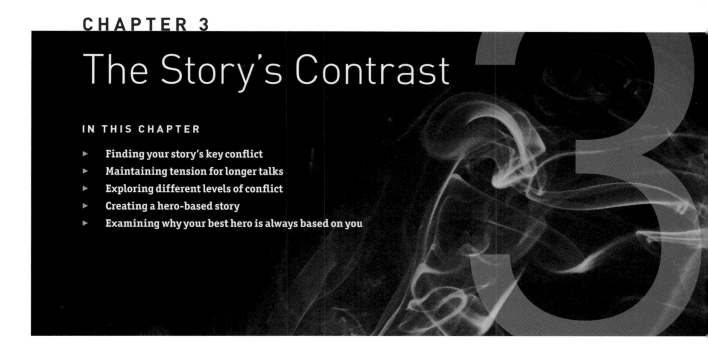

CHAPTER 3

The Story's Contrast

IN THIS CHAPTER

▶ **Finding your story's key conflict**

▶ **Maintaining tension for longer talks**

▶ **Exploring different levels of conflict**

▶ **Creating a hero-based story**

▶ **Examining why your best hero is always based on you**

This chapter explores something called "the controlling idea" of a story—the story's conflict, usually created by two or more contrasting agents. You will read about different ways to set up the conflict, ultimately learning about the most difficult, yet effective way: hero versus villain. The chapter covers two types of heroes used in presentations: the cartoons or stock characters and the heroes based on real people like you. Finally, you will learn about common pitfalls with personal stories and explore some workarounds.

PROBLEMS AND SOLUTIONS

What is the most important part of your presentation? Most people will say that it's a description of a product, a solution, or a finding. After all, this is what you are presenting, right? Wrong. I would argue that the most important part of your presentation is a problem. If you don't bother to describe the problem you are likely to lose your audience in the first 5 minutes. By defining a problem you create a conflict between two forces—a problem and a solution that makes your story interesting to follow. Defining a problem is a major prerequisite for a successful presentation.

No Conflict, No Story

So, now you have set your goals and have collected the initial information. Where do you go next? You come up with a main conflict. (For the purposes of this chapter I will be using the terms "conflict" and "contrast" interchangeably.) A *conflict* is an opposition between forces that creates tension and drives action. It is probably the single most essential element in fiction storytelling. Robert McKee, in his seminal book quite appropriately titled *Story,* calls conflict "the controlling idea." The action in the story stems from this core conflict. As humans, we need to see a struggle happening; a struggle without an easily predictable outcome (see Figure 3-1).

▶ Let me repeat this; it is very important. A conflict is the only thing that makes your story interesting. No conflict, no story.

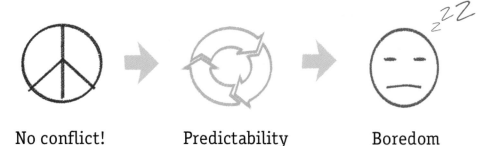

No conflict!   Predictability   Boredom

FIGURE 3-1: In storytelling, absence of conflict leads to boredom.

I don't think that in any form of storytelling you can get away without creating conflict.

I am asked all the time, "But why can't I just present the facts?" Well, you can. But as you learned in the previous chapters, humans are dramatically bad at digesting "just facts." Such a presentation will likely be tedious, difficult to follow, and ultimately ineffective. On very few occasions you can "just present the facts", but only when those facts are damn good. They should be mind-blowing. They should contradict other established facts. They should dispel myths. They must create conflict by themselves.

NOTE Again, if you allow me one more snippet of USSR nostalgia, all the low-level Communist Party meetings were famous for their extraordinary weariness because nobody was allowed to contradict "the party line." In the 1930s they used to shoot the people who contradicted the party line, and this message stuck. No discussions were allowed; there was just one right way to talk. The end result was a complete loss of grassroots initiative, an extreme formality of the proceedings, cynicism, and declining morale. It is true that people crave stability and certainty—but once those are achieved they start dying from boredom.

It is not an impossible task. If you want to see a purely fact-based presentation, go online and search for a YouTube video called "Did You Know?" or go to SlideShare for a non-animated version. This is one of the most popular presentations on the Web. It was originally prepared in August 2006 for a faculty meeting at Arapahoe High School in Centennial, Colorado. After being posted online, it "went viral" and a year later it had been viewed by at least 5 million online viewers. Today the different versions of this presentation have been viewed by at least 20 million people.

The first two sentences in the presentation are "If you're one in a million in China, there are 1,300 people just like you. China will soon become the number one English speaking country in the world." There's the conflict, right from the beginning. Most people might assume that the United States is the number one English-speaking country in the world. And they would be right, depending on their definition of "English-speaking." At the moment, it is either the United States or India, but certainly not China. This fact is in contradiction with most fundamental things we think we know—so it grabs our attention.

The next phrase is "The 25 percent of India's population with the highest IQ is greater than the total population of the United States. Translation: India has more honors kids than America has kids." Again, you see a conflict right there: India challenges the United States intellectually. Of course, it's not enough just to put India and the United States together on the same slide, the answer to the questions "So what? What's the problem? How is that important?" should be obvious to your audience.

Even in genres where storytelling is typically of secondary importance, such as with pornography, the "scriptwriter" (and I use that term loosely) has to establish some sort of conflict to hold all the sex scenes together. In *Logjammin'*, a one-minute porn parody of the 1998 Cohen Brothers' cult classic *The Big Lebowski*, a porn actor enters the scene saying, "My dispatcher says there's something wrong with a cable." This is a classic conflict: character vs. machine.

In this sense, business presentations can be worse than porn. The presenters are telling just facts and only pleasant facts, facts that could be interpreted in their favor. They shy away from controversy, from the dark side. They don't tell the truth. For instance, when talking about their company's history they present it as a string of dramatic successes, without mentioning any difficulties or even motivations for the achievements.

▶ In the heart of every motivation there's always a conflict!

This "success-only" history, number one, is very hard to believe and, secondly, comes dangerously close to a bad history lesson where all the drama is removed and the subject is reduced to memorizing dates. This is no way to go, yet we are still doing it. Why?

Bringing in conflict and controversy polarizes the audience. It produces love or hate relationships. This is risky, so we tend to settle for "just okay," which seldom results in anything interesting. The only way to get people on your side is to have a side, a position. And for every position there's an opposition. I believe that most conflicts could and should be solved with human creativity. I also believe that there's no way to solve the conflict without first uncovering it and bringing it to light. This is phase one; it's hard, but it's doable.

Establishing Conflict in Your Presentation

How do you establish conflict in a presentation? The easiest way is, of course, to take a value that is in a direct opposition to the value you'd like to promote and then illustrate it with concrete examples. Steve Jobs, whose values include "ease of use" and "beauty," contrasts his products with the competition, which he claims are visibly "hard to use," and "ugly." Figure 3-2 shows what a typical Jobs' slide might look like.

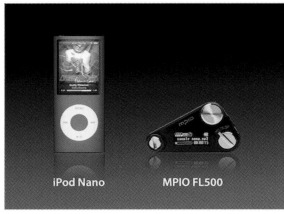

FIGURE 3-2: A typical comparison slide.

▶ If you want to get into more advanced storytelling, I suggest you familiarize yourself with the "four-corner opposition" technique from John Truby's The Anatomy of Story or read Chapter 14, "The Principle of Antagonism" from Story by Robert McKee.

It's simple but it works—at least for presentations and at least for now. It might not work in more developed forms of storytelling since this rule has become predictable, but as far as presentations are concerned, I think it's still okay.

But for most part, you don't even have to *create* conflict. The beauty of the genre is that conflict is already there, you just need to settle on it the way you settled on your goal. Ask yourself: What is the problem that I solved or intend to solve?

Initially, there has to be a problem (the conflict), which was the motivation for you to do the job. If you didn't solve a problem and there's no call to solve a problem, you aren't ready to be in front of an audience. If there was no problem, you have no solution, so you've got nothing to present! It's as simple as that. Recall the list of great presentations from Chapter 2; you can easily see a conflict in each one.

- Steve Jobs, *1984*
  - **Context:** Personal computing
  - **Conflict:** IBM PC versus Mac
  - **Problem:** "It appears that IBM wants it all"; where IBM is portrayed as a soulless corporation challenged by rebellious individuals

- Dick Hardt, *Identity 2.0*
  - **Context:** Identification over Internet
  - **Conflict:** Identity 2.0 versus Identity 1.0
  - **Problem:** "You can't see the person; you can't hear the person; in fact it may not even be a person"

- Guy Kawasaki, *The Art of Start*
  - **Context:** Entrepreneurship and startups
  - **Conflict:** Right way versus wrong way to start a business
  - **Problem:** "I made a lot of mistakes in my career" (and you might make them too)

- Dr. Martin Luther King, Jr., *I Have a Dream*
  - **Context:** Life of black Americans
  - **Conflict:** Dream versus Reality
  - **Problem:** "Black Americans are sadly crippled by the manacles of segregation"

- Laurence Lessig, *Free Culture*
  - **Context:** Copyright law
  - **Conflict:** Copyright versus Freedom
  - **Problem:** "Ours is a less and less free society"

Try creating a list like this for your own presentation. What is the problem? What is the conflict? What's at stake?

Four Types of Problems

You can find many different classifications of problems elsewhere in literature about storytelling; I came up with my own list based on my experiences. Here they are:

▶ **A moral or psychological problem.** This kind of problem is notoriously difficult to present. It's hard to observe an inner struggle from the outside. Besides, chances are that nobody cares about your inner problems. What you need is to show an outer problem and then demonstrate how solving the inner problem leads to solving the outer problem. Disclosing the inner problem is a very good—Guy Kawasaki in his speech does that brilliantly by admitting that he was a "bozo" himself—it's a great icing on a cake, but you can't serve the icing. You need a cake. I will cover this subject in more detail later.

▶ **A conflict with another person or company.** This is better. In a 2008 MacBook Air presentation, Steve Jobs started by saying that Apple took a Sony TZ series notebook as an industry standard and tried to improve on it. He then compares his product to the competition, winning almost every time. I have to admit it wasn't exactly fair because designers of TZ series obviously had different goals in mind, but it worked nevertheless. However, if your product is unprecedented, you have to take the closest precedent there is for comparison.

Now I know from my own experience that mentioning your competitors is psychologically very hard to do (it is also very hard to sell to your clients). It is more acceptable in the United States, but it is considered slightly unethical in Europe. Badmouthing competition is not a great idea and the line is thin. A lot of countries explicitly prohibit such comparisons in advertising.

> **NOTE** Again: the beauty of the genre. There are very few legal restrictions on presentations. Unless your speech will be broadcast live on national television, the risks of getting sued are minimal. Please note, however, that I'm not a qualified lawyer; this is not legal advice and "minimal" doesn't mean "nonexistent."

It takes time to learn how to critique competitors in this way. Apple has great experience in this sphere, but others are catching up. I was amazed to see Nokia's executives Anssi Vanjoki and Niklas Savander presenting at Nokia World 2010 and comparing the Nokia experience with the ones from Apple and Google.

Mentioning your competition is great. Most importantly, it shows that you are not afraid of comparisons. You might be thinking that your company doesn't have competitors because you are following a "Blue Ocean" strategy; you've found yourself a nice little niche. But if you want to explain what your niche is, you have to compare yourself to the others.

If you don't want to call them the competition, don't. Competing is not important but comparing is.

▶ **A conflict with a dominant paradigm, the status quo.** This, perhaps, is the best strategy. The easiest way to mention your competition without going into direct attacks is to bring out as many competitors as possible—or put yourself against a competitor that is bigger than you. It should be so big that any frontal attack seems suicidal. This way, you are opposing the status quo and presenting yourself as the underdog. You are telling a variation of a David and Goliath story, where the audience's sympathy is inevitably on David's side.

For example, take a closer look at Steve Jobs' 2005 keynote at MacWorld, or, more specifically, at his presentation of the iPod Shuffle—Apple's low-end MP3 player. Although it proved to be very successful (a market researcher NPD Group estimated that the Shuffle captured 43 percent of the Flash-based player market after only its second month of existence), I have to admit that I was initially very skeptical of this product. A screenless MP3 player? How the heck do I find my songs? After I saw the presentation I was totally convinced that it was a great product that I personally didn't need. I didn't buy one myself, but I did convince a number of my friends to buy one. So, how did Jobs do that? He kicked off with a short review of the market (of which Apple had exactly 0 percent) and then got to the problem:

So, we've taken a look at this market and it's a zoo! It's a zillion little Flash players and the market is incredibly fragmented; nobody has much market share, nobody's investing in marketing and growing the market. The products are all pretty much the same.

He then went on to describe some very specific aspects of the competitor's products he hates: tiny little screens, "tortured" user interfaces, and expensive AAA batteries.

NOTE And this is a lesson! You cannot fight an abstract status quo; it has to be represented by someone in particular. If you can name them, that's great. Otherwise you're stuck with abstract competition, like in advertising when a brand like Tide compares itself to those "ordinary washing agents." Admittedly, this is a very bad cliché, but if you play with it in a humorous way, it might work.

This is not the only presentation where Jobs takes this approach. As a matter of fact, he does this almost every time. In his 2007 iPhone presentation, he compares his product with Blackberry, Palm, and Motorola products; in his iconic 2001 iPod presentation he showed logos of Creative, Sonic Blue, and Sony just to say, "They haven't had a hit yet."

Whenever possible, Jobs brings with him on stage many competitors (usually sticking to no more than four at a time). His message—"this is the way the industry thinks right now and we are going to change it"—still works. This message works especially well when your company's slogan is "Think Different," which, in case you don't know, is itself a pun on IBM's motto "Think."

▶ **A conflict with "forces"—like nature, economy, trends, or even fate, the so-called "objective challenges."** How do we fit this processor into that case? How do we move a building? How do we fight obesity and/or starvation? The challenge with working with this sort of problem is that you need to evoke compassion for both sides. It's not just "Wow, great, Apple!", but it also should be "Oh, poor Sony" (or vice versa, depending on your personal preferences). If you think of any successful movie in which characters are pitted against forces of nature, such as *Titanic* or *Jaws*, there's always a conflict among human characters as well, which is what the film is actually about. Films in which most of the conflict is with the forces of nature and not between the characters don't get screen-writing nominations or become box-office hits.

It's the same with presentations. If you want to fight obesity, your best bet is to illustrate your point with a story of a guy who made it rather than the guy who didn't. Al Gore in his *An Inconvenient Truth* is not fighting global warming so much as he is fighting CO_2-emitting industrialists and climate change skeptics. On the level of values, it's the battle of the future versus the past. The last phrase of Gore's film is this: "Future generations may well have occasion to ask themselves, 'What were our parents thinking? Why didn't they wake up when they had a chance?' We have to hear that question from them, now." He is making it personal.

Objective challenges are difficult. They create a nice context—people suddenly have things worth fighting for—but the drama still happens between people. Consider Apple again: the "objective challenge" was to build a lightweight notebook. But look at the difference in approaches! This part is the one that holds audience's attention.

The last thing I want to say in this section is that the problem should be severe enough to worry about. The answer to the question "What happens if we don't solve this problem?" should be frightening enough. What if they don't build the lightweight notebook computer? Well, you have to continue carrying your six-pound monster on your back till the day you die! As a Russian scriptwriter Arif Aliev likes to say: "Your hero should have a problem that it is impossible to live with!"

So, again, what's the core problem and conflict of your presentation? Write it down.

Keeping the Tension

Let me admit one thing: having a problem in the beginning of your presentation is easy. It really is. Lot's of people do it. The thing is that most of them do it badly. They approach the task very formally. They announce the problem and then they solve it almost immediately. The tension disappears and the story ends, and then they proceed to tell the facts they think they need to tell. What a disappointment.

This is not unique to presentations. Movies (or rather movie-goers) suffer from it as well; it is called "the second-act syndrome." In a classic three-act structure, you introduce your heroes and establish conflict in Act 1, resolve the conflict in Act 3, and Act 2 is something in between. Even today, when lots of film and TV scriptwriters don't really use the three-act structure, the name for the problem, "the second-act syndrome," still holds.

So how does this manifest itself? Common manifestations of the second-act syndrome on the audience's side are:

- ▶ Glances at the clock or one's wristwatch
- ▶ Checking e-mail or Twitter on a mobile device
- ▶ Reading handouts (better) or unrelated printouts (worse)

On the presenter's side, it's:

- ▶ Increased monotony of voice and/or faster speech in the attempt to get to the end sooner
- ▶ Increased use of questions like "Where was I?" with an honest answer to that question being, of course, "nowhere."

The cure for this syndrome is to keep the problem unresolved until the very end; doing so will maintain an emotional rhythm like the one illustrated on Figure 3-3.

It doesn't mean that you should necessarily withhold information and keep the audience in the dark. But there always should be at least one important question hanging unanswered. For example, your presentation starts with a description of an urgent and serious problem in your department. Instantly, the question arises: did you solve the problem? If you hold an answer for 20 minutes, especially during a boardroom meeting, your audience might kill you. You need to say: "Don't worry, the problem has been solved". Next, you answer the questions: "But how did we do this? At what expense?" You have to keep asking the questions that lead the audience toward your ultimate goal.

The idea here is to make your presentation as close to a conversation as possible. This is the way to hold interest. Let's face it: Presentations are often cheap, wholesale alternatives to talking to each individual separately. But it's still a talk! Talking involves discussing points, asking questions, and establishing propositions. It's a dialogue, a conversation—not a one-way

▶ Make your presentation as close to a conversation as possible.

broadcast! You need to emulate discussion in your presentations whenever possible. One way to do so is to predict the questions that the audience is going to ask anyway—and ask them yourself. An even better way is to ask important questions the audience might not have considered. You need to split your major problem, the main conflict of your story, into several separate questions in such a way that the answers, when combined, create the bridge between the goal and the initial problem.

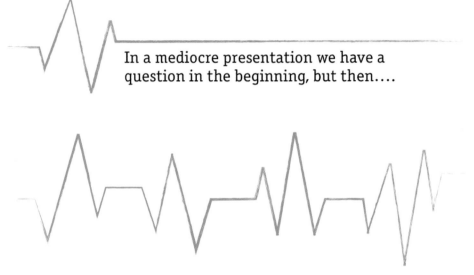

In a mediocre presentation we have a question in the beginning, but then....

Good presentation has an emotional rhythm like one of a heartbeat, a conversation.

FIGURE 3-3: Presentation's emotional rhythm.

How many questions should there be? If your presentation is a short two-minute elevator speech, one question is probably enough. There is no upper limit; I know people who even recommend using questions for slide headers instead of propositions. This way they have at least as many questions as they have slides. What really matters is that your presentation is memorable. For example, Guy Kawasaki's "The Art of Start" has 10 parts and each of those parts has a little "what's the problem" section. I'm pretty sure Guy knows that nobody is going to remember all 10 ideas. But he doesn't care. He is okay with the audience remembering three or four messages that are most personally appealing to them.

Steve Jobs traditionally has three parts in his "second act." If you consider his 2001 iPod presentation again, first he says that "nobody has a hit yet" (a big problem), then he makes a promise that the Apple brand is going to be fantastic in the area of digital music, and then he gives the audience the main tagline which is also his main objective challenge: "A thousand songs, your whole music library in your pocket." Then he proceeds to tell about three major breakthroughs:

- ▶ **Ultra-portable**. Problem: "How do we hold a thousand songs in your pocket?"

- ▶ **Apple's legendary ease of use**. Problem: "If any of you have ever used a portable music device or any portable digital device, a camera, or even a VCR, you know that consumer electronic devices are not known for their ease of use, right?"

- ▶ **Auto-sync**. Problem: "What happens when you add some new music to iTunes, you re-arrange your playlist, add new playlists, and so on?"

He then concludes that there is no other company that can put all those three things together, thus wrapping up his talk. He adds the price tag and shipping info (the call for action) and his trademark "the coolest gift" slide: "don't buy it for yourself, but for your loved ones" (the values thing). Those three questions hold the entire show together. Jobs even allows himself occasional departures from the main topic (after part two, he has a mini-presentation of iTunes' next version) and still gets back on track. So keep asking questions.

Now, consider this problem: I want to lead the audience from my central question to my presentation's goal. What questions will they need answers to in order to make this transition?

Select what seem to be the most important questions and then group everything else under those questions. You should have three logical levels of questions: the core question, several important questions, and everything else.

▶ Although questions are very indicative, you don't necessarily need to phrase problems as questions. Phrase them however you like. However, they have to put the audience in a "question-answering mode." This is when the audience is receptive and open.

Explaining the Solution

When you get to the lowest level of your presentation—the actual words, the slides, the fabric of your speech—you still need conflict. Remember, people understand things only by comparison to other things. Without context, a background, facts have no meaning. Let's look at the 2001 iPod presentation one more time, or, more specifically, at the "Ultra portable" part. Here are the levels of conflict:

Level 1 Problem: Existing MP3 players are largely unusable; nobody has a hit yet.
Solution: Apple brand is going to be fantastic; we will put a thousand songs in your pocket.

Level 2 Problem: If we want to hold a thousand songs in your pocket, how do we do this?
Solution: We start with an ultra-thin hard drive.

Level 3 Problem: But how do we get a thousand songs on this hard drive?
Solution: We use Firewire.

Level 4 Problem: Why Firewire? **Solution:** Because it's fast.

Level 5 Problem: How fast is it exactly? **Solution:** You can download an entire CD in 5 to 10 seconds. Let's take a look how it compares to USB. Here, on the lowest possible level he has a 2x2 matrix comparing USB and Firewire, with the latter clearly winning.

From the top level to the bottom, there is conflict, contrast, problems, and solutions. Ideally, you don't present a single important fact or opinion without a counter fact, a counter opinion, a background, or a comparison.

What's the difference between comparisons that work and comparisons that don't? Bruce Ching of the Valparaiso University School of Law suggested three criteria: familiarity, emotional resonance, and freedom from unintended associations. I am expanding this list with one more item: avoid avoiding the obvious.

▶ **Familiarity:** This is where your knowledge of the audience comes in. You need to make sure that that you are comparing an unfamiliar thing (the one that you are presenting) with something the audience is familiar with. For instance, if you are saying that your MP3 player is smaller than a pack of gum, you have to make sure they think of the right pack of gum. If you are saying that it weighs about the same as four quarters, you have to make sure that they know how much weight four quarters feel like. Being from Russia, I don't carry quarters in my pocket regularly (not unless I am in the United States, anyway), so I don't really know what it means on the experiential level. The knowledge should be tangible, not abstract.

▶ *make the difference dramatic. Make it twice as big (or as small)! Not only is our notebook generally thinner than the competitor's, its thick side is thinner than the competitor's thin side! Dramatize, dramatize, dramatize!*

▶ **Emotional resonance:** If they know how it feels, the comparison will produce at least some emotional resonance. One way to improve here is to connect to highly emotional topics like love, death, birth, sex, celebrities, religion, or politics. I credit at least some success of my presentation "Death by PowerPoint" to the dramatic title.

▶ **Avoid avoiding the obvious:** Sometimes it is good to compare apples to oranges. For example, many independent consultants (like me) don't compare the price of their online course to the price of other online courses. Rather, they compare it to the price of their live seminar or private coaching rate. However, there's always a fine line. When Apple's Phil Schiller was comparing a number of applications available for different mobile platforms, he listed Palm, Blackberry, Nokia, Android, and iPhone, but somehow failed to include Microsoft Windows. This is cheating.

▶ **Unintended associations:** This is another pitfall to be wary of; your comparisons may yield unintended associations in the minds of your audience. For example, bringing in sex or death will *always* produce unintended associations. There's no way to completely avoid it. You will likely upset somebody. Still, playing safe isn't what the presentations are about. Risk pays out. Just keep in mind that risky isn't the same as reckless. Try to be cognizant of the associations you might be stirring up in your audience.

Let me give you one final example here. On March 23, 1775, Patrick Henry, a Virginia politician and one of the founding fathers, gave one of the most famous speeches in the history of speeches. It is called "Give me Liberty or Give Me Death." The speech called for mobilization against the British and resulted in Virginia joining the War for Independence. This speech is really well-known and has been analyzed extensively, but it's worth looking at again.

The speech has a very strong beginning:

> *The question before the House is one of awful moment to this country. For my own part, I consider it as nothing less than a question of freedom or slavery; and in proportion to the magnitude of the subject ought to be the freedom of the debate. It is only in this way that we can hope to arrive at truth, and fulfill the great responsibility which we hold to God and our country.*

Right there, he brings in big things: freedom, slavery, truth, God. The ending is equally strong:

> *Is life so dear, or peace so sweet, as to be purchased at the price of chains and slavery? Forbid it, Almighty God! I know not what course others may take; but as for me, give me liberty or give me death!*

It's God and death and slavery again. You might think that your topic is not so hot and not worth such a fuss. But judging by the speech's beginning, there were a lot of folks at the Virginia Convention that day who didn't think this whole "revolution" thing was worth the fuss either. "Well, we have lived under the British for quite some time. Sure it's not ideal, but this is life!" I imagine some of them were thinking.

In the middle he poses some very difficult questions and makes great comparisons:

> *They tell us, sir, that we are weak; unable to cope with so formidable an adversary. But when shall we be stronger? Will it be the next week, or the next year? . . . Sir, we are not weak if we make a proper use of those means which the God of nature hath placed in our power.*

Again, he contrasts the present state with a hypothetical future state. He brings in God. Sure, he polarizes the audience. But he gets the job done, and this is what I wish most dearly for you and me.

HERO AND VILLAIN

One day in the early 1930s in England, a university professor was correcting some School Certificate papers. The task was a boring one. He got distracted, picked up a blank piece of paper, and scribbled the following sentence: "In a hole in the ground there lived a [hero]." The original sentence, of course, named the hero explicitly but for those of you who don't recognize the sentence, I will conceal the hero's identity for now.

▶ *Take note: There are 74 sentences in the speech and 22 of them, almost a third of the speech, end with question marks. About one third of the speech is questions. What percentage of your speech is made up of questions? 10 percent? 5 percent?*

In a couple of years the sentence was developed into a book, which was published by George Allen & Unwin, Ltd. of London in 1937. The critical acclaim was almost unanimous; the book was nominated for the Carnegie Medal and awarded a prize from the *New York Herald Tribune*. The publishers demanded a sequel, which took some years to complete, but eventually was published in 1954. It became one of the best-selling books of the 20th century and made it to first place in the BBC's Top 100 books. The screen adaptation became one of the most financially successful movie projects in history (currently the fifth highest-grossing series of all times) and won 17 out of the 30 Academy Awards it was nominated for. The missing word from that opening line, of course, is *hobbit*. It all started with a hero.

> NOTE There's a slight problem with the word *hero*; some people think it's too male-centered and that the image of the hero is one of a warrior. Let me assure you that this is not my vision, for me Juliette is as much of a hero as Romeo.

Believe it or not, I was once a hero of a somewhat similar story, although it lasted for only three days and never resulted in any Oscars. But I did a good presentation. My client was a facilities management company. I was creating a presentation that they needed to send along with their bidding application. The idea was to differentiate them from other companies, which provided rather unimaginative PowerPoint slides almost leaking with text. As usual, I gathered basic information, established the goal and the conflict, but was in doubt about the form. No, that's not true; I wasn't in doubt. I was clueless. My imagination decided to take a break this day; I was helplessly, desperately stuck.

I was browsing a photo stock website hoping to find a metaphor or inspirational idea, and then I saw my guy (see Figure 3-4).

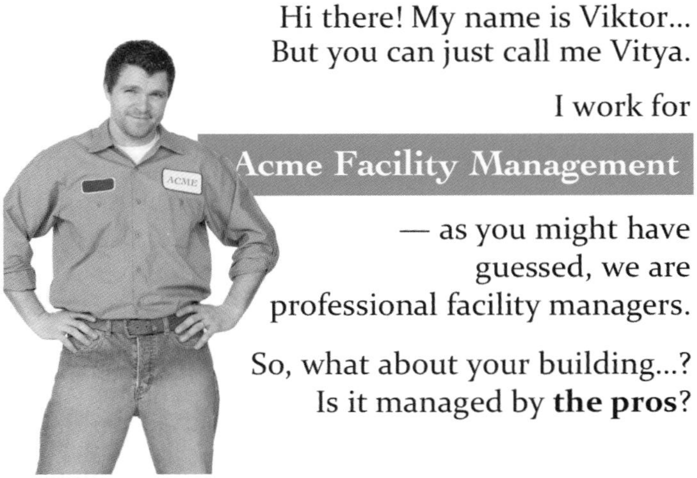

Hi there! My name is Viktor...
But you can just call me Vitya.

I work for

Acme Facility Management

— as you might have guessed, we are professional facility managers.

So, what about your building...?
Is it managed by **the pros**?

FIGURE 3-4: The main hero introducing himself.

This image just made the whole presentation for me. It just clicked, like a puzzle coming together. He became the host, the presenter, talking to the audience from the screen and telling them about various challenges and solutions. Most of the text he "spoke" came from word-by-word citations from the managers I interviewed. I also found other characters that complemented and contrasted with him (see Figure 3-5). In the end, it worked great.

Now let me warn you in advance: creating a hero for your presentation is not a trivial task. It could be quite difficult; it requires a lot of conscious effort. Personally, I don't do it unless the presentation is really, really important—or as a last resort. On the bright side it is really, I mean really, helpful. Some people even go as far as saying that "the hero is the story." I don't find it quite that way exactly; there are a lot of other story components that need to be done for the hero to really work, most notably, the villain. There is always need for a contrast and a pretty strong one. The general rule of drama is that the easier it is for the hero to overcome the villain and his own weaknesses, the less value there is in the drama. In the beginning, the villain has to be stronger and the hero's problems should seem overwhelming. If your hero is Superman, your enemy should be somebody like Lex Luthor.

▶ It would have worked even better if we had used actual employees. As usual, there wasn't any time. But it's something to keep in mind.

The main character

Other characters

FIGURE 3-5: The hero and other contrasting characters.

As you may have guessed by now, having a hero/character is most useful when you aren't presenting in person. Hero-based presentations work great over e-mail or via the Web, but they can be fairly useless when it comes to an actual meeting; there isn't much you can add to them with your voice. In this part I will analyze different strategies for using heroes and villains in your presentations. Basically, there are just three ways to use heroes and villains:

- ▶ Telling the client's story
- ▶ Telling your company's story
- ▶ Telling your personal story

Telling the Client's Story

Client-centric stories are very much like customer testimonials. They tell a story of a person who had a problem that was solved thanks to your solution. If you have a real person with a real name and address, great. Stress that. If not, no problem. Just tell what seems to you like a typical story. The pitfall to avoid here is that the fewer details you give about heroes, the more abstract they become. You know the problem with abstractions—they are hard to empathize with. You need to give your imagined heroes some very real traits, to "flesh them out," as some scriptwriters say.

The presentation most famous for taking advantage of this method is called "Meet Henry" by Scott Schwertly of Ethos3. It became extremely popular and produced a vast array of imitations and, as some of those imitations claim, started a whole new genre. It goes like this: on the very first slide we are introduced to a hero—Henry, a likable young man who lives in Vancouver, likes coffee, cheers for the Canucks, has an MBA, but sucks at public speaking. Why? Because of PowerPoint, his slides look awful. Ahh, poor Henry. Next, we are introduced to Erica (see Figure 3-6), who is described almost exactly like Henry except that she's female and, apparently, rocks at public speaking. Why? Well, thanks to the communications agency she understands content, design, and delivery. *Join Erica in the presentation revolution.*

Now, consider: Who is Henry in real life? He is, of course, your prospective client. Who is Erica? Erica is your existing client. She is also Henry's doppelganger, a double, whose sole purpose is to contrast Henry. She is the ideal Henry. She is what Sherlock Holmes is to Professor Moriarty: the same person with only one difference—he is better. But neither Erica nor Henry is evil, right? Then who's the arch villain, I hear you asking? It is, of course, PowerPoint.

The setup is really simple. You have a hero who is very nice, but has one serious personal drawback, the drawback that ultimately leads to problems in his career. He has a need and he might even not be aware of it. But you are. And you show him how to solve his problem with your solution. Genius.

FIGURE 3-6: Henry and Erica.

Sometimes people are afraid to give serious flaws to their heroes because they think that the audience will be reluctant to associate themselves with such a hero. "Oh no," they say, "clients will never recognize themselves in this person." Try it. It works. After all, you are not going for a full frontal attack. You are not saying directly to your prospective clients, "You suck at Power-Point (or whatever you are selling)!" The beauty of having a client-hero with a drawback is in its gentleness and indirectness.

> NOTE However, believe it or not, the second prize in SlideShare's 2010 annual presenta-
> tion contest went to a presentation titled "You Suck at PowerPoint!" Yes, it is blunt, but it
> works, too!

Let me give you even more stunning example from the world of advertising: the 2009 Coca-Cola's Super Bowl Sunday ad, a cartoon produced by *The Simpsons'* team. It starts off with the main character, Mr. Burns. Now, if you don't watch *The Simpsons,* let me tell you that there is no worse character than Mr. Burns. In a way, he is the best character because he is the most flexible one. He can do anything! No moral barriers whatsoever. But in this episode, he has some bad luck. Mr. Burns is broke; the financial crisis got him. We see shares of his company plummet, his property auctioned, and even his house removed by giant helicopters. He is now homeless. He walks to the nearby park and sees lots of people playing, conversing, and just walking around being ridiculously happy. Finally, one of them takes pity and offers him a bottle of Coke. At this point, Mr. Burns becomes ridiculously happy himself. "Coca-Cola: Open Happiness."

Now, why did The Coca-Cola Company choose to associate with the most unsympathetic character in the series? Because he became better in the end and contrast is the only thing that matters. Let's look at the setup: we have a hero who has a drawback (he is evil), a need (he is unhappy), and a problem (he is broke). Please notice that his problem is not even remotely related to the need and the drawback. He was rich before and we have no doubt that he will become rich again very soon (because this is who he is). But he must have some sort of the outer problem; otherwise, there's no motivation for change. By the end of this 30-second episode he becomes happier and more human and he acquires a new friend. (Recall the discussion of values and presentations in Chapter 2.)

I once created a presentation for an agency that was recruiting people for drug trials. (I am under the NDA here and I can't disclose too much detail.) I introduced a hero, a sympathetic old gentleman suffering from multiple sclerosis. MS is a quite severe condition without any known cure, but some companies are currently experimenting with different drugs. One day he went online to learn more about his condition and saw a Google ad. We walked him through all the perils of the drug trial recruitment process, of which there are many, we put him on some drugs, and in the end he was sitting with his wife on his couch and smiling. He was alive and maybe not completely well (he still has MS), but obviously better off.

Can you tell a story of your customer in that way? It's not too difficult, it's entertaining, and it works. Try it.

> *Remember that your audience shouldn't get what they want; they should get what they need. At the very least, they should get what they want but not the way they expect to get it. Otherwise, your story becomes trivial and predictable.*

Telling the Company's Story

In 1981, the Scandinavian Airlines company (SAS) was in turmoil. The management team lead by newly appointed CEO Jan Carlzon was preparing to implement many organizational changes. As a part of the effort, they produced a 25-page booklet called "Let's Get in There and Fight," soon nicknamed "the little red book" for its distinctive red cover. The booklet was distributed to all 20,000 employees of the company. Its goal was to present the management's overall strategy and, more importantly, their expectations of the employees. But it wasn't a typical 20th century corporate brochure, with lots of badly written texts and meaningless data. In fact, it was an ideal 21st century presentation.

There were very few words on each page and it was filled with cartoon-like drawings of airplanes. There was the main hero, a sympathetic and even sweet airplane guy who represented SAS. He was smiling at first, frowning as he was passing through difficulties, and even covering his eyes with his wings when he went into a nosedive. There were other airplanes representing

SAS's competitors, such as Delta and Lufthansa. The Delta guy was a tough-looking airplane wearing a cowboy hat and smoking a big cigar, whereas Lufthansa had clock dials where his eyes should have been obviously representing his fanatical punctuality (which the main hero sadly lacked). But in the end, the SAS guy prevailed. On the last slide there were two pair of hands supporting each other contrasted with another pair pointing at each other and the message was: "The customer doesn't care whose fault it is; we've got to work together!"

As Carlzon himself later recalled, "Many people thought the little red book was far too simplistic for SAS's many intellectual and highly educated employees. . . . [But] simplistic or not, the little red book was an effective communications tool internally."

This is one possible way to tell a story about a company. If you are presenting live, you probably don't need to draw a character but can get away with a collective "we," "We thought," "we did," and so on. Essentially it's the same as "me" but much more humble (but also less personal). Steve Jobs does it all the time; the main hero of his presentations is, of course, his team, Apple. But of course, this is just a variation of the presentation.

So, you start with a hero who has many good features. And you put him or her against a great problem, a challenge. You introduce other worthy characters competing for the same goal. You can also give the hero some defect, some inner psychological problem, a weakness that he or she should be solving throughout the presentation. Don't focus on it too much: it's very hard to observe the inner struggle. But remember to get back to it in the end; this is your "values" part. This is what the hero really gets. Your hero may or may not solve the problem you've started with; maybe he or she will end up solving some entirely different problem. What's important is that the hero is successful and changed.

Again, you don't need to invent anything. Stories mimic life; this is how life actually works. All you need is to remove excessive information and do some rearranging.

Telling Your Own Story

Now to the most interesting type of hero-based story: a story about you, about your experience. There's an important principle in scriptwriting that says "always pick your best hero, a hero you are most passionate about." It is very likely that the hero you are most passionate about is based on you. You can always tell when a speaker is talking about his personal experience and not about some abstract conceptions or facts.

This is not news; this concept was introduced by Demosthenes, a famous Greek orator of the 4th century B.C. What troubles me is why after all those centuries people still prefer to talk about something other than themselves? Why do they prefer to hide behind objective data, such as quotes from other people or somebody else's stories poorly retold?

▶ Make it about the values, not about the facts. The facts are just illustrations for what you are trying to say on a deeper level. Don't skip the facts either, but always put them into context, compare them to something else.

▶ By the way, if you aren't passionate about your company, don't try to tell a story about it. Your insincerity will be evident and will only make things worse.

If you look again at the great presentations, most of them are highly personalized:

Steve Jobs: He is probably the greatest egomaniac around. His computer calls him "my father"!

Dick Hardt: Whose identity do you think he takes as the prime example? "This is what I like to wear, this is what I like to drive; this is my identity."

Guy Kawasaki: The whole presentation is about his experience as an entrepreneur and venture capitalist.

Dr. Martin Luther King, Jr.: "I have a dream." Not "my clients have a dream," not even "black America has a dream." I. Have. A. Dream. He shares his personal vision.

I think the main reason people are afraid to make it personal is because for every position there's an opposition. They shy away from telling what they think because they are afraid to be personally criticized. The workaround is to accommodate criticism as a part of your presentation; it will only make it better. The next problem is that you probably don't know what they are going to criticize you for. Well, there's one way to find out.

Secondly, people are afraid that nobody's interested in them unless they are somebody famous, which is true. No, really, I think it is true. Why do I have to listen to you? And I think the only feasible answer to this question is this: I am a storyteller. I am an artist. I am the one who puts a lot of energy and effort in crafting the stories; I made it so it's a present for you, my audience. People seldom refuse presents. It is considered impolite. They also feel obligated afterward: reciprocity at work.

The third problem is that there's actually very little you can tell about yourself. Your experience is limited; how many truly different stories you can tell? The good news is that your compassion increases your ability to tell stories about other people. For example, when telling a story of a person suffering from MS, I tried to "put myself in his shoes," imagining how it was to have a life-threatening disease and be participating in a drug trial.

▶ *If possible, go for first-hand experiences; they are priceless.*

One of my clients, a marketing manager of a major telecommunications company, told me once how their department suspended their employer-paid cell phone accounts and opened accounts like regular customers. Within a couple of days they had dozens of suggestions on how to improve client service. For example, while trying to pay for the cell phone from their own bank accounts (something they never did before), they realized that the minimum payment was too high. So they lowered it. It was easy to convince the management to do it because they spoke from their experiences and were persuasive. The increase in number of payments was dramatic and now more than 40 percent of the payments the company receives via bank transfers are below the former limit.

Presenting Your Strengths and Weaknesses

The biggest problem of "me" presentations is lack of humility. I think there are probably many people who don't speak from their own experiences (or do it poorly) not because they are afraid, but because they simply think that this is a bad thing to do. Nancy Duarte, the principle of Duarte Design and the author of a best-selling book on presentations called *Resonate,* is 100 percent right in saying, "Audience detests arrogance and self-centeredness."

The problem with me presentations is when people talk only about their strengths. Here's the secret: you are not your own hero. You just happen to have the same name. That doesn't make him (or her) you. Your hero is your brand. Your hero is your *persona*, just one of your many faces, one of the versions of a mask that you're wearing while you're on stage. The word "mask" is a bit discomforting, I know. But still, it's a mask. It's just an image of you with similar features. If you don't construct it yourself, the audience will gladly do it for you, and I don't think you should trust them with this. This is your job. After all, this is your mask.

▶ Your hero is your story, but you are not your story. You are a storyteller. Do you get the difference?

You are the author, not the actor. This is very important. This stance allows you to manipulate your hero in a way that suits you. Again, you don't need to lie or invent anything. Be as transparent and as honest as you can. I think it's a very noble task to attempt to get your mask as close to "real you" as possible. I don't know why but by default it becomes really skewed. Fixing this mask is probably my premier interest in this life. Still—it is a mask.

What's even more important is that this stance allows you to have clear-cut opinions on your issues. The real Arnold Schwarzenegger probably doesn't really have clear-cut opinions on anything—he is a live human being, he has doubts like the rest of us. But his mask, the Terminator (or the Governator) can. Do you get it? Your "real you" is just too complex for a presentation, whereas your hero, who is a simplified image of you, is perfectly fine. You don't even need to hide stuff; just keep in mind that the show time is limited, the clock is ticking, there's only that much you can show anyway, and you need to show your most important stuff. Now what are you going to show?

Remember that traditional Greek theater masks always come in pairs. There's a sad one and a happy one. Your hero can be both. Moreover, your hero *needs* to be both. This is how you solve the conflict problem as well as the humility problem. It can be painful, but the fact that it's just a mask somehow eases the pain.

One of the best presentations I ever attended personally was a speech by Marat Guelman, a Russian-Jewish contemporary art dealer and political consultant. He was speaking at one of the Russian TEDx conferences, an independently organized TEDx event.

> **NOTE**   TEDx is a franchise project of a popular American conference TED, which is perhaps the best conference in the world—at least as far as presentations are concerned. More that 850 presentations from this conference are freely available to watch online at **www.ted.com**, and by the standards of any other conference most of them are outstanding.
>
> Visit **http://www.ted.com/tedx** for more details about TEDx.

In 15 minutes he told seven stories about various people taking advantage of his ignorance and foolishness—all of which allowed him to become who he is. Here are things he told about himself:

I was easily fooled because if you're a son of a famous person it's extremely difficult to be a common engineer.

I couldn't go back because my ego would have never survived it.

When I was 45, I had a midlife crisis and didn't know what to do.

His was the best presentation I saw live. He was passionate, he was charming, he was candid and he was humble. He had a point, he was easy to follow, and he was interesting to listen to. It was an adventure story. There was a hero, there were villains, and by the end of the presentation the hero was victorious and was transformed. Was that "the real Marat Guelman"? Hardly. The real Marat Guelman is much more complex. Was he lying? I don't think so.

If that's not enough (and I know it's not), watch Al Gore's 2006 presentation at TED. Before getting to his main subject, which predictably was global warming, he spent several minutes talking about his experience as a loser in the presidential race. He presented himself as a loser in the beginning—only to come as a winner in the end.

Finally, have a look at the first entry of Google's corporate history (http://www.google.com/corporate/history.html):

> *1995: Larry Page and Sergey Brin meet at Stanford. According to some accounts, they disagree about most everything during this first meeting.*

We can only imagine what the word *disagree* means here. Did they fight? If you scroll farther down there's even more fun stuff. The first check was written to an entity that wasn't even registered; they started off in a garage (which by now has become acceptable and even hip)!

What this all means is that you don't have to present yourself or your company as an equivalent of Superman. It's not necessary, and most people are far more forgiving than you think. I hear you saying: "But hey, now when they are rich and famous, they can have this luxury." It doesn't matter. If you demonstrate growth, people will trust (believe) that you will grow more. And by growth I mean inner growth, not just acquiring fame and wealth. So, humility works. Change matters.

SUMMARY

The key points to remember from this chapter are as follows:

- ▶ **No conflict—no story.** If you want to evoke emotions, you need drama, and there's no drama without conflict. No conflict attracts as much attention as a conflict between actual people. It is even better if the challenge seems overwhelming at first. A greater challenge elicits more drama.

- ▶ **Keep the conflict alive.** Don't resolve your conflict prematurely, but if you do set up the next conflict right away. Ask yourself: "If I want to lead my audience from the problem to my goal, what questions do I need to answer for them?"

- ▶ **Keep comparing—even at the most basic, factual level.** Always put your facts, your data, in context; otherwise they have no meaning.

- ▶ **Heroes win.** Creating stories with heroes is a difficult yet very effective technique. Come up with a hero, and give him or her a problem to solve, and then introduce the solution step by step. If you want to make a great presentation, give your hero an inner moral or psychological problem, which he or she overcomes in the end. This inner problem should be related to the values you are ultimately promoting.

- ▶ **You are not your hero.** Your best hero will always be based on you, but it is not exactly you. You are the storyteller, not the actor. This position allows you to control the image that you project and leaves space for humility.

CHAPTER 4

The Story's Unity

IN THIS CHAPTER

► Finding the gestalt of your story
► Choosing how many parts to have
► Recognizing why balance is important
► Applying L.A.T.C.H. to presentations
► Considering some case studies

This chapter is concerned with arranging the information you have in a dramatic story. It covers what should be in the beginning, the middle, and the end; it covers the problem of balance between different parts of the story and ways to organize your middle part—which is the longest and thus the most difficult part to present. This chapter also examines the structure of some of the world's most famous presentations and covers what you can learn from them.

MAKING YOUR STORY UNIFIED

When talking about a story's unity, I mean the psychological satisfaction derived by both presenter and the audience from the completeness and internal consistency of the speech. A story is whole when all the important questions are answered, all the information is in its rightful place, and any implications of the story are clear. It's the gestalt effect in action. When answering the question of what makes a story whole, you actually need to get back to the question, "What's story?"

According to John Truby, the author of *The Anatomy of Story,* whom I referred to in Chapter 3:

> *All stories are a form of communication that expresses the dramatic code. The dramatic code, embedded deep in the human psyche, is an artistic description of how a person can grow or evolve.*

So what's a dramatic code? In short, dramatic code consists of a character with a desire. While pursuing his or her desire, the character encounters obstacles, and while trying to overcome the obstacles, he or she changes irreversibly. This is the one part of the equation which I pretty much covered in the previous chapter. It is known in Russian playwriting school as *fabula.*

Next, there's a second part known as *syuzhet;* it's the dramatic arc or dramatic structure, the emotional trajectory that the story follows. The closest plain English word to *syuzhet* is "plot" (although it is arguably very ambiguous by itself). So, what makes a good *syuzhet*? The best and the oldest answer to this question can be found in Aristotle's *Poetics* circa 335 BCE, "A whole is what has a beginning and middle and end," to which the 20th-century French film director Jean-Luc Godard famously replied, "A story should have a beginning, a middle, and an end . . . but not necessarily in that order."

Godard's comment notwithstanding, I suggest that you stick with the sequential order, at least for now, but having these three essential parts is something that I 100 percent agree with: the beginning, the middle, and the end. Most of the presentations I see (and I see a lot of them) have just one part: the beginning, or the middle, or the end. Now what do I mean by the beginning, the middle, and the end? What should be there?

Acts and Parts

Different parts of a play are called acts. There's a classic structure called the three-act structure. This is how Syd Field, author of *Screenplay* and *The Screen Writer's Workbook*, outlines contents of the acts:

1. **Exposition and inciting incident:** The characters are introduced and placed in a context. Something happens that upsets the balance of things.

2. **Rising action:** The character is working his (or her) way to resolve the problem, but that way is complicated by problems to the point where the character begins to look like he (or she) is going to snap.

3. **Climax:** The play reaches dramatic culmination and the conflict is resolved. The state of equilibrium returns but the situation is changed irreversibly, for better or worse.

This sequence seems to be universal; it has many similarities in other genres. For example, in a classical sonata the main musical theme is introduced in an *exposition*, contrasted in a *development,* and resolved in a *recapitulation*. So if you listen to Bach's fugues or violin concertos, you will find the same pattern there. Although many contemporary pieces of art deviate from this sequence (hence Godard's "not necessarily in this order"), as far as presentations are concerned this structure is underused rather than overused, so it's best to stay with it for now.

Now, what's an "act"? In theater, an act starts when the curtain goes up and ends when the curtain goes down. Presentations don't have a curtain. In classical Greek theater there was no curtain either; acts were divided up by a chorus coming onstage. The Romans had five acts. If you write for today's television format, there will be as many acts as there are commercial breaks. None of these has anything to do with a story itself, but are just different ways of breaking the story into parts.

I would argue that for the purposes of presentation, you have four parts in something I call the *classical structure*:

1. **Exposition:** This is where you lay out the groundwork, establish the context, and introduce yourself and your heroes.

2. **Problem:** Here you ask questions and introduce the conflicts, constraints, and challenges.

3. **Solution:** This is the largest part, which is typically divided into several sub-parts. In a strict sense, this is the actual presentation. Everything else is auxiliary.

4. **Conclusion:** Here you summarize, discuss the morals of the story, and ask your audience to do something.

The reason the first two parts, exposition and problem, are usually grouped together in Act I is because the exposition is usually quite short. Granted, in a Woody Allen script we may be well 15 minutes into the film before any problem occurs. But mostly scriptwriters want to get to the problem as quickly as possible; after all, this is where the action starts. If you consider a fairy tale as an example, the exposition might not even be a complete sentence:

> *One upon a time there was a prince who wanted to marry a princess; but she would have to be a real princess.*

This is the beginning of a classic Hans Christian Andersen fairy tale "The Princess and the Pea." In a single sentence we are introduced to the hero and we now know that he has a problem—not just any random princess will suit His Royal Highness, only a real one. This is the beginning. But short doesn't mean unimportant. Exposition is really important; it establishes an initial backdrop, a frame for everything you are going to say. So I suggest adopting a four-part approach instead of a three-part one.

Japanese film director Takeshi Kitano brilliantly illustrated these four parts in his 1970 screenplay. The script is really short; in fact it is so short that I can actually quote it here in its entirety. It's called "Samurai on a Toilet":

(>_<)

(o_o)

(0_0)

(^_^)

That's it. That's the film. It's 20 characters long. It may be a little off color, but it's great! Look, it has everything a movie—and a presentation for that matter—should have: a beginning, a middle, and an end. First, you have a hero: (>_<). Next comes the problem (o_o). He is Japanese; his eyes shouldn't be like this; they are way too big. He obviously has a problem. But our hero is persistent (0_0). He doesn't run away; he's bold; he's a samurai. Next, we see him smiling calmly again: (^_^). The peace is restored. What a solid film! I really suggest you adopt this structure for your presentations.

OTHER STORY STRUCTURES

There's also Gustav Freytag's five-piece structure from the 19th century, which consists of Exposition, Rising Action, Climax, Falling Action, and Denouement. There is also Joseph Campbell's *monomyth* or hero's journey, which consists of (wait for it) 17 different stages. Lajos Egri in *The Art of Dramatic Writing*, one of the most influential books on the subject, argues that we should avoid exposition and start straight with the conflict, and the Japanese Jo-ha-kyū structure puts emphasis on the speed of action: slow, speed up, rapid. These are all interesting points of view and I encourage you to read a book or two on scriptwriting. Although the topic might initially seem inapplicable to business presentations, I can assure you that such cross-pollinations frequently produce interesting results.

This structure is not the only one in existence. But I think especially for the beginners (and still I consider myself a beginner in art of storytelling) it serves as solid training wheels. When you master the art, you can go beyond this structure. In fact, you'll need to. After all, at a certain point, the words "classic" and "cliché" begin to mean the same thing. For now try and play with this classic structure. It works.

Emotional Arc

Suppose you have those four parts. Is that all? Hardly. You have to arrange them in a sequence to demonstrate your hero's transformation from one state of mind to another. This has to do with the goals of your presentation. How is it that you want to transform your audience? Do you want to move them from ignorance to knowledge? From inaction to action? From cynicism to participation? You are the speaker; it's your call.

If you succeed in establishing emotional rapport with your audience from the beginning, they will be going through all those emotional states—the journey that ultimately results in a change. Have a look at Figure 4-1; I am pretty sure you've seen somewhere. It's "the S-curve," one of the most widely recognized patterns of change. This is more or less how the story progresses in terms of emotions. You start out fine, then have a crisis (which is the motivations for change), then have a period of boom, and finally hit a plateau. Notice that the second plateau is slightly higher than the first one. If you need to take people from one level to another, this is exactly how you do it.

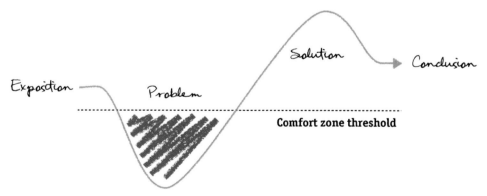

FIGURE 4-1: The S-curve applied to a story's emotional arc.

The dotted line represents the comfort zone threshold. Both you and the audience need to step outside this narrow line of your comfort zones for the change to happen. Outside of the comfort zone you talk about your mistakes and your pain and dissatisfaction with the present state of affairs. If your problem part is emotional enough and, again, if you have rapport with your audience, they will follow you. But it starts with you. It's like in comedy: one of the core principles is that you can't laugh at other people before you have laughed at yourself and gotten the audience on your side.

How emotional should the different parts of your presentation be? You can see my opinion on this matter in Figure 4-2. You start relatively cool, then you get excited about the problem, then you say (sometimes literally), "Don't panic, I have the solution"—that cools things off—and you end with crescendo again.

RELATIVE EMOTIONALITY

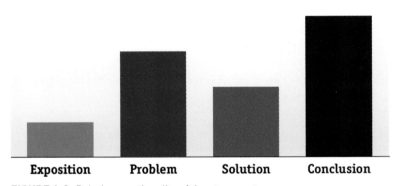

FIGURE 4-2: Relative emotionality of the story parts.

CASE STUDY: THE STORY OF TOMATO SAUCE

Let's analyze a presentation by Malcolm Gladwell, the *New Yorker* columnist and best-selling writer who is widely renowned both as a master storyteller and presenter. This is a speech he gave at a TED conference in 2004. I first saw it in 2006 and fell in love with it instantly. I watched it dozens of times and even reproduced it on a number of occasions (giving full credit to Mr. Gladwell) in order to understand how it feels to give a presentation like this. It influenced both my speaking style and my story design style profoundly. It's about 17 minutes long. So, without any further ado . . . Malcolm Gladwell.

Gladwell starts by talking about what he is going to talk about. He states that he thought of talking about his then-new book *Blink!* but since it had nothing to do with the overall theme of the event (which was happiness), he decided to change the subject and talk about his "great personal hero," a guy named Howard Moskowitz. (Time: About one minute.)

▶ You can easily find it online at www.ted.com/talks/malcolm_gladwell_on_spaghetti_sauce .html or http://goo.gl/kDB2r.

He then describes Moskowitz's appearance in great detail and explains that he is psychophysicist and that his job has to do with measuring people's perceptions of different foods. (Time: About one minute.)

Next, he gives his hero a problem. Or, rather, Pepsi, Inc. gives Moskowitz a problem: to find a perfect taste for Diet Pepsi. The hero failed; he was unable to come out with the perfect taste despite the seeming obviousness of the task. The data he collected from test drinks were a mess; they "were all over the place." (Time: Two minutes.)

However, after a period of deliberation, he finally figured it out. It turns out there's no such thing as one perfect Pepsi, there are several perfect Pepsis. This didn't make any sense to the audience, so Gladwell spends another five minutes telling the story of Moskowitz and Prego and a revolutionary extra chunky tomato sauce that was discovered while searching for the perfect tomato sauce. (Time: Five minutes.)

"Why is that important?" asks Gladwell. He then proceeds with revealing three implications of his story:

1. People don't know what they want, so it's bad idea to ask them. He illustrates with an example of "milky weak coffee" which virtually everyone is drinking but nobody would admit drinking. (Time: Three minutes.)

2. The discovery of horizontal segmentation: putting products not on a hierarchical scale, where there are superior products and inferior products but on horizontal plane, where there are just different products for different people. He illustrates this with a story of Grey Poupon, a mustard brand. (Time: Two minutes.)

3. Finally, he argues why pursuing universal principles in food is wrong, illustrated with research done by Moskowitz for Nescafé. (Time: Three more minutes.)

He concludes with a phrase, "In embracing the diversity of human beings, we will find a surer way to true happiness." Applause.

Have a look at Gladwell's timeline in Figure 4-3. This talk is somewhat unusual in a sense that his conclusion is very long. I can also tell you that this part was the most difficult for me to remember. I do not recommend making your conclusion that long; it is a sign of moralizing, but since Gladwell illustrates all his points with additional stories and examples, his talk goes together rather smoothly. All you need to remember is the sequence of the three points. A more typical presentation would have a much shorter conclusion part, which would be broken into three points, but as you can see, Gladwell's design is also a possibility. Watch your favorite presentation and try to break it down it this way. How many pieces does it have? What are they?

FIGURE 4-3: Timeline of Gladwell's speech.

THE PROBLEM OF BALANCE

Most presentations I attend suffer from a problem: one of the main parts is way too long and the others have been shrunk accordingly to fit the time frame. You cannot predict which one it is going to be. It's almost like a horoscope; there are certain types of people who are comfortable presenting the exposition part all day long, some who prefer to discuss the problem part, others who enjoy the middle part, and finally those who over-discuss the call for action part. However, to have a complete story, you need to do all of them. Let me tell you what exactly is wrong which each of these approaches and how to deal with it.

Exposition

TOO MUCH

The vast majority of the presentations I see have just an exposition. Sadly, this has become the gold standard of corporate communications. Why? Because this approach requires a minimal amount of emotional labor. If you don't want to invest emotionally, just give them a very long introduction and nothing else.

Here is a sequence of slides from an actual corporate presentation I was once asked to re-create (I know it's hard, but please bear with me):

1. About [company name]

2. Mission and vision statements

3. Key corporate values

4. Worldwide headquarters

5. Regional offices

6. International presence

7. Quality statement

8. Products of [company name]

9. Broad-based brand portfolio

10. Key facts and figures

11. Award-winning brands

12. Competitive advantages of [company name]

The last slide included the company's name again. That's it. Not even a "thank you" in the end. Are you still here?

This is known as a "What's your point?" presentation. Apart from being an utter bore, this approach has another problem: It's hard to believe. When people just lay down the facts, the audience knows they are laying down only the facts that benefit their argument. The presentation becomes sterilized. It's dead. "Okay, so you have all those major international clients; I know you are big and serious. Now tell me something interesting," I always want to say at this point. They never do. The idea of bigness and seriousness can be communicated in one slide. Maybe two. Maybe even five if you are really big and serious about being big and serious. Not 12!

The problem is not that the presentation is about the company. We expect it to be. Introduction is important. And the problem is never that the speaker says something about himself in the beginning. I know some people in the industry are seriously against this—I'm not. After all, when I listen to a speaker I do want to know who he is. The problem is that these are just facts; there are no emotions attached. I'm bored and disengaged. These types of presentations go on and on for what seems like an eternity.

TOO LITTLE

I have to admit that this is a rare problem, but I'll cover it anyway. Speakers jumping right into the action signals one of two problems: either they are really short of time or they are so absorbed in whatever problem is on their mind that they don't care about the audience. They don't care about establishing common grounds, they don't care about the context, and they don't care if they are going to be understood. Maybe they are right, and they shouldn't care. I don't know. But I usually do care, and I'd suggest that you do, too. Before the bus departs it's good to know your passengers are on the bus, buckled up, and that they know where they are going. It just seems like a reasonable idea.

JUST RIGHT

Why do we even have an exposition part? The main goal of this part is to be a mini-presentation of a bigger presentation. Here's a short list of what you can do in the exposition part. Remember, none of these items is obligatory.

▶ Not all these questions need to be answered, obviously, but it's good to place yourself in your audience's shoes and think about what they'd like to know first.

1. **Introduce the ground rules.** How long is your speech? Will there be a break and, if so, when? Should the audience hold the questions until the end? Should they interrupt you? If they interrupt you, should they raise their hands first? And so on. Obvious, yet frequently overlooked, ground rules. These are especially important if you are going on a long journey together.

   Figure 4-4 shows a typical second lecture slide (the first presumably contains the speaker's name and topic of the speech).

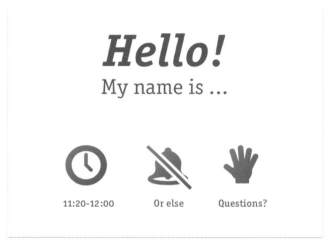

FIGURE 4-4: A typical welcome slide.

▶ The golden rule is that you should only say things that are relevant. People hate when presenters start with lengthy lists of their qualifications and experience.

2. **Introduce your hero.** Again, the hero is the story. If people in the audience don't know you, it may be appropriate to introduce yourself. Your words will have more impact if the audience sees you as an authority figure and not just some random person sharing his/her opinions on the subject. If you have any relevant qualifications, experience, awards, and so on, be sure they know about it.

   The best approach, of course, is to tell a very short personal story that mentions some of those positions and awards. Also, if you intend to show your hero's transformation, this is the place to reveal your hero's weakness. "At the time, we were thinking that..." This is the place where you plant a seed that you want to grow and blossom in the future parts.

3. **Introduce the situation.** Give the audience some context so they can appreciate the problem you will be talking about. Most of the time you cannot just say "the situation is bad"; you have to say "the situation was fine but then it went bad." This is the way people appreciate how bad it became. Show some statistics. This gives your audience some factual background and also establishes an emotional baseline. Things will go downhill from this point (but only for some time).

4. **Introduce your story.** If there's any ambiguity about the subject of your talk, you can clear it up right away, especially if you have a long presentation. Here comes the "I will be talking about this and I will not be talking about that" slide. But again, do it only if you think ambiguity exists. Otherwise "I have something great for you today" is perfectly sufficient. If you have three stories just say "I have three stories, the first one is about..." and then go straight to the story. If you have some overarching concept for the presentation, you might mention it here. But again, this is not the place for too much detail.

AGENDA SLIDES

Some people always have those "agenda" slides in their presentations, and what's even worse is that some corporate standards mandate that you have one! I don't think these slides are necessary, and they are often boring. Have you ever seen an agenda set forth in a movie? No, not only would it be pointless, it would also harm the plot! You know what really needs an agenda? Dictionaries, reference books, and manuals. Things you don't read from the beginning to end. Most of the time an "agenda" slide indicates bad structure or simply tells your audience when they need to wake up to catch the important parts. It's a promise to be boring. If you have a lengthy solution you might need to give the audience the plan for it, but only after you've presented the problem. More on this later in the chapter.

Exposition is an important part; it's really just a couple of minutes long, so you can think it through. Remember, you will never get a second chance to produce the first impression. There's a widespread notion that you need to do something spectacular within a couple of minutes, to produce a joke, to grab the audience's attention. I honestly don't think that's the case. For the first couple of minutes the audience's attention is sharp anyway, the novelty effect: "Whoa, somebody new is on stage! (Thank God it's not me!)" It's also quite sharp in the end; it's the middle that gets speakers into trouble.

▶ The keyword for this exposition part is "short." The key question is, "Do they really need to know this here?"

Problem

TOO MUCH

Imagine one day you're surfing the Internet and you see a flashing banner with a sign such as "Your computer is in danger! Free virus check!" Well, everyone likes a free virus check, right? So you click on it. Next, you see a website with a realistic-looking progress bar and some status messages implying that a virus check is running on your computer. In a minute—it's really quick!—viruses (Trojans, worms, whatever) are found. Now you are being asked to download and install a free Trojan removal tool. This is how you get an actual Trojan into your system, the one that steals your passwords and turns your computer into a botnet node. This is also a typical script (approach) for a great many business presentations.

It isn't the worst script ever. After all, scare tactics like this do work. Whatever it is, it's not a bore. You are engaged. The idea spreads. If you go to a website called www.Snopes.com (no, there aren't any free virus checks there!), you will find a great collection of urban legends. Click Random, or better yet, click Hot 25 for the hottest, most popular legends. Read any of them. There's more than 95 percent chance that the story you'll find will be about something frightening, about a girl who foolishly went to the park at night and was dismembered by a maniac with an axe wearing a bunny rabbit suit . . . Ah, the thrill! It will be a horror story of a sort, with a very simple, straightforward moral: don't be stupid. Don't go there. Don't talk to strangers. Don't . . . A very simple solution. This use of simple scare tactics is the way urban legends work.

Al Gore's *An Inconvenient Truth* is structured like this. Don't get me wrong, it's a great presentation. It is probably one of the greatest presentations ever delivered. You might not agree with it, but it is hard to deny the impact. As far as I know, this is the only presentation that won an Oscar and got the Nobel Peace Prize at the same time. But if you look at it, it is structured the way most urban legends are. Gore spends about 90 percent of the time discussing the problem. He spends about 90 percent of the time trying to scare his audience. It's a horror story. Less than 10 percent is spent offering solutions. It's not his fault. He is not a scientist and even if he was, there aren't that many good solutions to the problem he is concerned with.

There's a notion in the personal development industry: "The easiest way to make people happy is to make them unhappy first and then get them back to normal." Some people take that a bit too literally. And it does not only go "back to normal"; more often it's "better than before"! However, very few complex problems have simple, straightforward solutions. Yes, discussing the problem is absolutely essential. Every decent presentation begins with discussing a problem. And sometimes you have to go to lengths for the audience to admit the problem. But this is just the first step in a long journey. Offer a plausible solution next. There are already way too many people running around crying wolf. You need to differentiate yourself.

▶ If you see a business presentation structured like this, beware. Either something has indeed gone terribly, terribly wrong or you are being manipulated.

TOO LITTLE

This problem is covered in detail in the previous chapter. If you don't answer the question "Why bother?" no one will. Not answering this question presupposes a motivated audience, which in my experience is a very rare occurrence.

JUST RIGHT

Again, this issue is covered in the previous chapter, but let me recap here. The problem part serves two main purposes:

▶ **Provides a logical explanation for any further actions.** Here you explain why are you are going to do what you're going to do. What's the problem and why is it important? Why bother?

▶ **Serves as an emotional "hook."** It upsets the balance of things so the audience cannot rest until the balance is restored, until the gestalt, the pattern, is restored.

This is where you introduce your antagonist (if you have one); this is where you present your character with a moral choice. "You can have it fast, cheap, and high-quality—pick any of the two." What will your hero choose? And next you work toward resolution of this conflict, trying to find a win-win situation or aligning with just one side.

The main difficulty here is to say something the audience doesn't really know and that is actually true, something that will resonate with their experiences. I've seen a number of presentations in which the speakers spent too much time discussing a problem that the audience was already familiar with. There was no reason to do this—other than to follow the rules they were recently taught at a Presentation Skills workshop. This part should be surprising. (Again, telling personal stories is usually a fun and effective approach.)

If you intend to show some statistics at this point, be sure to dramatize them. As always, go for contrast. For example, in his TED 2009 speech about malaria, Bill Gates said that "less money is being spent on researching malaria than baldness," getting lots of laughs but also lots of concerned nods.

Note that time is only a relative measure of importance. What also matters is how much emotion you show during each of those parts. The problem part is a very emotional part, second only to the conclusion. Again, if you watch Bill Gates' speech, you can see right from the beginning that Mr. Gates is not a very emotional person (which is a polite way of saying that he sucks as a speaker), so he needed to do something to produce this emotional impact. He ended up releasing live mosquitoes so the audience "can have the experience" poor people have. The mosquitoes weren't actually infected with malaria but he waited for several seconds before revealing this information. It doesn't take a lot of time to pull a trick like this, but the impact is tremendous.

▶ If you can't find an interesting angle to look at the familiar problem, just make sure the audience is really familiar with the problem. "As you might know, we are currently experiencing..." Be ready to expand this part on the spot during your presentation if you're not getting nods of agreement from the audience here.

Solution

TOO MUCH

They start from nowhere and go to nowhere. They could have started five minutes later and ended five minutes earlier; nobody would ever notice. It's just an endless list of things they have. It's either statistical data or numerous products with nearly identical characteristics. No emotions, just facts. They are here to pass on the information. Again, it's an over-exposition, albeit done a different way.

"Just the solution" people don't talk about the problems because problems are obvious and time shouldn't be wasted on such nonsense. Or so they say. It reality, they are simply afraid to inflict any unpleasant emotions upon the audience. They are afraid that if the solution fails, they will be left with an unsolved problem, which is much worse than no problem. Of course, they are right. The problem is that if there's no risk, there's no revenue.

▶ If you are afraid to make your audience worried, afraid, or angry, you will fail as a presenter.

TOO LITTLE

It has been argued that the best presentation is the shortest one; why say more if you can say less? To which I usually reply that the shortest and, arguably, the most affective presentation is the classic "Got some change?" I would imagine that throughout history variations of this pitch have raised more money than any other presentation. It's short, the goal is clear, and to save time the problem is communicated non-verbally as well, via tone of voice and looks. It could be delivered hundreds of times a day. The only problem is that it is not very comfortable to deliver or to listen to. Actually, this is one of those few instances where you are being paid to stop delivering your presentation. This is not a good story.

Let me repeat myself here: if you don't have a solution, you have no right to be in front of the audience. The only exception is when your goal is to draw attention to some really important and formerly unnoticed problem, but this is a rare occasion. I am personally very proud of the fact that about 30 of the 60 slides in my "Death by PowerPoint" presentation actually contain direct advice on how to deal with the problems raised by the other 30 slides.

JUST RIGHT

Typically, the middle part, the solution, is the longest. After you've created emotional charge by unveiling the problem, your audience is ready to listen. Not forever, but you've bought yourself some time. What you need to do first is plan the journey. Also, this is the place where you can actually share your plans with the audience. If you are telling a personal story, this is where you say how you planned to deal with the problem (the way that ultimately didn't work, of course). If you are presenting a future solution, you discuss your roadmap.

> **NOTE** This is where you can actually have "the agenda slide" with several items. I am putting the quotes here because this is not a plan for the whole presentation; this is a plan just for the middle part. Also, you need to outline your plan explicitly only when the middle part is longer than 10 minutes or when you absolutely want them to remember your main points.

MANAGING THE TIMING OF YOUR SOLUTION

Why is that? First of all, research[1] shows that after about 10 minutes, the audience's attention drops sharply.

"You must do something emotionally relevant at each 10-minute mark to regain attention," says Dr. John Medina in his bestselling *Brain Rules* book. I had two problems with this statement: first of all, it is based on just one research article from 1978. Secondly, it's difficult to time your presentation that way. However, I was surprised to discover that most of the presentations that I like do, in fact, follow this rule. Maybe not exactly every 10 minutes; sometimes it's 11, sometimes it's 12.

Have a look at the Figure 4-5. I've plotted several presentations here; this is relative time devoted by the presenters to each part of their speeches. The five presentations are:

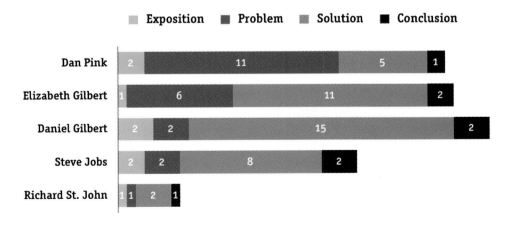

FIGURE 4-5: Timelines for five presentations.

> ► **Dan Pink's 2009 talk on motivation**, which, according to www.postrank.com is the most forwarded TED presentation ever (based on social network analysis at http://blog .postrank.com/2010/05/and-the-most-engaging-ted-talk-is/ or http://goo.gl/wsb38).

[1] See Hartley, J., & Davies, I. "Note-taking: A critical review." *Programmed Learning and Educational Technology*, 1978, 15, 207-224.

The secret of its popularity? 11 minutes spent discussing the problem and only five minutes spent discussing the solution. During the talk he mentions that there's a longer version of this speech where the solution part has three sub-parts: "autonomy, mastery, and purpose." But at TED he spoke about only one of them! He didn't shrink the problem part, he shrank the solution!

> **NOTE** All of these talks (except for Steve Jobs' talk) are on the TED's own Top 20 list, which can be found at `http://blog.ted.com/2011/06/27/the-20-most-watched-tedtalks-so-far/` or `http://goo.gl/tTZ1X`.

▶ **Elizabeth Gilbert's 2009 talk about creativity** is also one of the more popular talks, and ended up being on lots of top 10 lists. It's also as of this writing #14 in postrank's list. Notice the reverse pattern compared to Pink's discussion. Less of a problem, more of a solution. Still, 30 percent of the speech is dedicated to the problem.

▶ **Daniel Gilbert** (no relation) is a Harvard professor of psychology. His speech about happiness was one of the first TED talks ever posted online and thus one of the first talks I saw. The long solution part was actually split into two sub-parts. He discussed two points and illustrated them with two experiments. One experiment took nine minutes and the second was six minutes long. And there was a small problem part before the six-minute part.

▶ **Steve Jobs' 2005 iPod Shuffle presentation.** A classic composition, very fair and balanced. The solution part is also split into two sub-parts: hardware and software.

▶ **Richard St. John's three-minute TED talk about success** (the longer version is two hours). It's also very popular, and it's good to see how even the shortest presentation basically follows the same pattern. Richard has eight sub-parts in his solution part.

If you have one or two sub-parts making up your solution or if your speech is short, you don't need to bother announcing the plan. But, as Guy Kawasaki says, if you are going to suck, it's good for people to know how long you are going to suck for. Also, if somebody is browsing your slides without you it is always good for them to understand two things: how did they get there and what are they doing. So it can be a good idea to share your plan and show a way to track progress. It is also a good idea to have a unifying metaphor; something that holds the different pieces of your story together.

ORGANIZING INFORMATION VIA L.A.T.C.H.

Richard Saul Wurman, an architect and graphic designer (probably best known as the founder of the TED conferences), created a unifying metaphor for unifying metaphors. I know; it does sound a bit confusing, but bear with me. He proposed that there are five possible ways of organizing information, and he organized those five possible ways with the acronym L.A.T.C.H. (Location, Alphabet, Time, Category, and Hierarchy).

▶ **Location:** Information can be organized spatially, as on a map. What you see on Figure 4-6 is a simple idea for a unifying metaphor, the chair. It has three legs, which are the three spatial locations assigned to three things. The metaphor is quite clear. Steve Jobs once used it while talking about Apple, and the legs were "Mac, iPhone, and Music." Figure 4-7 is slightly more sophisticated: it's a wheel. If your list has five or more items, you can arrange them this way. I have no evidence that it improves retention, but it's a little more entertaining than just a list.

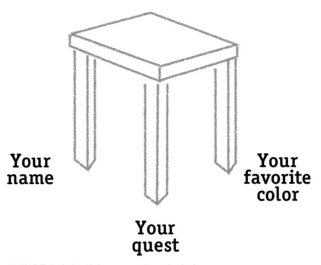

Your name

Your favorite color

Your quest

FIGURE 4-6: Unifying metaphor: A chair.

You've probably seen the house like the one shown in Figure 4-8. I know it's a cliché. However, I was surprised how once at Mercator we were able to "sell" a house like this as the organizing concept for an investor relations film (see Figure 4-9). The client was Vimetco, one of the largest aluminum producers in the world. Their core competence is smelting (the central piece), but in order to have profitable smelting, you need to have access to cheap resources like electricity, which is about 50 percent of the total cost, and coal, for the power plants, alumina, and bauxites. If you have all this you can create high-end products such as alloys for the aerospace industry where you have a much higher added value. I have to admit that I was initially skeptical of this idea, but the house unifying metaphor worked perfectly for this presentation!

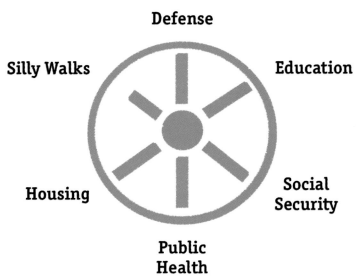

FIGURE 4-7: Unifying metaphor: A wheel.

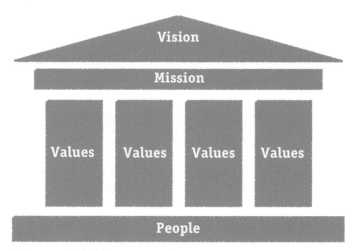

FIGURE 4-8: Unifying metaphor: A house.

NOTE One point to remember about this L.A.T.C.H. list is that these organizational approaches are not mutually exclusive; they might intersect. For example, Figure 4-10 shows a diagram describing the process of opening a retail outlet for a foreign brand in Russia. The process is quite long so it is split into three stages: Planning, Legalization, and Launch. In this figure, you see three of the organizational approaches appearing simultaneously: Location (it's a diagram), Time (the events happen in a predetermined sequence), and Category (the stages).

This pencil was marking the progress.

FIGURE 4-9: Vimetco film unifying metaphor.

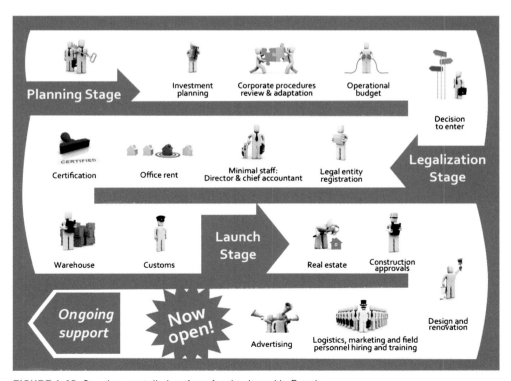

Planning Stage

Investment planning

Corporate procedures review & adaptation

Operational budget

Decision to enter

Certification

Office rent

Minimal staff: Director & chief accountant

Legal entity registration

Legalization Stage

Warehouse

Customs

Launch Stage

Real estate

Construction approvals

Ongoing support

Now open!

Advertising

Logistics, marketing and field personnel hiring and training

Design and renovation

FIGURE 4-10: Opening a retail shop for a foreign brand in Russia.

▶ **Alphabet:** Alphabetical order is a very common way of organizing directories, but presentations? Keep in mind that "Alphabet" can be interpreted liberally. What's important is that the letter order makes sense. One way to make sense is to arrange the letters in a sequence that resembles an actual word—the acronym! Chip Heath and Dan Heath in their book *Made to Stick* make an excellent list of criteria for ideas that stick, ideas that survive the evolutionary race. The list consists of six items—Simple, Unexpected, Credible, Concrete, Emotional, Story—and provides readers with a nice acronym: S.U.C.C.E.S.

In "Death by PowerPoint," the agenda was outlined on slide 12, right after the problem (see Figure 4-11): Significance, Structure, Simplicity, Rehearsal. The acronym doesn't quite work in English but in Russian it reads basically as USSR. I was later tracking the progress in the agenda of the presentation with little numbers, as shown in Figure 4-12.

And of course, as I said, L.A.T.C.H. itself is an example of this strategy.

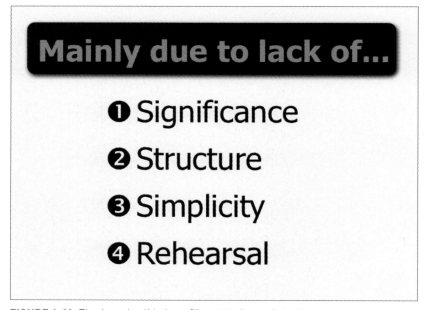

FIGURE 4-11: The Agenda slide from "Death by PowerPoint."

And speaking of the alphabet, I once heard a wonderful lecture entitled "Storytelling from A to Z" which was in fact organized as a journey from A to Z. There was an appropriate term assigned to each letter (such "P for plot") and the lecturer just went from A to Z for an hour and a half talking about different storytelling concepts. As you might imagine, some of the letters were tricky (such as X), but overall the concept worked.

▶ **Time:** Now this is important, at least as far as storytelling is concerned. Time is one of the most important parameters of the story. Time can run forward, but can also run backward. There can be jumps, flashbacks, and so on. It can be cyclical, which is a great way to present life cycles. In the most basic form of storytelling, time runs exactly like we live through it—the past, the present, and then the future. For example, if your narrative has three important events, three stages of the process, or three attempts at experiments, then this sequence is the easiest and the most natural way to organize your story.

FIGURE 4-12: Tracking progress in "Death by PowerPoint."

There can be different graphical representations for timelines. Figure 4-13 shows the simplest and Figure 4-14 shows one of the most complex. Your timeline is likely to be something in between; remember that simpler is better. Charles Minard's diagram might look cool but it really takes a lot of time to grasp (hint: thickness of the line represents the size of Napoleon's army).

▶ **Category:** This is probably the easiest, although definitely not the best, way to organize your solution. If you break topics into categories, you just come up with a list of issues and you are back to square one where you need to organize this list. This process works best when your list is short. Let me give you an example. In his 2001 iPod presentation, Steve Jobs says that Apple made three major breakthroughs. He doesn't then list each of them; he just goes straight to the first one: "It's ultra-portable." The slides marking the sub-parts of his solution had just numbers in rectangles with rounded corners. Nothing else. They were simple, but unmistakably different from the rest his slides.

▶ *Most people can remember a list consisting of four items without external help; this is more or less the limit for our short-term memories. Any more is a problem. It's hard to memorize anything more than four. Just keep that in mind.*

> You can, however, spend a lot of time searching for the right way to organize your middle part. I'd say there's nothing more important here.

▶ **Hierarchy:** Figure 4-15 shows a concept for a motivational presentation. It goes from the top down, first describing the Big Hairy Audacious Goal (in Jim Collins' *Good to Great* terms) the company's management aspires to and then describing specific targets and milestones for this department. Finally, it asks: "What can you personally do to make it all happen?" Apart from pyramids, for graphical representations of hierarchy you can use trees with trunks, branches and leaves, tributaries and rivers, and so on. Again, hierarchy is a great (and very natural) way to organize information; just keep in mind the KISS rule ("Keep It Simple, Stupid!").

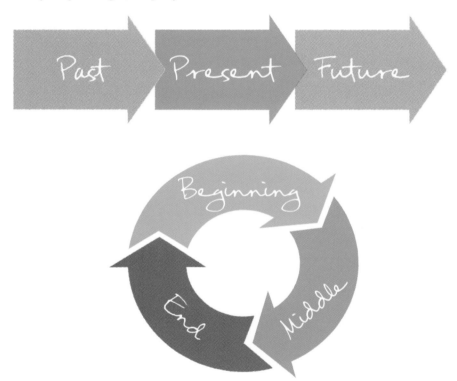

FIGURE 4-13: Unifying metaphor: Process diagrams.

NOTE One final point: I strongly suggest drawing unifying metaphors by yourself and never using specialized software (like Microsoft PowerPoint's SmartArt diagrams). Don't spend more than 15 minutes on them, either. This way only the simplest will survive.

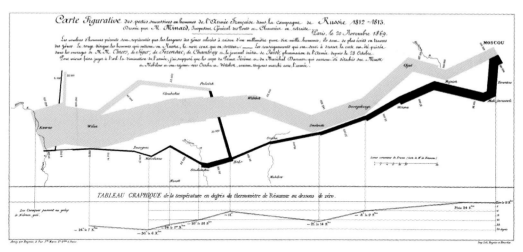

FIGURE 4-14: Napoleon's campaign in Russia; diagram by Charles Minard circa 1869.

FIGURE 4-15: Unifying metaphor: A pyramid.

Conclusion

TOO MUCH

A long conclusion part is usually a sign of unsupported and highly abstract moralizing that audiences just hate. "We all should not be bad; instead we should be good." That's cool philosophy, but how exactly? This is a classic beginner's mistake. Some people can do long conclusions, most notably, of course, Malcolm Gladwell, whose speech I deconstructed earlier. But what he actually does in conclusion is create three mini-presentations with their own dramatic arcs. His core story about Howard Moskowitz is so powerful that it allows multiple morals to be drawn from it; not every story is that potent. Unless you know what you are doing, I recommend you keep the conclusion short.

TOO LITTLE

This is known as the "now what?" presentation. I was shocked to discover that otherwise great presentations could be easily killed by a bad conclusion. "So, this is our solution," the speaker says and leaves the podium. The audience now has to determine what to do next. Should they call him? If so, why didn't he show his number? Heck, let's just listen to the next guy.

"The end is important in all things," so says *Hagakure*, an 18th-century book of samurai wisdom. Presentations are no exception. The attention of the audience rises just before the end. This an additional opportunity to say your most important words. Don't miss it.

JUST RIGHT

There are three sub-parts to consider including in the last part:

▶ *Use no more than one slide—just one slide, seriously. And have no more than four items.*

- ▶ **Wrap-up:** You have a chance to repeat the most important points that you want your audience to remember. You can get back to the unifying concept (1-2-3, From A to Z, or whatever). Never end with a wrap-up, though.

> **NOTE** I am very tempted to say that the wrap-up structurally belongs to the middle and not the end of the solution part of your presentation, but I will not go so far as to say that. Let's just agree that you will not end with a summary. It's just a waste of a good story.

▶ *This is the most important sub-part of the conclusion.*

- ▶ **Call for action:** Here you ask your audience to actually go and do something. If you've constructed your dramatic arc properly, if you've harnessed your logic and the steps are clear, you can ask the audience to make a move in the same direction as your hero did. Be concrete. Who exactly should do what by when? Look at the last slide of your last presentation. What does it say? Are you just thanking them for coming and taking questions? If so, this is a very weak ending. There should be a call for action somewhere in the end.

► **The moral:** This is the coolest sub-part to your conclusion. This is where you can say, "Let's all be peaceful," and be effective in it. If your story is any good, you've bought yourself some time for preaching. It's not much: you have just one, maybe two, sentences. Really think them through. There's probably no way to measure the impact of this part. The change might not translate directly into any observable behavior. But if there's any way to influence people's values, to adjust corporate culture, this is the way. In the end, people act one way or another not because we motivate them with incentives, but because they believe in what they do or they don't.

> *If we repair this mismatch between what science knows and business does, if we bring our notions of motivation into 21st century, if we get past this lazy, dangerous ideology of carrots and sticks—we can strengthen our businesses, we can solve a lot of those problems and maybe, maybe, maybe . . . we can change the world.*

This is the end for the most popular TED talk, the presentation by Dan Pink.

CASE STUDY: A COMPANY INTRODUCTION

This presentation was developed during an executive training session for one of my clients, a company specializing in the factoring business. Factoring involves certain types of financial transactions akin to loans. It's actually quite complicated. We presumed that our audience consisted of business owners who were familiar with bank loans but not with factoring. However, if they wanted to grow their business they needed to understand these more complex financial concepts. We needed to explain to them what factoring is.

We took a typical corporate presentation prepared by the marketing department (You know this stuff: We were founded in this year, we have offices all over the place, we have this and that, a bare listing of facts—the "too much exposition" problem) and made a story out of it. After about 2 hours of work it looked something like this:

► **Exposition:**
  ▷ Who are we? Our company is a bank that was founded 1999 (back then factoring operations required a banking license). We now have 21 offices all over the country.

  ▷ Who are our clients? Our clients are companies that also want to develop and grow their businesses. They are mostly in wholesale, but also in manufacturing, construction, and retail.

▶ **Problem:**

▷ Suppose you own a business and you need working capital. You have clients who are willing to pay you, but they ask for deferment. But if you don't get their money now, you will have no cash to pay salaries or make payments to your own suppliers. Where can you get the cash?

▷ You can apply for a bank loan. But what if your credit limit is overdrawn? What if you have nothing to offer as collateral? You will also need to collect a lot of papers and spend a lot of time for every loan you get.

▷ Case study: We once had a client, a small company specializing in selling pet products. They weren't able to secure a bank loan since they had almost no property to offer as collateral. They went for factoring and in 5 years they grew so much that we are now borrowing money from them. How is this possible?

▶ **Solution:**

▷ Factoring works like this: You deliver whatever you're selling to your client and immediately get your money (minus the bank fee) from us. Next, we collect money from your clients without bothering you. That's it; it's very simple.

▷ You are getting the cash you need. Your client gets the deferment of payment they need. We are getting our percentage. As an added bonus, we also manage your accounts receivable for you! You don't have to call your clients if they delay payments; we do it. We know some companies have people who do nothing but bill chasing. No more.

▷ We have three simple criteria for this process to work. Your business has to be at least one year old. This doesn't work for one-time deals; only for recurring deals with your regular clients. We don't work with monthly turnovers less than a certain amount.

▶ **Conclusion:**

▷ What's the cost? Well, it depends on two factors: how long the deferment is and how many of your clients are participating. (We showed a table with three possible situations at this point.)

▷ If you calculate the daily rate, it might seem a bit high, but keep in mind that you are paying only for the days you are actually using the money. When you take a bank loan, you are paying for the whole term at once! Call us and we will calculate the cost in different scenarios.

▷ So, this is it; this is who we are. We help our clients to develop and grow their businesses.

Now, this is probably not the greatest story ever told. But it was way better than the presentation they had before. It is more memorable, more dynamic, and the person who delivered it . . . well, it looked like she was actually proud of the company she's working for. Her eyes started to glow. To me, this is the main goal and the main result of this whole storytelling affair. If the speaker is transformed in the end, I have no doubt the audience will be transformed too.

Go back now to your mind map or outline you made in Chapter 2. Arrange its contents in a sequence. Go for the flow. Build a story arc. If you find that anything is missing, add it. It's time to create your story.

SUMMARY

The key points to remember from this chapter are as follows:

- ▶ **The plot follows "the S-curve."** The goal and the conflict are two major components of the story. The last component is called the plot, the dramatic sequence. There are many ways to look at the plot, but for most part it follows the "S-curve," the common change pattern. It starts with an exposition, which is an introduction for the speaker and the hero. It continues with the problem and the solution. It ends with the conclusion.

- ▶ **Timing matters.** It terms of time, the shortest parts are the exposition and the conclusion. The solution is typically the longest and the problem is the second longest. However, if you want to draw attention to the problem, don't be afraid to take more time for it. The conclusion is the most emotional part. Then follows the problem, solution, and finally the exposition.

- ▶ **The solution is the most difficult part to present.** Too often the middle is too long and thus easily becomes the muddle. If this happens, you probably need another unifying idea, just for this part. The most obvious is a timeline, but you can also use visual metaphors and acronyms. For presentations longer than twenty minutes, you should give your audience a way to track the progress. I highly recommend you have no more than four key ideas in the middle section of your presentation.

- ▶ **If you've constructed your emotional arc properly, in the end there will be an opportunity to change the world.** Don't miss it.

PART II

SLIDES

CHAPTER 5   The Slides' Focus
CHAPTER 6   The Slides' Contrast
CHAPTER 7   The Slides' Unity

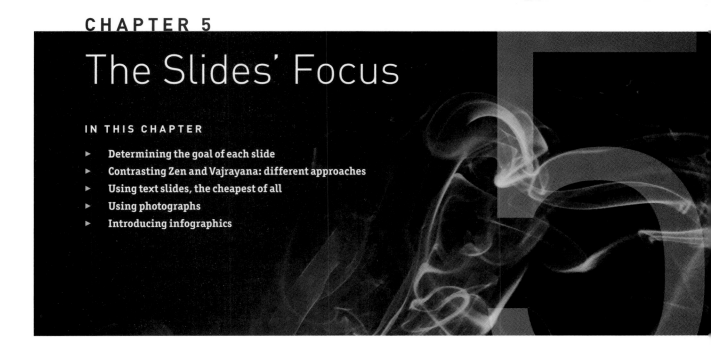

The Slides' Focus

IN THIS CHAPTER

▶ Determining the goal of each slide
▶ Contrasting Zen and Vajrayana: different approaches
▶ Using text slides, the cheapest of all
▶ Using photographs
▶ Introducing infographics

This chapter discusses the fundamentals of slide design. I will walk you through the first part of the design process, which mostly has to do with answering the question, "What am I trying to say?", and you'll see the choices you have. The chapter also looks at the most basic slides, which have only text, and more advanced slides, which use photos or abstract images. Expect lots of examples.

PRODUCING YOUR SLIDES

Suppose that by now you have your story as an outline or as a mind map, or maybe just written as plain text. What's next? Now you get to the slides. This is the process that I typically follow:

1. **Reproduce the story in your presentation software—PowerPoint, Keynote, or whatever you are using:** One slide per message, text only.

2. **Decide what you want to see on the slides on a very basic conceptual level:** Text or visuals? What kind of visuals? Some people sketch their slides on paper at this stage. I don't, but only because my drawing skills are terrible and my Keynote skills are very good, so it makes more sense for me to sketch in Keynote, or a similar program.

3. **Define the overall style for the presentation:** Colors, fonts, backgrounds, textures, and so on.

4. **Finalize the slides:** Draw the diagrams, find the pictures, place the text, and so on.

Before you get to the process, however, I want to address one very important question first: Why design slides at all? Why can't you just say what you need to say and be off? Why spend hours tinkering with fonts and line widths when this time could be spend on other worthwhile activities?

There are four functions for the slides, four reasons why they are well worth your time. (There may be more, but these are the most important.)

▶ First of all, slides are used to **remind** the speaker what to say next. If they are passed to the audience after the talk, they also remind the audience what the speaker said. Text slides usually do this job well enough.

▶ Second, slides **impress**. As you know, images have a bigger impact than words, and they are more memorable. That is why people sometimes use photographs and drawings to illustrate their points.

▶ The third function of slides is to **explain**, so diagrams are used to simplify complex processes, relations, and so on.

▶ The last and the most important function is to **prove**. There are many types of evidence—of which statistical data is probably the strongest. We use data visualizations to make comparisons and draw conclusions.

▶ Strongest doesn't mean the most convincing; it means "the closest to scientific evidence." In my experience, the most convincing evidence is anecdotal rather than statistical. People still prefer listening to stories rather than making sense of data.

Figure 5-1 illustrates different functions and different types of slides. These are just examples, all the possible slide types simply won't fit into one diagram, but I hope you get the general idea. This is yet another way to look at the process of creating your slides. First you come up with a message, and then you decide what you need in order to communicate it successfully. Decide what the slide will do: remind, impress, explain, or prove. Then come up with a concept of a slide, and finally with the slide itself.

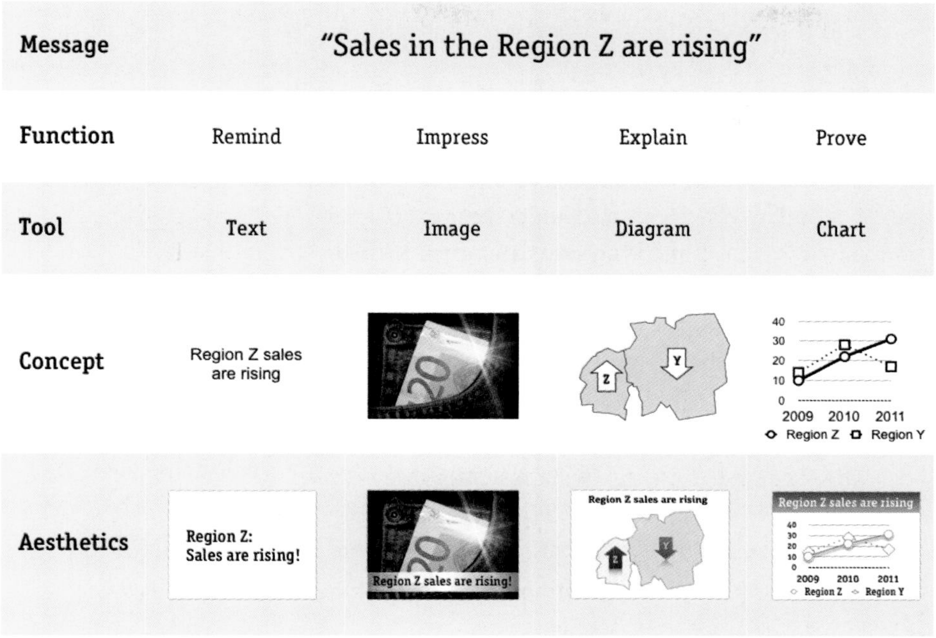
Message
"Sales in the Region Z are rising"
Function
Remind
Impress
Explain
Prove
Tool
Text
Image
Diagram
Chart
Concept
Region Z sales are rising
Z
Y
40
30
20
10
0
2009 2010 2011
Region Z Region Y
Aesthetics
Region Z:
Sales are rising!
Region Z sales are rising!
Region Z sales are rising
Region Z sales are rising
2009 2010 2011
Region Z Region Y

FIGURE 5-1: The slide design matrix.

There are three chapters in this part of the book. The chapter you are reading now is mostly about conceptual design; it's about sketching basic contents of your slide. You'll start with text-based slides and illustrations and try to answer the question, "What am I trying to say?" Chapter 6 is dedicated mostly to diagrams and data visualizations and covers the different ways of explaining and presenting your visual evidence. I think that these things are important enough to deserve a separate chapter. The last chapter in this part of the book, Chapter 7, covers artistic design and discusses bringing all these elements together: overall style, fonts, colors, and so on.

ZEN AND VAJRAYANA

In the beginning, slides were slides. I mean, they were real, physical slides. They really did slide. And they were projected through a slide projector. They were mostly pictures or illustrations. There was almost no text: all the text was spoken out loud by the presenter from notes or memory. You were not able to send those slides via e-mail. They were expensive and took a long time to produce.

These were Slides 1.0. Then came "foils," which were projected transparencies. They were much easier to write on, so speakers began putting brief outlines of what they wanted to say on them: more text and fewer graphics. Then PowerPoint came along and changed everything. Slides became electronic, cheap, and very quick to make. However, manipulating graphics was still very time-consuming and required advanced technical skills. So we ended up with mostly text slides, maybe some charts and occasional clip art. It was a disaster.

People started to complain. Seth Godin in his e-book *Really Bad PowerPoint* called the prevailing style a "dismal failure." Edward Tufte, a Yale professor of statistics and one of the most influential figures in the field of visual communication, questioned whether we should be using PowerPoint at all. Gene Zelazny, Director of Visual Communications for McKinsey & Co., in his books *Say It with Charts* and *Say It with Presentations,* made a call for simplifying business communication. Nobody, including the majority of McKinsey & Co. consultants, seemed to listen.

Figure 5-2 shows what I find to be a more or less typical slide from a modern corporate presentation: cryptic, overloaded with text and data, and almost impossible to interpret. I know, I know, it could be much worse. It could also be much better. Things have changed over the last couple of years thanks to Garr Reynolds and many other great presenters practicing "the Zen approach," the path of minimalistic slides. Their slides look more like Figure 5-3. These slides are clear and concise; most of the time they have only one picture and/or only one sentence, quite like Slides 1.0, surprisingly.

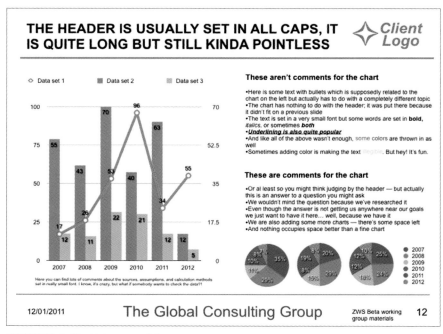

FIGURE 5-2: The Vajrayana slide.

FIGURE 5-3: The Zen slide.

A lot of marketers adopted the Zen approach, but overall it was not very well received in corporate environment. From what I see, many large corporations still prefer a completely different approach that I call *Vajrayana presentation*.

> **NOTE** Vajrayana is a very complex system of Buddhist thought and practices, which in a way is in a direct opposition to Zen. Zen is essential Buddhism; there are very few texts and methods that you have to learn. Vajrayana, on the other hand, is like a Buddhist supermarket, offering an innumerable amount of different practices, teachings, texts, and so on.

This approach can be summed up in the following sentences: "I will put everything I have on the slide because I might need it. Also, my boss told me to put everything in five slides, maximum. So I will squeeze everything I have in five slides. Sure it will be a bit messy, but I have a five-slide limit."

It is still a mystery to me why people estimate their presentations using slides as units of measurement. I guess it's a legacy from reports, when you had certain expectations about how much text can one fit onto a single page. But slides are so much more free-form than reports! Why do we keep counting presentation length in slides? I once decided to count the number of slides in Steve Jobs' talks. It turns out his rate is approximately three slides per minute, which means that in 15 minutes he would show 45 slides. Isn't it too much? When I ask it like this it does sound a lot, doesn't it? However, it doesn't *look* like too much when he actually presents it. Time is the limit, not the number of slides.

▶ Measure your presentation by time, not by number of slides.

It is argued that the Zen presentation works well with live presentations but doesn't work as well when you put your slides on the Web or send them through e-mail. This is a very important difference, but it's not about Zen at all. Yes, it is true that if you put Zen slides from your talk on the Web, people may hardly able to make sense of them. But again, this is not a presentation problem; this is an expectations problem. When I put my slides on the Web for the audience, I include a disclaimer that these slides were not designed to be viewed without a speaker. This solves the expectations problem.

PRESENTATIONS WITHOUT PRESENTERS

There are many Zen presentations that work perfectly well without a speaker. Consider Garr Reynolds' *Brain Rules* presentation (`http://goo.gl/ecqSo`), Scott Schwertly's *Meet Henry* (`http://goo.gl/zIoZ4`), and—hey!—*Death by PowerPoint*! "Why don't you make all your presentations like *Death by PowerPoint*?" I am sometimes asked. "It works both with and without the speaker!" No it doesn't! Do you know how many times I presented *Death by PowerPoint* live? None. Zero times. Never. I was never asked! And, if fact, what's the point? If it's all very clear without me (and it is), do I really need to say anything?

Providing Choice

Andrew Abela in his book, *Advanced Presentations by Design,* suggested that there are two separate environments and thus two separate presentation styles:

▶ **Ballroom style:** intended to "inform, impress, or entertain" with hundreds of people sitting in the audience

▶ **Conference room style:** intended to "engage, persuade, and drive action" among maybe 10 or fewer people

I disagree. First of all, I don't think that the goals are any different for these two types of presentations. I don't believe that "inform, impress, or entertain" are worthy goals for any presentation. You can drive action in a ballroom quite the same way you do in a conference room. I think there's another important distinction that differentiates Zen presentations from Vajrayana presentations. It is called choice.

Zen presentations are about controlling choices available to the audience. They are about guiding the audience's attention towards an outcome that is sought by the speaker and (hopefully) beneficial for the audience as well. Vajrayana presentations let the audience's attention roam. The words "controlling choice" might sound manipulative or patronizing; however, an important distinction should be made here. In presentations there are two types of choice: one is about the process and the other is about the substance.

▶ An example of decision about the process is: "Should I listen to the speaker or just read the slides?" The speaker should guide the audience's attention. I don't believe anyone would think that leaving the audience in doubt here is a good idea. This would just create confusion without achieving anything.

▶ An example of decision about the substance is: "Should we invest or divest?" This decision lies solely with the audience. But the speaker must leave no doubt about his or her intentions and preferences. Also, the speaker should try to limit the available number of choices because this vastly increases the odds of any choice to be made at all. We often think that more choices are better but that's not always the case. Barry Schwartz, a professor of social theory and social action at Swarthmore College argues in his bestselling book *The Paradox of Choice* that although no choice is bad, having too much choice causes indecisiveness. Our cognitive abilities are limited and putting excessive strain on them is a bad idea.

WHAT DO YOU WANT THEM TO SEE?—DECISIONS ABOUT FORM

As far as form is concerned, I don't think you should be leaving your audience any choice.

"I have lots of information on my slides so if somebody finds me boring, they can just read my slides," one participant actually told me at one of my workshops. Whoa, what a great excuse to be boring! By adding a noisy background, this person is creating a powerful distraction, which diminishes his effectiveness as a presenter. There should be no choice about where to look. You direct the audience's attention. You can focus them on slides or on yourself, but you have to focus them somewhere. Your job as a presenter is to manipulate people's attention. During every second of your speech, your audience should be absolutely sure where you want them to look.

▶ If you need a laser pointer to show your audience where to look on every other slide, that's a clue that your slides are overloaded.

Some people say that the focus should be on a presenter and that the slides are in the background supporting the presenter; they are just the prop and not the act. However, there are numerous examples that prove otherwise. If you watch presentations by Larry Lessig (http://goo.gl/kY7nO) or Dick Hardt (http://goo.gl/BJBDR), what you see is mostly slides; the speaker just provides commentary. In many other excellent presentations you won't see a speaker, just the slides. Why? Because there's a lot of effort put into creating those slides. They convey much more information and with great emotion; they clearly outweigh the speaker. This is perfectly fine! After all, the goal is to have the impact and not to show yourself off. So, this is about the form. What about the content?

DO YOU WANT THEM TO THINK?—DECISIONS ABOUT SUBSTANCE

Denying people any choice sounds oppressive. However, if you have a solution to a problem and you want to implement it, or if you have a product to sell, your audience has few choices to begin with. It's either buy the product or don't. Notice that these choices aren't very creative either. You don't want them to come up with a funny third option. Also, you mostly want them to buy! Granted, you don't want to sell the wrong project to the wrong client (this can have disastrous consequences). However, for the most part, you want to sell your product or idea. That is why all your slides should be doing one and only one thing—selling.

But what if it's not a sales presentation? In business consulting, there are roughly four stages in a project:

1. Formulate the questions
2. Acquire the data
3. Analyze the data
4. Present the findings

What's the biggest problem with Vajrayana presentations? People don't do stage three properly. They don't have any interesting findings to present. So they hide behind the cloud of data in hope that nobody will notice. This is not a presentation problem; this is a management problem. They either didn't do the job, or the job was pointless to begin with. These people are not presenting their ideas; they are not trying to convince the audience of anything. They don't have any strong opinion on the subject.

Instead, they just show their slides so the audience can have a good look and draw their own conclusions based on the data. This is perfectly fine as long as it matches expectations of the audience. Sometimes data is the main result of your work. For instance, one of my clients works for a polling agency, and guess what: She's expected to provide poll results. But most of the time, this approach doesn't match the audience's expectations: People expect to see "a presentation." If you don't properly analyze the data, I don't think you can call it a presentation. You have nothing to present. Call it a meeting, or a discussion. Call your slides "fact sheets"; this is what they are.

The point is that it is very hard to design focused slides if you don't have any focus in the first place. So, the biggest difference between the Vajrayana presentation and the Zen presentation is that with the Zen presentation approach, you are forced to have a strong opinion—something many people are deeply uncomfortable with. Of course, sometimes having strong opinions is not in your job description.

DO THEY WANT TO THINK?

Sometimes people come to your presentations expecting to think hard. Sometimes they are in a fairly critical mood, and they want you to provide a lot of data to support your judgment. This typically happens if the audience is:

▶ **A client:** This especially applies to complex technology or consulting projects. They want to know what they are paying for. Some people believe that there's no point in hiring consultants you don't trust in the first place; others believe that trust is something that should be earned. Some clients demand lots of data—not to really make sense of it, but to have it "just in case."

▶ **Your boss:** Again, some bosses are comfortable with their subordinates making independent decisions; they just want to know what the decision is and the general rationale. Some bosses are ready to scrutinize and demand lots of explanations.

▶ **Members of the scientific community:** It seems that a scientific presentation is deemed credible if you have a complex diagram on every other slide. Doug Zonker's *Chicken Chicken Chicken* (http://goo.gl/aGzpw) is a great satire on this whole genre. Granted, cognitive limits for scientists are probably not the same as cognitive limits for line managers (although some line managers might disagree). But I still think most presenters at scientific conferences overstretch it.

Sometimes you need to have a lot of data in your presentation, but even so, don't dwell on it! Your data is not your presentation. Data is just a way to prove your point. The good news is that if you do have a point, if you know what you want to say, there are many great ways to present your data beautifully and without overloading the audience. I will talk about them in the next chapter.

DESIGNING ZEN SLIDES

Both PowerPoint and Keynote (pretty much any slideware) have Master Slides, which is another name for slide templates. They are used to give your presentation a uniform look. They establish fonts, colors, backgrounds, and positions for various elements of the canvas. If you choose your template wisely you increase the chance that your presentation will look decent. So, before discussing any actual slides let's have a look at some templates. I think that the choice of template is a good indicator of the general approach to design.

▶ *I have to note that a good template does not guarantee good slides; I have seen people ruin great templates with their "creativity." However, following a bad template will definitely lead to poorly designed slides.*

Slide Templates

Even if you work for a large company in which slide templates are set in stone, it's still important to understand how templates are supposed to look. I have noticed that people in large companies get tired of standard templates very quickly and start customizing them to suit their needs and personal taste. I am not saying that's a good thing. Most of the time, they end up creating something that's worse than before. But since you do have this ability, why not use it well? If there's a real need to modify the template, I doubt anyone would object.

I've seen quite a few corporate style guidelines in my life. I came to the conclusion that most of the time those templates are designed by people who don't have a clue about how to design presentation templates. Designers often don't use PowerPoint and don't often deliver presentations themselves. Therefore, they just try to marry the overall graphical style they've developed (which is good!) with any "conventions of the PowerPoint genre" as they understand them. The result is inevitably disastrous. Unless your templates were designed by somebody specializing in designing PowerPoint templates, they are likely to be subpar.

Figure 5-4 shows my impression of a better than average slide template. The biggest (and most common) problem with this slide is the logo, in the corner which makes about 15 percent of the overall slide space unusable. I call this pattern "a slide within a slide" because the slide space is divided between a couple of different frames. For some reason, the designer thinks one slide is just not enough; they have to create an additional frame to achieve a look of sophistication and style. But I guess it's not entirely the designer's fault. If you look at many templates by Microsoft (see Figure 5-5), you will see the same "slide within a slide" pattern there. Designers just copy what they see elsewhere. They just don't get how precious space is in this medium.

FIGURE 5-4: A typical presentation template.

FIGURE 5-5: PowerPoint templates by Microsoft.

If the print is too small on a piece of paper you are reading, you can just bring the paper closer to your eyes. But slides are different. If you're sitting in a conference, your audience might not be able to just stand and walk closer. By closing off space, such "slide within slide" templates just require that everything else on the slide be smaller, thus alienating some percentage of the audience. Do you really need that look at that cost?

Look at the last template on Figure 5-5, the dark blue one on the bottom right. It's obviously a copy of Apple's template with a dark blue gradient background. This background is simple yet looks cool, especially in large rooms, where it blends with the darkness of the ceiling, producing an impression of a never-ending slide. Microsoft's version, however, has a bright white line on the left with some red patterns, supposedly mimicking film. Why? Do you really need that line? Second, if you have a closer look, the fonts for header and body are not the same. That's cool; you are supposed to have a contrast between header and text. But it is such a weak contrast! The difference in size is okay, but the difference in color is barely visible. Why have two colors when you can have one? What's the point?

And why have two nearly identical fonts when you have one? The header font is called Consolas, and if you look at Figure 5-6, you will see that it looks very much like Corbel used in the rest of the presentation. However, this is a monospaced font, much like typewriter fonts where all letters have the same width. In most fonts, different letters take different amounts of space. There are thin letters like "i" and wide letters like "w". In Consolas, however, all letters have the same width. It's not as legible. Unless you have some serious technical or aesthetic reasons to use monospaced font, don't. What's the point of using one here? There is no answer except "because I can."

Whatever　Consolas

Whatever　Courier New

Whatever　Corbel

FIGURE 5-6: Consolas vs. Courier vs. Corbel.

What's the big deal, you might ask. This variety makes the slide more stylish and less boring, doesn't it? First of all, it doesn't. If your presentation is boring and you think some fancy background and frames can improve it—think again. This is not a design problem, this is a content problem. When people ask me, "Where do I find a suitable background image for my PowerPoint template?", I think they 1) don't need any background at all and 2) most certainly need to work on their structure and not on design.

▶ *The biggest problem with "stylishness" is that it's a waste of attention.*

Paul Watzlawick, an Austrian-born American psychologist, philosopher, and theoretician in communication theory, had one famous communication axiom that went, "*Man kann nicht nicht kommunizieren*" or, "You cannot not communicate." (It sounds much cooler in German.) That means *everything* you have on your slides says something: every line, every border, every shadow, and every background. They communicate some information. Because human capacity for processing information is limited, you must ensure that everything on your slides communicates your message. A complicated design wastes not only your time but also the audience's attention.

Design is not decoration—you've probably heard that one somewhere. A good design communicates and solves problems. Look at the Figure 5-5 one more time, the first template in the upper left. Can you see that the header text has a shadow? Have you ever wondered why it is there? What's the point? Well, the point of a text shadow is to add contrast. Without a shadow, it might be hard to read the orange words on the gray background. But why have this background in the first place? Why not tweak the colors and lose the shadow? This is the biggest problem with slide design: people don't ask those kinds of questions.

So what makes a good slide template?

▶ **Clarity:** There are no unnecessary decorations. No huge borders. No logos except for the first and last slides. All the branding you need is accomplished with fonts and colors. No noisy background. No rotating cogwheels in the background, no human faces, no faces of any kind, in fact. Here's a good description for your background: "It's white." No unnecessary shadows for headers, no word art, and no stroking and 3D effects for fonts.

- **Good contrast:** The body text is clearly visible on the background. The header text is clearly distinguishable from the body text.

- **Consistency:** Different elements of the template "belong together," thus producing a consistent reality. For example, if the slides produce a scrapbook effect, there should be no 3D objects. (I discuss more on consistency in Chapter 7.)

Figure 5-7 shows an Apple Keynote template, which I think is a good one. Not all Keynote templates are perfect, but this one is. Why do I think it's so good?

- First of all, there are no superfluous design elements. There's only one font and there are no borders! (Note that the border you see is just an element of the interface; it's invisible in the slideshow mode.)

- Second, the header font is huge and bright while the body font is smaller and paler. I know what's important and what's less important right away here.

- Third, the background is just "grid paper" (and nothing else) and it matches the font. The bullets also match the font and the paper. By the way, strictly speaking asterisks are not bullets and you are not supposed to use them for bullets. However, in this case you can bend some rules without fear of reprimand. In "real life" you can actually see these kinds of "bullets" and this font on this kind of paper. This is truth.

▶ Here's a rule: If you can describe your background in more than one sentence, replace it.

▶ Remember, the main focal point of your text slide is almost always the header!

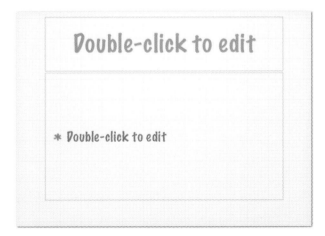

FIGURE 5-7: Keynote template by Apple.

Text Slides

Text slides have one unbeatable advantage over more complex, graphic-driven slides: In terms of time they are really cheap. I mean dirt cheap. You can create a decent-looking text slide in a couple of minutes. These slides won't wow the audience much, but at least you will not be afraid you might forget what to say next.

▶ Watch Tom Peters reading his slides at http://goo .gl/kp1uf and other related videos. Even though you've read the text ahead of him you still want to hear how exactly Tom will say it!

> **NOTE** Don't, however, make a classical mistake of actually reading your slides to the audience aloud; there's nothing worse than that. Dave Paradi at **www.thinkoutsidetheslide.com** conducted a survey that asked for all the things people hate in presentations. 69.2 percent of those polled reported hating it when the presenter read his/her slides aloud. "The font's too small" came creeping in second at 48.2 percent. There are a few people who can read their slides and still look passionate and entertaining—most notably Tom Peters, perhaps world's greatest business speaker—but it's difficult to pull off effectively.

What you really need for a text-based slide (moreso perhaps than for any other type of the slide) is focus. The biggest problem with text slides is that they are distracting. A little bit too much text and you're dead in the water. And you don't want people to read your slides ahead of you. However, the good news is that people don't want to read your slides. People don't even read documents anymore; they don't have time. Instead they try to quickly scan them to make sure they aren't missing anything important. So if you design your text slides for scanning rather than for reading, you will get more attention as a presenter.

▶ To get more attention from your audience as a presenter, design your text slides for scanning rather than for reading.

Look at the Figure 5-8, which shows three slides from President Barack Obama's State of the Union address in 2011. This is the exact order they appear in the speech and they provide excellent support for the speech that an audience can easily scan. (They are perhaps too short for a handout, but that's another issue.)

FIGURE 5-8: Obama's text slides.

NOTE You will see more of the Obama slides later in the book; they are good examples. Let me admit, though, that they are not really slides; the audience didn't see them during the actual talk. They were broadcast during the enhanced Web version. However, they are very similar to what the slides should be. The only difference is the orientation—portrait instead of landscape—which isn't important here. They have an advantage of being mostly good but not perfect, which gives me opportunity for critique.

What's the focal point of these slides? I am sure you have no trouble answering this question. It's in the center, where the big numbers are. The rest of the slide is set in a noticeably smaller font. You can surmise that "how much?" is the most important question here, and that the speaker is emphasizing numbers with his words in his speech. Any problems with these slides? Setting text in all capital letters reduces readability. It is probably okay for a short header, but not for the whole slide.

Figure 5-9 shows an even shorter slide, which separates one part of the speech from another. Those kinds of slides are sometimes called "bumper slides" because they act like a buffer between different parts of the presentation. Notice that the name of the part—REFORM—is set in much bigger type than the name of the speech—Winning the Future. Why is that? Typically, the whole speech is more important than one of its parts, right? Well, not here. The audience already knows the name of the speech; they need to know the name of the next part at this point.

FIGURE 5-9: Obama's bumper slide.

LISTS

What's the text limit on a single slide? Figure 5-10 is a slide from *Death by PowerPoint,* trashing the once-classic 7×7 rule. I understand that coming up with a 4×4 rule as a replacement wasn't probably very creative but a slide from the same presentation (shown in Figure 5-11) proves that it probably works. Seven is too much, but four is fine.

Now look at the next three text slides shown in Figure 5-12. The first slide is not very imaginative but isn't bad either. It has a clear focal point in the header and clearly spaced bullet points underneath. We know what it's about the instant we see it. The template is good. The background is just a gradient blue; the white text is clearly visible; the header is set in a larger font.

FIGURE 5-10: "Classic" 7×7 rule debunked.

FIGURE 5-11: Suggested 4×4 limit.

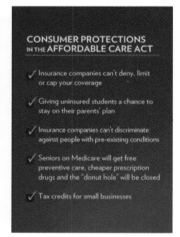

FIGURE 5-12: Obama's lists.

▶ Remember, the header is the most important element of the text slide. Ideally, people should be able to make sense of your presentation by reading just your headers. Practice writing clear and concise headers.

The second slide is much worse, though. First of all, it has the same header. If your next slide has the same header as the previous one, this is a signal that something is probably wrong. The audience loses the focus here. You knew where to look before for the main point; now you don't. The audience has to orient towards a new focal point, which will be the center of the slide, where figures set in heavy type are. But the focus is not there. The numbers in the list don't make any sense before you move up and read the word "HELPED," which is set in much thinner type. Also, the phrase "for less than 1%..." set in smaller type looks like a footnote. And footnotes, as you probably know, have a really bad reputation; avoid them whenever possible.

The third slide is a disaster. Its goal is to remind the audience of something that the speaker is mentioning only briefly. It is giving people a choice—to read or to listen. If they choose to read, they miss part of the speech, and they cannot read it quickly enough, because there's too much text. They don't have time to digest this information.

Bullets recently got a bad reputation. The purpose of the bullets is to create strong focal points so you know where the next thought begins. This is especially helpful when scanning, when you don't read to the end of the sentence and jump right to the next sentence to see what's there. Unfortunately, the only situation when you need to jump like this is when you have a list that is way too long.

Figure 5-13 shows that bullets actually do help; the top left slide is clearly better than the top right. However, if you take some time to think about what you are really trying to say, you can do it well without bullets. If your list has just four points, or you can pare it down to four points (as in Figure 5-13 along the bottom), bullets bring no advantage. If you have another strong focal point on your slide—such as a picture—you are better off without bullets. Clear spacing is essential for lists. Notice how in Figure 5-13 the list takes all available space on a slide by adding extra space between paragraphs, versus cramming all the text in the upper part of the slide—as usually happens if you just use default spacing.

▶ Lists are notoriously hard to process and too much text is frequently the kiss of death. So use bullets with caution.

Dogs perform many roles:

* Hunting
* Herding
* Protection
* Companionship
* Assisting police and military
* Aiding disabled individuals

Dogs perform many roles:

Hunting
Herding
Protection
Companionship
Assisting police and military
Aiding disabled individuals

4 key roles for dogs:

Hunting

Herding

Protection

Companionship

4 key roles for dogs:

Hunting

Herding

Companionship

Protection

FIGURE 5-13: Using bullets.

Also, make sure your list has a clear order, with either the most important or the least important issues covered first. For example, the last slide about dogs in Figure 5-13 goes with these spoken words: "Historically, dogs were mostly used for hunting and herding. Now their main roles are protection and, most importantly, companionship—which is what I am going to talk about." The dogs' roles on the slide are placed in historical order.

Using Slides with Photos

The most elementary function of slides is to remind you what to say, and text slides do this very well. If you don't need any more support (or you don't have any more time), you might as well stop here. However, if you do have time, you can go to the next stage. Here you decide which messages need which kind of support. Again, the most basic distinction I use is "illustration" versus "explanation" versus "evidence." Illustrations provide emotional impact and retention. Explanations explain. Evidence proves.

▶ **Illustration** is important when you need to add emotions in order to bring more life to your slides. You can ask the audience members to picture the dog in their mind's eye, or you can show them a picture of a dog and have a bigger impact.

▶ **Explanation** helps if you want your audience to understand some complex, abstract idea, concept, or scheme.

▶ If there's a trust issue between you and the audience, if they might not believe what you say, you need **evidence.** But remember that there's a notion in the legal profession called "the burden of proof." This burden is two-fold; you make an effort to submit the evidence while the audience makes an effort to process it. If you produce too much evidence you will overload people with insubstantial details. If you don't produce enough evidence, your presentation will seem superficial and lack substance. So evidence is important but not every slide is about evidence.

Let's deal with other types of slides first. A slide with a large photo and a short statement is an archetypal Zen slide. Photos are very powerful; they are great way to reinforce your point and they don't take much time for the audience to process. There are just two challenges when using photos: finding them and combining them with your text.

CROSSREF This chapter focuses more on finding appropriate photos, whereas combining photos with your text has more to do with artistic design, which is covered in Chapter 7.

First, if you have your own photos—great. Nothing could be better. Seriously. Using your own photographs shows that you care enough to take a picture for your audience to see. People appreciate that. Also, unlike stock photos, your photographs are authentic. They are really connected to the presentation, which is also appealing. And don't worry too much about the quality. Photo quality was an issue several years ago but now even pictures taken by cell phones look decent. (My first digital camera back in 2002 had just 2 megapixels in resolution; my current cell phone has an excellent 5 megapixel camera, more than enough to snap a casual photo whenever I need one.) Most of us are lousy photographers (I am no exception), but on the bright side your audience's expectations about your artistic abilities aren't high. Just make sure the images are visible and they, in fact, illustrate what you intend. I won't go much into photo editing here, but if there's an Enhance button somewhere in the software you are using (as there is in Apple Keynote) try pressing it. It might just do the trick.

▶ Whenever possible, try using your own photos—they will give your slides a much-needed authentic look and feel. They communicate caring, and creating decent-looking digital photos is easier than ever now.

Let's talk about stock photography next. There are many excellent websites selling photos or even offering free downloads. The problem is that it takes an enormous amount of time to find a suitable image. Time just flies! You look at the clock and see that you've just spent an hour and a half and found only two photographs out of the approximately 15 you need. Here are some hints to save you some time:

▶ **Hint number one:** at whatever stock photo site you are searching type into the Search box whatever you think, exactly how you think it. Don't try to rephrase it for the search algorithm, and don't be politically correct. What are you really trying to say? If you are looking for a secretary, ask for secretary. This is very easy and sometimes it works.

▶ **Hint number two:** try visualizing in your mind's eye the picture you want and then "describe" it to the Search box. Be as specific as you can. If you see her as blond, search for "blond."

▶ **Hint number three:** if you have trouble visualizing your ideas, use the Google image search instead of your mind's eye.

WARNING   I am not suggesting you use images found using Google image search for your presentation! It is probably one of the worst presentation habits that I encounter. Never use images from a Google/Bing/Yahoo! image search. First, they are most likely to be copyrighted. Second, they are likely to be optimized for the Web, so quality will be an issue.

It is quite easy to illustrate concrete ideas like events, places, or actions. It's hard to illustrate abstract concepts like trust or values, and this is where illustrations are especially powerful. If you have trouble visualizing abstract ideas, tell Google what you need. If you like some of the pictures you see, "describe" them to a stock photography website. Determine how people solved this problem before on Google, and if you like one you find, just create an image more or less the same.

But please don't ever use a handshake to illustrate "partnership." To me, there are very few things that hurt partnerships more. You see, the biggest problem with stock imagery is that people produce pictures that they want to sell. How exactly is this a problem? If you want to sell a photo, it has to illustrate some behavior, emotion, or concept that frequently occurs in life—essentially, a stereotype. Stock photography is stereotypical. People sell clichés; that's their business (see some examples in Figure 5-14). You're probably seeing those images in every other presentation: a handshake, a blue globe, stacks of coins, hands holding sprouting trees, unbelievably diverse teams with members of every race, age group, gender, and sexual orientation.

▶ You can, however, use cliché stock images to produce humorous effects. Stereotypes work well as grotesque comic exaggerations.

I don't really believe in originality. I think there's nothing wrong with illustrating a concept of a car with a picture of a car. It doesn't matter how many times that was done before me. The problem with the handshake is *not* that it's not original; it's that it is not authentic, it's fake. It doesn't really represent partnership. Partnership maybe starts with a handshake but it's not a handshake. Shaking hands doesn't automatically make people partners. What does? I don't know. It really depends on the context. Now if you take time and think what makes people partners in your case and illustrate that, it will be a great illustration. So, what are you really trying to say?

FIGURE 5-14: Stock clichés.

Let's have a look at how Obama's team solved the task of illustrating his speech. I will leave out statistics and visual comparisons for the next chapter and just focus on using photographic images. Figure 5-15 shows some very typical photographs used in the 2011 State of the Union address. Overall, there were about 30 photographs used and they were mostly used toward the end of the show, during the emotional crescendo.

FIGURE 5-15: Obama's use of photos and words.

The first thing you might notice is that President Obama can afford the luxury of having his own photographers. Most of the pictures are good, and this one is no exception. Speaking to the workers from the loader is certainly very cool, but to me there's too much car on the right. Make sure your picture focuses on what you are trying to say. Apart from Obama's own pictures, there was also some other imagery used. When he was talking about wounded congresswoman Gabrielle Giffords, we saw her picture. When he produced a quotation from Robert Kennedy, we saw a photograph of Kennedy with a personal quote on the slide. Most of the time pictures were used in conjunction with words, but not always (as in Figure 5-16). Sometimes the event is so famous, like the moon landing, that text would be pointless.

FIGURE 5-16: Obama's use of photos only.

Once during the speech pictures were used as bullet points: while describing American achievements like railroads, highways, and the telephone system, black and white pictures were shown of the past. Notice how black and white pictures—of Kennedy and of U.S. achievements—are about the past whereas color images indicated the future. (The moon landing picture is in color, and that's probably because space always seems like the future, even if was 50 years ago.)

To summarize:

▶ **Illustrate actual ideas or events**. Don't insert pictures just because "using pictures is good."

▶ **Use pictures to highlight**. Pictures carry a powerful emotional charge. Don't let that go to waste. Use pictures to evoke emotion and to motivate, in the beginning and in the end. The middle is more about explanations.

▶ **What's the most important (read: big) point of your picture?** Does it display what you are trying to say? Make sure your picture is cropped so that important points are big enough.

NOTE Try the following sites to find good stock images:

Paid images can be found at:

▶ www.istockphoto.com

▶ www.fotolia.com

▶ www.shutterstock.com

Free images can be found at:

▶ www.sxc.hu

▶ www.photl.com

▶ www.morguefile.com

Free European art can be found at:

▶ www.wga.hu

Using Abstract Illustrations

If you need to explain rather than to impress, there are different types of images for that. Have a look at the Figure 5-17. The first picture is a photograph of a man wearing a uniform and smiling. This is an actual person with a name. His face produces an emotional response. We might like it or not. The next picture is much more abstract. It may even represent the same person, but a lot of details are gone. There are no facial expressions to interpret; this person is more generic and replaceable. It's not a person anymore; it represents the workforce. Far fewer emotions are engaged by this illustration. However, you can still see his hairstyle, a badge, and his basic shape. The last picture is as abstract as it gets. It's not entirely clear whether this is a male or female. Can you go even more abstract than that? Well, actually, you could—it just wouldn't be a picture anymore. You could just write "a person."

FIGURE 5-17: Levels of abstraction.

Sometimes less emotion is what you need. If you need to illustrate a process, draw a map, show relationships, or explain an abstract concept, photos aren't the best way to go. Instead, use pictograms, contours, and geometric shapes. Welcome to the wonderful world of infographics. The oldest human writing systems—cuneiform and Egyptian hieroglyphs—were based on how things look rather than how they sound. However, over time visual representations were largely replaced by phonetic ones as western civilizations developed alphabets. Oriental characters, while originally quite pictorial, lost their apparent meaning to an untrained eye. In the 20th century when information overload became serious problem, a new visual language was developed.

What you see on Figure 5-18 is a page from a Soviet book dating back to 1932. Now, even if you don't know any Russian, you can guess that the drawing illustrates different proportions of... well, something related to people in different parts of the Soviet Union. These are in fact per capita budgets, where each red circle represented five rubles. You can see a lot of money being poured into southern parts of the USSR (these are now independent states Uzbekistan, Tajikistan, and Turkmenistan). This isn't to say that the Soviets developed this language; it was in fact based on an approach by the Austrian professor Otto Neurath called "the Vienna method." But you can also see that those stick figures have very limited flexibility. They can only stand; there's no simple way to make them do other things. In 1972 a German designer Otl Aicher created the iconic look (pun intended) of stick figures and the foundation for the modern pictorial language was established. Figure 5-19 shows an excerpt from the United National Park Service cartography symbols vocabulary. Much more flexible! You can tell stories using those figures!

In the history of presentations there was a period when something called "clip art" was used for much the same purposes. Presenters now have much better options. If you use clip art, please stop already. It was quite cool about 20 years ago; it's passé now. Better have a look at how modern 3D rendering software makes stick figures prettier without adding insignificant details (see Figure 5-20). Now you can create some really cool stuff! So, what's the use of all this?

First of all, icons and pictograms are great addition to your bulleted lists. They are probably the cheapest way to make your lists friendlier. See Figure 5-21. But I think that as far as presentations are concerned, the prime use of pictograms is with process maps. Figure 5-22 shows different business units within an Internet retail company.

FIGURE 5-18: Soviet infographics from 1932.

Winter Recreation

  Chair lift/Ski lift

  Ice fishing

  Ski jumping

  Snowboarding

  Snow-shoeing

 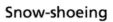 Winter Recreation area

FIGURE 5-19: Stick figures from the National Park Service.

FIGURE 5-20: 3D rendering of stick figures.

And Figure 5-23 is even more complex; can you guess what's going on there? This is an offshore programming process. It starts with discussing the project scope. "What is it that we are trying to achieve?" Notice how the concept of scope is notoriously hard to visualize. The client is the guy in a blue suit; the account manager is in the red T-shirt. Throughout the diagram, blue is always the client's color and red is always the business's color. Blue arrows represent parts of the process visible to the client, whereas red arrows indicate that these parts are internal. Next, the account manager discusses the project with a programmer and they come up with a proposal. After the proposal is signed, the actual work begins. I won't bore you with any more details; I think you get the idea. There aren't that many secrets in drawing those maps: keep them untangled, use consistent language (only one meaning per icon and per color), emphasize important stuff, and don't include the unimportant. For example, it would be a mistake to make arrows very bright because icons are obviously much more important.

Exercise:

 Brainstorm ideas   20 min.

 SMART **Make them S.M.A.R.T**   5 min.

 Present them   3 min.

FIGURE 5-21: Using icons to illustrate a bulleted list.

Call center & IT   Inventory handling   Delivery & cash collection

FIGURE 5-22: Internet retailer's process map.

Apart from the process maps, you can use pictograms in more or less the same way you use photos—for illustration. There is, however, an important difference: you use them for concepts rather than for actual events or people. Figure 5-24 shows some of President Barack Obama's slides again. The first slide's focus is on the $1,000 figure, but in the background we see a silhouette of a family receiving those benefits. It would be a mistake to use the photograph as the focus because it's not a particular family; it's an abstract family, hence the abstract picture. On the next slide the emphasis is on the figure "$630 per year"—it's bright orange—as well as on the plug and the thunderbolt representing electricity. The last slide is a mistake because this is where they could have shown a photograph of the school. It doesn't matter that much where it is located, and seeing actual students who had improved their reading scores would be more effective.

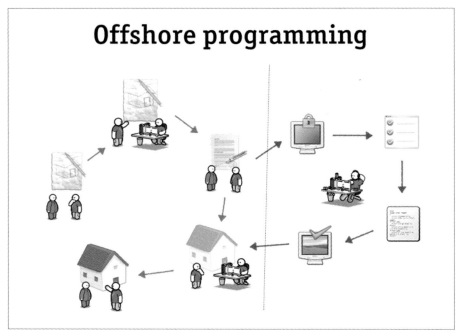

FIGURE 5-23: Software outsourcing process map.

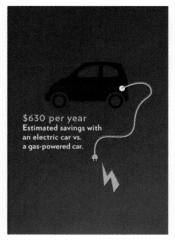
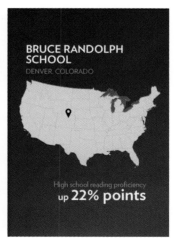

FIGURE 5-24: Obama's "infographics."

Last but not least: if you can draw, draw! There's something about hand-drawn pictures that just wins hearts. Even if they are crude, they have a lot of emotional warmth.

That's it! The next chapter continues the discussion of infographics but in the context of visual comparisons, to make and prove points.

To summarize:

> ▶ **Illustrate abstract ideas or events**. Try not to use photographs for those kinds of illustrations; they give too much unnecessary detail.

> ▶ **Use icons for process diagrams, flowcharts, and so on.** This is a universal language and is easily understood.

> ▶ **Icons are a great addition to your bulleted lists**. Even in the most basic form, pictures have some emotional charge.

> **NOTE** To find some good pictograms, check out `www.iconfinder.com` and `www.findicons.com`; these search engines find mostly free icons. Also check out `http://helveticons.ch`, which is a rather pricey but extensive and wonderfully universal icon set.

▶ Hand-drawn presentations inevitably turn out to be the best presentations I see at any conference.

SUMMARY

The key points to remember from this chapter are as follows:

> ▶ **Much like everything else in your presentation, slides should have a goal.** Moreover, elements on your slides should have goals. "What's the purpose of this slide/element?" is the single most important question to answer as far as slide design is concerned.

> ▶ **Don't design slides for reading, design them for scanning.** Separate important information from the less important. The most obvious way to do this is to make important elements big and bright and less important elements smaller and faded into the background. If you want to highlight more than one concept, you might be losing your focus.

> ▶ **The most important element on a text slide is the header.** Make it big and clear. Ideally, people should be able to make sense of your presentation by reading only your headers. Try not to make lists with more than four items.

> ▶ **Use photographs to produce emotional impact and to illustrate concrete events, things, and places.** Use stock illustrations with caution: avoid clichés entirely or use them in humorous ways. Use abstract icons to illustrate abstract concepts when you don't need much detail. Avoid clip art.

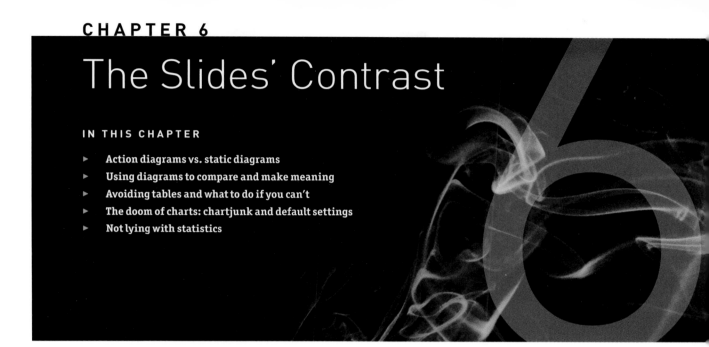

CHAPTER 6

The Slides' Contrast

IN THIS CHAPTER

▶ Action diagrams vs. static diagrams
▶ Using diagrams to compare and make meaning
▶ Avoiding tables and what to do if you can't
▶ The doom of charts: chartjunk and default settings
▶ Not lying with statistics

In Chapter 5 you read about illustrations, the purpose of which is to inspire emotions or to give quick hints to both the speaker and the audience about the contents of the speech. But what if you don't want to entertain or impress, but rather want to explain and persuade? This chapter deals with the basics of infographics, the art of visual explanations. A special focus of this chapter is using charts to produce powerful visual comparisons.

ENERGIZING LIFELESS DIAGRAMS

When I see a diagram in a presentation it usually looks like the one shown in Figure 6-1. A bit dull isn't it? Still, I think it's a wonderful diagram. I know the author was feeling a sense of accomplishment when he finished making it. I know that to him, it made total sense. It answered all those nagging questions, like "how?" and "who?" and maybe even "why?" Unfortunately, wonderful as it is, it is entirely unfit for the purposes of a presentation.

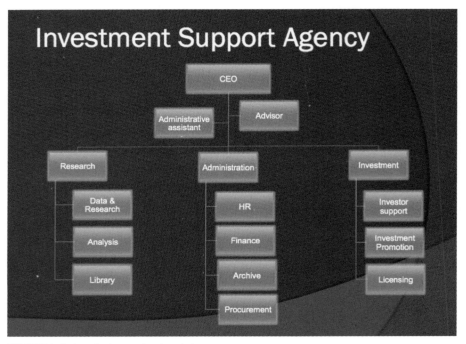

FIGURE 6-1: A typical organizational chart.

The problem with most diagrams shown in presentations is that they could probably work as an analytical tool, but they need too much explanation to be of any use. They are not pictures that are worth a thousand words, they are pictures that require a thousand words to comprehend. But that's not even the worst problem with a slide like this. Although people do need time to digest information, you can set up the animation and show the slide gradually, layer by layer. As long as the whole picture makes sense, it will work. The main issue here is that the picture is senseless and lifeless. The chart lacks drama. It's not going anywhere. It's too static.

Like a good story, every good diagram needs some simple contrast, some conflict. It needs a hero and a villain. It needs some action. Okay, this is a structure of something—so what? Where are the challenges? The deadlines? What's important and what's less important? Where's the

▶ A good diagram is like a good story—it has conflict, it has a hero and a villain.

goal? These are the questions that ultimately make us study and understand things. This chart doesn't answer any of those questions in any meaningful ways.

Consider some examples. Figure 6-2 is a diagram designed by NASA. It shows the flow between different convection zones at the sun. Even though the diagram doesn't make much sense without a legend—can you see (I'm tempted to write "feel" here) how much more dynamic it is? Do you see the inflow and the outflow? Something is happening! There is a clear opposition between + and –, the picture is divided into three main parts, and there's something going on between them.

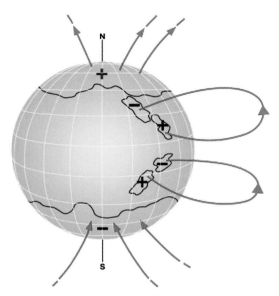

FIGURE 6-2: NASA diagram of the sun's flux-transport dynamo.

"Yes," you might say, "but this is a process diagram whereas previous one was an organizational chart, which represents structure rather than actions!" Well, that is precisely why you should be avoiding "structure" diagrams whenever possible. In 2000 Henry Mintzberg, a renowned management theoretician, together with Ludo Van der Heyden in their article, "Organigraphs: Drawing How Companies Really Work" published in *Harvard Business Review*, suggested replacing organizational charts with something they called "organigraphs." The latter show how a company works rather that how it is structured. They've suggested replacing static charts with action charts, which is what I am suggesting you do with your slides.

Figure 6-3 is essentially the same chart as Figure 6-1, but redrawn in a more action-oriented way. Do you notice any differences? See how the organization works now? Do pictures help? It took me about 10 minutes to draw the first chart (mostly struggling with SmartArt alignments) and about 40 minutes to draw the second. Was it worth it? You decide.

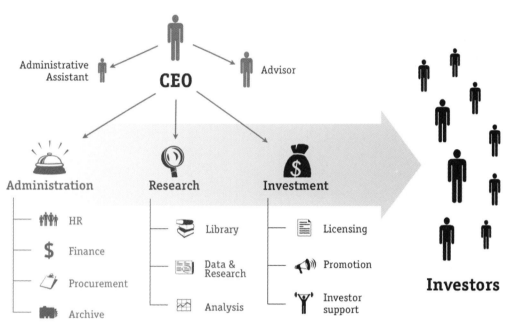

► By the way, I used only freely available symbols from the Windows Wingdings font to build Figure 6-3!

FIGURE 6-3: Organizational chart redesigned.

To create the chart in Figure 6-3 required me to do more up-front thinking. I had to understand the overall point of my chart and draw it accordingly. You can't draw these kinds of diagrams mechanically. Try drawing your structure as a process and feel the difference. It is said that if it can't be drawn, it can't be done, which means that if you don't have a good visual representation for a project you will have a hard time making it reality. When you are drawing, you have to answer a number of crucial questions like, "Who is going to do what in what sequence?" Equally important is to realize what *not* to draw on diagram. It is hardly possible to do the drawing without setting your priorities straight.

USING COMPARISONS

Most good diagrams I see either move somewhere or compare something to some other thing. This is the secret. Right now only one type of static visual explanations come to mind that really works—cross-section diagrams—and this is only because of the implicit opposition between the surface view and the internal structure. Difference. Change. If you want change, you must show it.

Figure 6-4 shows what is probably one of the most famous diagrams in the world: the Brookes print. It was designed in Plymouth, UK, in 1788 by the Plymouth Chapter of the Society for Effecting the Abolition of the Slave Trade. Its sole goal was to explain the horrific conditions on board a typical slave ship. Since 1788 it was reproduced many thousands of times in print, found its way into school textbooks and museums, and some might say even became the symbol for the abolitionist movement itself. What's the secret; why did this picture suddenly become so popular and powerful?

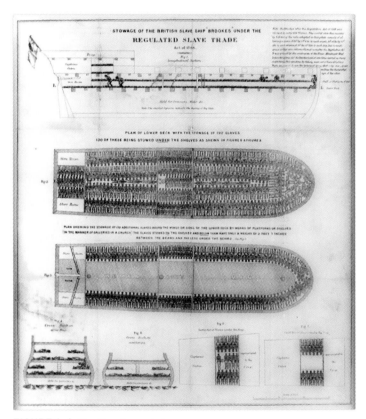

FIGURE 6-4: The Brookes print.

First of all, it lifts the veil. It showed what was happening inside a seemingly harmless ship. Why do we almost immediately realize that the things going on are torturous and inhumane? The diagram displays two aspects: free space and occupied space. The point is there's almost no free space. And that's very efficient, but that's also very inhumane. Live people were reduced to the status of cargo here. That's torturous and inhumane. "What's the juxtaposition? What's the change?"—these are the questions you should ask while designing slides in general and explanatory slides in particular.

Scale Slides

Figure 6-5 shows another NASA chart comparing different planets of the solar system. Just in case you are wondering, 2003 UB is what later was named Eris, a dwarf planet behind Pluto, also larger than Pluto. Its discovery eventually lead to Pluto being stripped of its planetary status—because apparently it was easier for astronomers to remove one planet from the list than to add another one. We can appreciate things better in comparison, and we can better appreciate the true size of a planet by placing it next to other celestial bodies. Using this approach, Pluto is too small to be a planet.

FIGURE 6-5: The planets compared.

NOTE Of course, diagrams like these are nothing new. They've been around for centuries, helping us to understand the real magnitude of things we never saw. I don't know why but I seldom see slides like this in presentations. Why? Most of us don't understand all those thousands of miles, pentaflops, billions of dollars, and so on. How much is it really? These sorts of slides can help.

Steve Jobs famously used this type of method to explain size and weight of his MP3 players in a whole array of presentations. Both size and weight matter a great deal in MP3 players, because people carry them in their pockets all day long. How do you know whether this one will be too heavy, too light (this also can be an issue, especially with cell phones), or just right? In 2001 Steve Jobs compared the size of the first iPod to a deck of playing cards. He also described it as being "lighter than most cell phones." In 2005, while presenting the iPod Shuffle, he compared its size to a pack of gum and its weight to four quarters. In both cases he didn't just say it, he actually produced slides showing a deck of cards, several different packs of bubble gum, and four quarters stacked nicely on top of each other.

The problem with creating slides like these is not that people don't take the time to make them. Making them is relatively obvious. You just place two pictures (your object in question and another) next to each other, so that the comparison gives your object scale. The problem is that presenters slack off and choose instead to go the easier (and less effective) route of just giving out the numbers. "It's just 14 ounces," those presenters might say. And the audience is then left to think, "How am I supposed to know whether 14 ounces is heavy or light? Is it that a good weight for an object like this?" They have nothing to scale it against unless you give it to them.

▶ Comparing a certain object to other everyday objects is a great way to make connections for your audience that might be otherwise hard to for them to grasp.

Change Slides

In 1840 a French engineer Charles Minard—also recognized as one of the information visualization pioneers—was asked to investigate the cause of the collapse of one of the bridges on the Rhone. In his report, he included a diagram (shown in Figure 6-6) that explained it all. As you see, the riverbed beneath the bridge had washed away on the left side so the bridge just had no other choice but to collapse. The beauty of this diagram is that it really is worth a thousand words. Notice how the "before" state is juxtaposed against the "after" state. That's change.

> **NOTE** There were many more great charts produced before the 20th century. Edward Tufte, a Yale statistics professor, is an avid collector of those masterpieces and features them in his books on visual communication. Those dinosaurs of the past might seem irrelevant now in the age of Facebook and Twitter. Indeed they were designed for paper rather than for screen, and the information density is therefore much higher. They might not have clean sans serif typefaces that became commonplace later, but nevertheless, they provide excellent demonstration for why visualizations became so popular in the 20th and 21st centuries. We still have much to learn from these examples.

Figure 6-7 shows a couple of Barack Obama's slides again. Let's analyze the one on the left first. What's the point of the slide? "Between 2000 and 2009, U.S. annual income declined"—that's the message. When I face a task like this, I am tempted to produce a trend chart with all the years between 2000 and 2009. I would probably even include years before 2000, just in case. As shown here, that's not always necessary. Maybe all you need is a sort of before and after. Why say more if you only need that much? The decline is shown with a downward arrow and the difference is marked with bright yellow. Although it doesn't look that sophisticated, this is not a bad slide at all. It gets the point across.

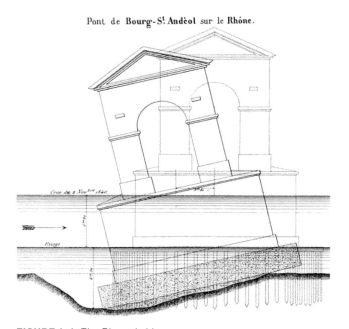

FIGURE 6-6: The Rhone bridge.

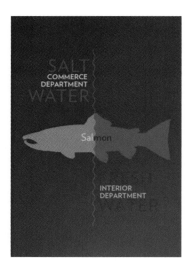

FIGURE 6-7: Obama's comparison slides.

The hero of the slide on the right is salmon, traveling from fresh waters (presumably rivers) to salty waters (presumably oceans) and changing jurisdiction from the Commerce Department to the Interior Department. One salmon divided. The absurdity of the situation is communicated quite clearly and within White House style guidelines.

Venn Diagrams and Matrix Slides

The salmon shown in Figure 6-7 brings the topic dangerously close to Venn diagrams, which I have no doubt you've seen hundreds of times. They look like overlapping circles and visualize relationships and contrast between two or more sets of data or abstract concepts. I used Venn diagrams in this book, for example, in Chapter 2, Figure 2. I don't even need to produce another Venn diagram here; you can easily draw one in you head. Imagine two overlapping circles, one marked as "Education" and another as "Entertainment". What do you get in the middle? (Answer: "Edutainment"). Portmanteau concepts like this one can be easily visualized using this kind of diagram. A close relative of the Venn diagram is a matrix slide, also known as "the four quadrants." Unlike Venn diagrams, which have only one axis, typically horizontal, matrix slides have both horizontal and vertical axes.

Both are very simple forms that have potential to amplify your message, make it clearer, easier to understand. Be aware, however, that as a visualization tool they work a bit like a megaphone: they only amplify the message but not improve it in any fundamental way. If you start with an interesting but somewhat unclear message, they will work beautifully. But if the message is banal it will be like a banality is being shouted very loudly. People hate that. Please don't use these instruments if you think they will make your point more interesting or give it more weight. They won't. They just make the point more obvious. So if there's no point, it will just be more obvious that there isn't one.

Take a look at a couple of examples. The matrix shown in Figure 6-8 was produced by Steve Jobs at the 2006 MacWord Conference. He was presenting iWeb—a simple program for creating websites for people who don't know any HTML (like me). This is probably the best comparison slide I have ever seen. That's the whole philosophy of Apple in just one slide! Notice how in the lower left corner there was some space left for the competition—I think it was Microsoft Front-Page or maybe Microsoft in general. The audience laughed, and he got the response he wanted.

Jobs also produced a very similar diagram while seriously explaining the iPhone positioning. This time axes were "smart—not so smart" and "easy to use—hard to use" with iPhone being in the upper right corner: both very smart and very easy to use. You see, that's a heck of a promise. Only because he had such a great reputation of actually fulfilling his promises he was able to get away with that.

▶ Notice, however, a mistake on the part of a designer. While trying to differentiate two waters, the letters of fresh water became almost illegible. Your juxtapositions need to be clear.

▶ The upper right corner of the matrix reserved for "us" (as well as the 2 × 2 matrix itself) is a stereotype. But what do we do with stereotypes? We make jokes about them.

	Ugly	Beautiful
Easy	X	iWeb
Hard		X

FIGURE 6-8: iWeb matrix.

You can combine Cartesian coordinates and Venn diagrams together and produce something like an approximation bubble chart, as shown on a Figure 6-9. This slide was created during one of my own projects as an attempt to explain the company positioning for potential customers. Note, however, that this diagram is too complex to be presented in one piece; it needs animation to reveal it slowly, layer by layer.

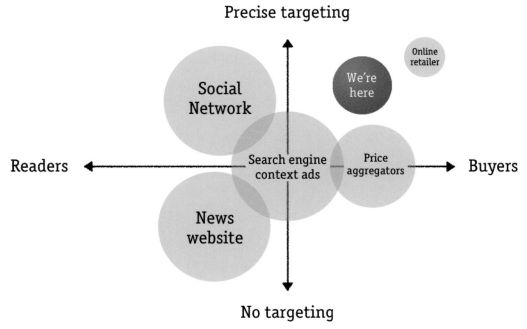

FIGURE 6-9: Startup positioning.

AVOIDING SMARTART IS THE SMART THING TO DO

Sometimes people use "diagrams" just for the sake of using something. They think, "Whatever it is, at least it's not just a list!" They are afraid of showing a simple list and think that a diagram will give their idea a sense of sophistication. It won't. Microsoft PowerPoint has a whole array of SmartArt "diagrams" dedicated to the purpose of glorifying lists (see Figure 6-10). Avoid them. The attempt is futile; it's still a list. Note that this applies only to the List type of SmartArt, not to other types like Process, Cycle, or Relationship—which are true visualizations and might be useful—especially if limited time does not allow you to draw a diagram especially for the occasion (which is always better than using a template).

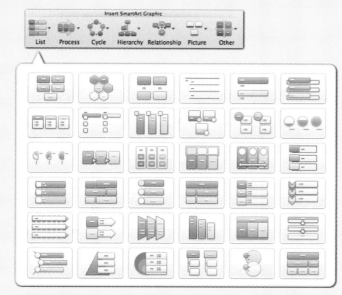

FIGURE 6-10: Microsoft SmartArt.

Tables

Do you have you more than a 2 × 2 matrix? It's a table! In fact, a 2 × 2 matrix is a table, too, albeit a very small one. Now I have to warn you: tables are a great analytical tool. You can probably use the terms "financial analysis" and "spreadsheets" interchangeably. However, they are dramatically bad for the purposes of presentations. Tables just have too much data for a quick glance. They demand thinking. People study tables, which takes time. Do you really want them to think that much?

Maybe you need to show an excerpt from a report. Let me give you a couple of hints on how to deal with that:

- ▶ Make your headers really stand out (contrast headers and contents).
- ▶ Group related ideas together and introduce a sensible order wherever you can.
- ▶ Delete everything you don't really need.
- ▶ Use alternating colors to improve contrast between rows. Don't show gridlines unless you really need to. Seriously, try it; the table won't fall apart if you turn your gridlines off. Alternating colors do the same job much better.
- ▶ Visualize everything you can.
- ▶ Use animation to show the table gradually or use semi-transparent masks to guide the audience's attention.

Figure 6-11 shows more or less the same table, before and after. We eliminated some rows we didn't need and created four sensible categories. The table still takes time to comprehend, but much less so than before.

I once had a client who was a regional manager at a major international corporation. He had to present at a meeting using the same standard template managers from other regions used so there was no unfair advantage to anyone. When I say "standard template" I don't just mean colors and logos. I mean there was a fixed amount of slides with charts and tables already embedded and all he was allowed to do was to fill the tables with his data. And those tables were probably the worst tables I have ever seen!

In the end, we formulated a single message for every slide and highlighted the most important numbers, which reinforced the message (we made the font visibly bigger and changed its color to red). So when the next slide appeared my client paused for a while allowing the audience to grasp the slide and then proceeded to talk only about the most important figure. It was a success.

To recap: Avoid tables whenever possible. If you need a table, answer the question "what is my message?" before designing anything. Delete any extra information that nobody really needs. Guide the audience's attention by highlighting key figures.

DATA VISUALIZATION

Now, if you have a table full of numbers, it's time to get to the subject of data visualization. This is an extremely wide and complex subject. I wouldn't even dream of trying to give you a comprehensive overview of this subject in the small amount of pages I have here. However, I do understand that next time you're working on your presentation, you probably won't have enough time to conceive an ingenious and novel visualization anyway. So I will just touch on the most popular diagrams and most common mistakes people make.

Function	Base (2010)	Target (2011)	Status
Customer reviews	None	Customer interacts with web-site	100%
Customer loyalty program	None	Major impact for cross sales (bonus program)	90%
Information - news	Limited	News engine	70%
Affiliate program	None	Significant rev driver	50%
Mobile native apps	None	iPhone, Symantec, Andr, BB	40%
Product search on site	Limited	Best in class	40%
Customer engagement	None	All major social media, including built in shop and aggregator	30%
Professional consulting	Call center	Cosmetics, medical, etc dedicated	30%
Customer database	70k	500,000 (3m by 2015)	10%
Foto	500 per month	Professional studio: 5,000 products per month	10%
Personalization	None	IoT and Semantic web (Web 3.0) as applicable. Context engine ready	10%
Email management	1 blast email	Clear segmentation and customization, template ready	10%
Remarketing	None	Context advertizing	5%
Video	None	Active and regular (including education and PR)	5%
Live chat	None	Best in class	5%
Pricing tracking & update	Manual	Automated	5%
Retargeting	None	Decrease abandoned cart	5%

Purpose	Function	Target (2011)	Complete
Attract new clients	Information / news	News engine	■ ■ ■ ■
	Mobile native apps	iPhone, Symbian, Android, BB	■ ■ ■ ☐
	Video content	Active and regular (including education and PR)	■ ☐ ☐ ☐
	Affiliate program	Significant revenue driver	☐ ☐ ☐ ☐
Improve conversion	Product search on site	Best in class	■ ■ ■ ☐
	Professional consulting	Cosmetics, medical, etc	■ ■ ☐ ☐
	Email management	Clear segmentation and customization, template ready	■ ☐ ☐ ☐
	Live chat	Best in class	■ ☐ ☐ ☐
Increase empathy	Customer engagement	All major social media, including built in shop and aggregator	■ ■ ☐ ☐
Improve ROI	Pricing tracking & update	Automated	■ ☐ ☐ ☐

FIGURE 6-11: A table redesigned for presentations.

Discerning between Analytical and Presentational Charts

Just as with tables, charts are used for two purposes. First and foremost, people use charts for analysis. They visualize data to uncover hidden patterns, find dependencies, and make sense of numbers. However, charts are also used for presentations. These are two different goals. What's the difference? Analytical charts are open to interpretation. You can study them and draw multiple conclusions from those charts. Presentation charts are usually optimized to carry one and only one message. If you need to illustrate another message, you just draw another chart. Trust me, most of the time it is far easier to design two charts than to design a chart that carries two clear messages.

▶ *You shouldn't be using analytical charts, charts designed for analysis, for presentations and vice versa.*

Analytical charts are meant to be "zoomed" by the viewer. If it's on paper, you can bring it closer to your eyes. If it's on a screen, you can press a zoom button. The audience can't do any of those things during a presentation. They just don't have enough control. Therefore presentations have a much smaller resolution capacity. That is why, when you are designing slides for a live presentation, it's important you don't make stuff smaller; instead, you must delete it. Of course, you can also use some sort of highlighter to guide the audience's attention. You can magnify important stuff, make it brighter, or use the laser pointer.

▶ *However, generally speaking, if you have to use the laser pointer, that means your slides need optimization.*

Have a look at the Figure 6-12, which shows two variants of Minard's famous chart describing Napoleon's march to Russia in 1812–1813. The top diagram is wonderfully multi-purpose; it has everything you need, including the size of the army in numbers, the rivers, towns, cities, temperature, scales, and so on. The bottom chart looks far less sophisticated, but it gets the message across. The point is that you don't really need to see every single Russian river out there to realize that Napoleon wasn't defeated in any major battle.

I have no doubt that some people will find the lower chart a horrible violation of Minard's masterpiece. Likewise, sometimes people distrust simple charts; they come to a presentation expecting to think. Don't make the mistake of showing presentation-style charts when your audience expects analytical ones. Know your audience and their expectations.

As far as chart design is concerned, there are three important points to remember:

▶ **A presentation chart must affirm something.** The credit for this brilliant advice goes to Gene Zelazny, the author of the book *Say It with Charts: The Executive's Guide to Visual Communication*. Take any existing chart of yours and look at the header. It is very likely that the header is descriptive rather than affirming. It probably says something like "Third Quarter Results," but it doesn't say what the results are. Are they positive or negative? If you know what you are trying to say, it is much easier to draw a clear chart that says exactly that and nothing else. If you don't know what you need to say, get back to the analysis; it's too early to present your ideas. Again, this is one of those obvious things easily overlooked. *Say it with Charts* was first published in 1985, yet I'm still seeing those vague and unfocused charts in every other presentation.

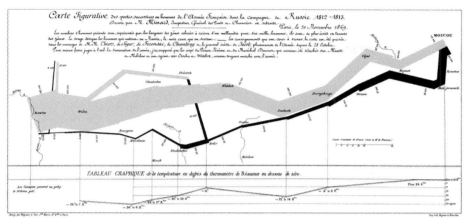

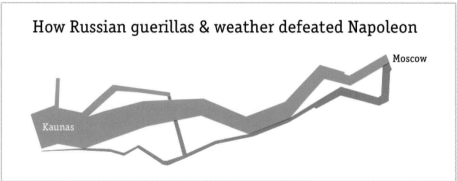

FIGURE 6-12: Two approaches to Minard's chart.

▶ **If you want to affirm something with a chart, you have to show the difference.** You
have to compare something with something else. Ask yourself: What is the comparison?
What's the difference? What chart will be best to display this comparison? For example,
the third quarter results are good, but compared to what? When you are trying to compare too many things on one chart, you are likely to produce a bad chart. The comparison
should be very clear; avoid fancy, uncommon charts, unless you really need them. They
take time to explain, and you have to educate the audience before using them.

▶ **Once you've visualized your message, delete everything else.** The credit for this advice
goes to Edward Tufte, the author of many wonderful books, including *The Visual Display
of Quantitative Information* and *Beautiful Evidence*. Although he is a known hater of presentations as a genre—mainly due to their low resolution and unsuitability for "serious

analysis"—he proposed one of the most radical simplifications for charts, called *sparklines*. He writes the following in *Beautiful Evidence*:

> *Whereas the typical chart is designed to show as much data as possible, and is set off from the flow of text, sparklines are intended to be succinct, memorable, and located precisely where appropriate.*

A sparkline is a type of line chart that shows nothing but the line. No axis, no numbers, nothing. Just the beat. Radical as it is, it works. Sometimes you don't need anything else to visualize the trend or to compare two trends. Microsoft even included sparklines in its latest edition of Office and now tries to patent the idea.

So, for every element of the chart ask yourself, "Is this thing really necessary? Or is this chartjunk (Tufte's term)?"

But you know what's best about chartjunk? No recycling necessary. Just press Delete.

Visualizing Percentages

Suppose you have this message: "25 percent of American students don't graduate from high school." You could simply note this as text on a slide. You could also, however, make it more visual. Since you already know what you want to say, the next thing to decide is, "What's the comparison? What's the juxtaposition?"

Twenty-five percent already lends itself to a comparison—it's 25 percent versus 75 percent, or simply put 1 versus 3, right? Figure 6-13 shows two slightly different approaches to visualizing the same simple set of data. Which one do you prefer? The slide on the right was produced by me; the other one was designed by Obama's team.

▶ You can always distinguish my slides from Obama's by the font. Can you see the difference?

FIGURE 6-13: One in four don't graduate.

I prefer my own version because it's much clearer and it actually does show 25 percent. You can see it straight away. Obama's slide certainly has its charm and looks more sophisticated. There was much more effort put in it. But was it worth it? I have doubts. Without looking closely, can you really see if it is 1 in 4 or 1 in 5? Hardly. I think designers themselves were having a hard time getting it right. I'm almost tempted to count whether they blew the proportion or not. Still the designers would have benefited from a little more simplicity.

The next chart by Obama's team (shown on the left in Figure 6-14) is almost perfect though. Its intent is to show that there's parity between the Democrats and the Republicans both in the House of Representatives and in the Senate, and it does the job beautifully. I drew a more traditional pie chart for comparison next. Is it better or worse? I think it's worse. Obama's slide is not a chart, it's a diagram. It shows how things actually look; it gives us an overhead view of the House of Representatives and the Senate. It is closer to truth. Arguably, drawing it required much more effort than just hitting "Insert Chart" and inputting data, but I think this time the result pays off.

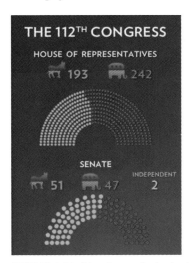
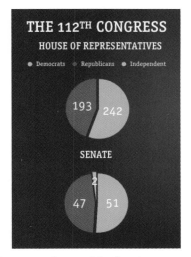

FIGURE 6-14: Showing parity in the House of Representatives and the Senate.

NOTE Please don't get me wrong; I'm not against pie charts per se. I know that lots of people—including Edward Tufte—recommend avoiding pie charts altogether. Why? They argue that it is very difficult to compare sections within a given pie chart and that bar charts would be much more effective in these cases. Pie charts are seldom used in science; they are considered too "pop." This is all probably true, but I still recommend using pie charts precisely because they are "pop." They are intuitive, and when you're comparing one part to a whole, nothing beats a pie chart.

Figure 6-15 shows a couple of charts; the left one is from Obama's deck and the right one, designed by myself, show the typical errors. Although the right one might look like more fun, which one is easier to grasp? A couple of thoughts here:

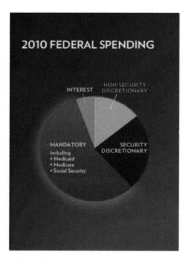 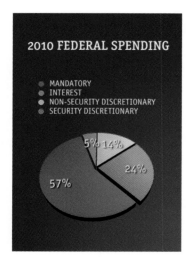

FIGURE 6-15: 2010 federal spending.

▶ Think twice before using 3D for charts; doing so distorts proportions way too much. 3D charts might look cool, but what's the point? Does it really help to get the message across?

▶ Try putting the legend as close to the chart as possible, preferably on the chart itself. Use callout lines if necessary. Draw them by hand if necessary! Don't force the readers to jump back and forth, comparing different colors.

▶ Don't use all the colors available. Use one bright color to create strong contrast. Notice on the left side of Figure 6-15, the callout "Non-security discretionary" is in bright orange while everything else is in varying shades of blue. You have no problem telling what the chart is really about.

Column Charts

The chart shown in Figure 6-16 is yet another one that made history. It was designed by Florence Nightingale, an English nurse, writer, and (surprisingly) statistician. It's a bit hard to decode, isn't it? The message is that far more people were dying from lack of sanitation than from wounds during the wars in the East. Do you get it now? Anyway, this diagram did the job: It convinced the Queen and the members of Parliament to improve sanitary conditions in British hospitals. It was a very successful chart. My only question is, "Why not draw a simple column chart instead?"

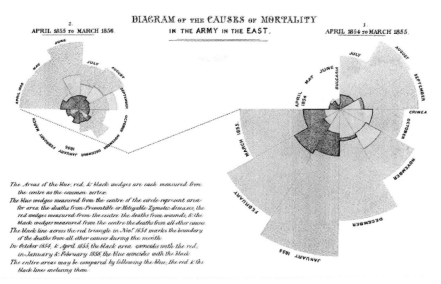

FIGURE 6-16: Florence Nightingale's coxcomb chart.

Florence Nightingale might have had her reasons. After all, statistics in general and information visualization in particular were in their infancy at the time. But look at the Figure 6-17; it's the same data on a column chart. It is certainly much clearer. Is it any less dramatic? We want to compare diseases and wounds. We get that! We can also probably sum everything up in just one pie chart, but then people might ask, "But what about the months where all the fighting happened?" On a column chart it is clear that in June and up to September of 1855 there are many more deaths from wounds and injuries than before, but still fewer than from disease.

▶ I do have to tip my non-existent hat at Florence Nightingale for merging all the other causes into "All other causes". We don't need to know what exactly those causes were, and she wisely knew that.

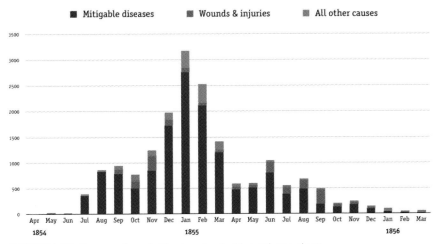

FIGURE 6-17: Causes of mortality visualized with a column chart.

So if you need to compare data on a timeline, use column charts. They are, perhaps, the most common charts you see. They are exceptionally easy to read. However, at the same time, no other type of chart suffers from chartjunk more than column charts. Figure 6-18 shows some very common mistakes.

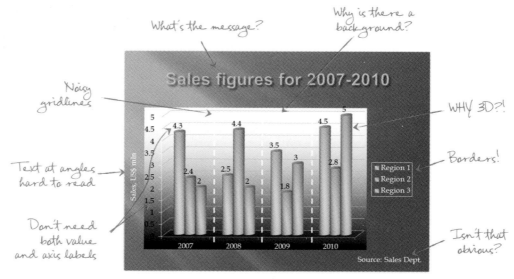

FIGURE 6-18: Common mistakes with column charts.

Why is that? For one thing, admit it, most people aren't terribly obsessed with optimizing our communication. If the software we use (whether it is Keynote or PowerPoint) creates a chart, they are most likely to just leave as it is. Unfortunately—and especially with older software—those charts are far from ideal. Another impulse people often give into is to obsess with optimization but in a wrong way. They try to make the chart communicate everything and anything. Inevitably they produce too much noise.

Take a look at Figure 6-19; isn't it a bit difficult to read? I have to tilt my head. Placing text vertically is a bad idea; it makes it impossible to read quickly. I don't know why people keep doing this. Well, actually, there's only one possible explanation: they don't need to read it themselves, because they know it already. And the audience ... who cares about the audience, right? But if you do care, why not simply turn the chart, as shown in Figure 6-19 on the right. Doesn't turning it make the chart more readable?

Bar Charts

But wait, turning the column chart produces another type of chart, doesn't it? Actually, they are more or less the same. Both PowerPoint and Keynote create a distinction between these two charts, but I think it is largely artificial; for most purposes bar charts and column charts work exactly the same way. I can recall only two instances when it's not a good idea to turn your chart axes: when you display data across time—because time goes from left to right for most people—and when you display a probability distribution (histogram). Other than those two exceptions, feel free to turn the axes whenever your text becomes unreadable.

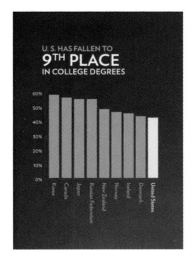

FIGURE 6-19: Changing text orientation improves comprehension.

Figure 6-20 displays two rather complex bar charts, one of which looks messier and the other looks somewhat cleaner. Actually, if you look at it, it's the same bar chart with some alterations done by me. First of all, the top chart is ordered by alphabet and the bottom chart by the counselor's score. This was done with a press of a button, very simply. And it worked! Ranking people alphabetically is not what the chart is about. The chart is about star performers and outsiders, and both could be identified easily now. Suddenly, the chart makes much more sense. Why did the author arrange people alphabetically? Most likely because this is what was suggested by PowerPoint by default and he or she never really thought about the slide's purpose. Arranging alphabetically could be useful in a large printed table where people scan to find just one person they are looking for. But this is not what they do during a presentation.

Secondly, the original bar chart (Figure 6-20, top) used a rather weird color scheme. It is very contrasting, but the end result is confusing. I chose a calmer scheme with colors for Good and Excellent closer to each other while highlighting Average. Lastly, I deleted everything deemed unnecessary; everything that didn't fit in the overall scheme of things. Focus, contrast, and unity.

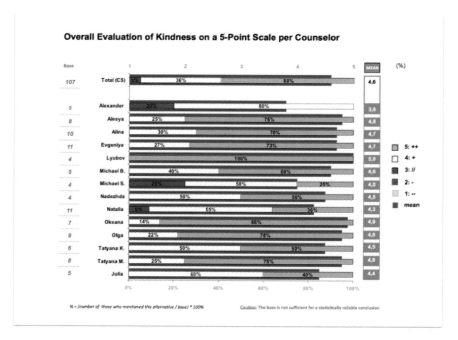

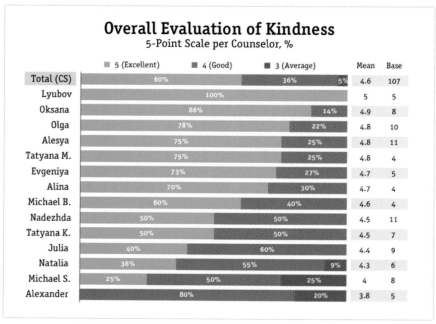

FIGURE 6-20: Bar chart makeover.

Line Charts

Line charts are line column charts specifically for trends. Their main doom is, again, chartjunk and using the default settings. I understand that tweaking the default settings in the program you use to make your slides requires thinking, time, and manual labor. Sometimes you have to delete automatically inserted legends or axes and draw others that better suits your message. The only question is, "Do you care about your communication that much?" If the answer to that question is yes, all the other questions come very naturally. Figure 6-21 shows a bad line chart (top) and its improvement (bottom). Do you need both value labels and axis labels? Do you need those bright gridlines? Shouldn't you fade them or remove altogether? Do you need full dates or will months suffice? These are the questions you should be asking yourself about the top line chart to make the improvements displayed in the bottom line chart, which is cleaner and clearer.

Figure 6-22 shows several of the best line charts I've ever seen. They're beautiful. We see a trend going in one direction and then we see it turn. Right at the tipping point in bright yellow: "President Obama Takes Office." Most of us know that correlation doesn't necessarily mean causation. Most of us also know that the U.S. economy has a huge inertia and that these trends were probably turning well before President Obama took office. Still, I am totally stunned by the clarity of communication here. They are all very persuasive. These examples show what your line charts should aspire to.

> **NOTE** One final note on charts: please make sure your chart doesn't resemble anything else to the point of looking silly. For example, there's a running joke about 20 percent of pie charts looking like Pac-Mans. Figure 6-23 shows how Obama's designers are capable of making that mistake, too. Whenever I show this chart at my workshops, the audience exclaims almost in unison: "Ties!" Indeed, these do look like a pair of men's ties. Don't let the form distract from the serious content.

LIES, DAMNED LIES, AND STATISTICS

The middle circles shown in Figure 6-24 are the same size, although they definitely don't seem so. I know it for sure because I drew them myself; they are both 80 pixels in diameter. But "80 pixels" might not mean anything to you. It's just a number. We can only make sense of this number in comparison.

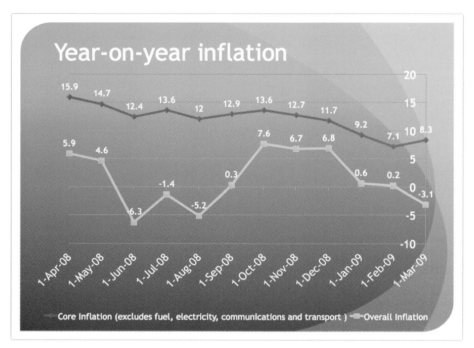

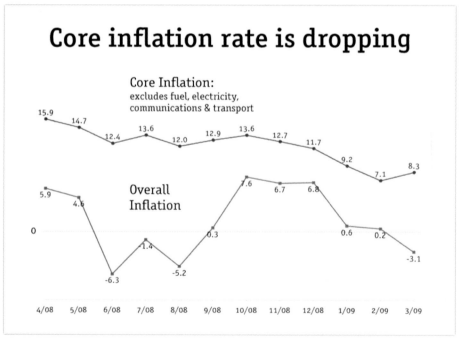

FIGURE 6-21: Line chart makeover.

This looks like a column chart but essentially it's a line chart

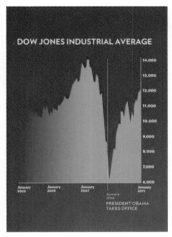

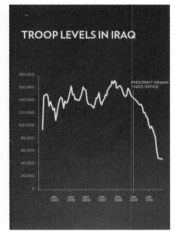

This looks like an area chart but essentially it's a line chart

Finally: a line chart!

FIGURE 6-22: Obama's line charts.

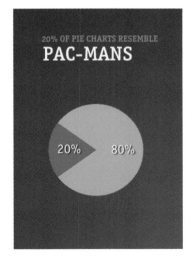

FIGURE 6-23: What does your chart resemble?

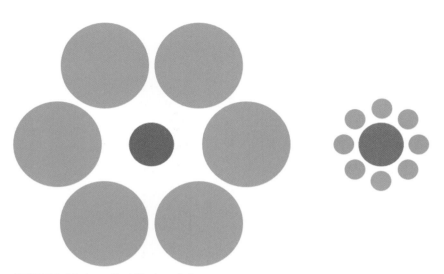

FIGURE 6-24: An optical illusion of size.

▶ I don't exactly know where to draw the line, so I will just repeat my advice from Chapter 3: avoid avoiding the obvious.

If you're surrounded by giants, you will seem small. If you're surrounded by pygmies, you will seem tall. We can try to be "objective" and not surround ourselves with anything or anybody, but then people have a hard time coming to any judgment at all. We can surround ourselves with giants, pygmies, and tons of average-sized people, but then we run into the risk of overloading the audience. So, where's the fine line?

I am assuming that you have neither the intention nor the pressing need to lie. What you want to do is amplify your message using reasonable means, which I think is okay.

If there's a very obvious comparison that you should make, make it. If it's not in your favor, don't amplify it, don't be your own enemy, but still make it. Then make another comparison and show the difference. If there's a very obvious type of chart for your type of data, use it! Otherwise, people will notice, and you will have done more harm than good by trying to avoid the obvious. Always assume that there will be at least person in the audience who read *How to Lie with Statistics*. At the very least, be prepared to make the obvious comparison. You may not have to show it, but you should have it as a hidden slide just in case.

Figure 6-25 shows one of the last slides from Barack Obama's speech. The message was that the United States is still the largest economy in the world, but other folks are catching up. This chart type is appropriately called a "bubble chart," and it is notorious for the distortions it can introduce. This is because the bubble's radius is not the same as the bubble's area and by proportionately lengthening the radius you blow everything else out of proportion. On the right you see the same data represented by a simple column chart, which is a much more reasonable choice. The difference suddenly doesn't seem all that dramatic, does it? That bubble is deflated. Again, avoid avoiding the obvious.

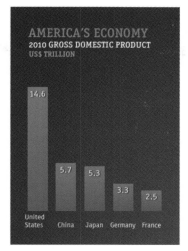

FIGURE 6-25: Obama's bubble chart, deflated.

A WORD ON ANIMATION

Animation is a great way to show change and guide the audience's attention. Unfortunately, it is frequently misused to the point that most books on presentations recommend avoiding it entirely. The problem, of course, is that people add animation to "pimp their slides," to make them "sexier." What they achieve, invariably, is the reverse effect. Flashy effects aren't really enjoyed by anyone since most of the time they have nothing to do with the content itself. However, I think that by banning animation altogether we are missing many opportunities to improve our presentations.

> Presenters use animation with intention to attract more attention, but since animation has no real meaning, it doesn't attract—it distracts.

I think there are a number of situations where animation is not just permissible, it is obligatory. For example, if you have a complex diagram (which is not a great idea but sometimes there's no other choice) or a chart, you can show parts of it in a sequence, explaining them as you go, so the audience has a chance to keep up with you. If you have multiple bullets (also not a great idea, but still) you can show them one by one, so the audience doesn't read ahead of you and thus doesn't lose interest in what are you going to say next. Even Steve Jobs does that sometimes. Finally, if you have to show a transition from one situation to another by moving an object on a slide from one place to another, do it! It is a great way show change. What shouldn't you do then?

> ▶ **Avoid complex effects.** Use "Dissolve", rather than "Spinner" or "Blinds". Unfortunately, most effects employed by currently slideware look amateurish and cheesy. This especially applies to PowerPoint. The latest version is an improvement, but there is still a lot to be

done. Keynote currently has much better effects than PowerPoint. Apple even markets Keynote effects as "cinema quality", which I find not very far from truth, at least for some of them. They have high frame rate, and you don't see sudden jumps that many people find irritating with PowerPoint animations. Still, most of those "spectacular" effects are inappropriate for serious occasions. I mostly use them to achieve humorous effect. If you watch presentations by the Apple team, they use quite a few effects themselves, but keep in mind that they are also showcasing their own presentation software at the same time.

▶ **Don't use an animation just because you can.** Treat objects on your slides like they are physical, like they are made of atoms, not bytes. This will help you to understand which animation is appropriate and which one is not. For examples, a "typewriter" animation, where letters appear one by one like they are being punched in, goes very well with a typewriter font like Courier or American Typewriter. The combination of a typewriter font and a typewriter animation creates a solid, consistent reality. Typewriter animation is entirely inappropriate with fonts like Arial or Calibri because no typewriter uses any of these fonts in reality. On the other hand, text set in a typewriter-style font cannot "Fly in" or "Grow and turn": no typewriter I know works that way. Also, once you've established a typewriter reality you cannot have 3D-objects with gradients and shadows swooshing around. You can only have effects that are appropriate for paper and ink.

CROSSREF   Remember there's more about creating a consistent reality within your slides in Chapter 7.

▶ **Don't make it painfully slow.** For most PowerPoint animations an appropriate speed is "Fast" or "Very fast." Try to keep the animation within one second unless you really know what you are doing.

WHAT ABOUT SLIDE TRANSITIONS?

There is a difference between slide animation and slide transition: the latter is applied not to a single object but to the whole slide. Transition is the way one slide changes to the next one. Should you use them and why? Rapid change from one slide to another is unnatural and irritates the eye; it doesn't give the audience time to adapt. As far as I am concerned, for most cases short and simple "Fade" ("Dissolve" in Keynote) looks much better. For most situations I recommend avoiding complex transitions, especially in PowerPoint. Again, PowerPoint 2010 (or 2011 on a Mac) is an improvement, but unless you have the latest version don't even dream of using anything more complex.

The point is that even with quality effects, you need to think about the content first. When you reveal the slide people were really waiting for, the "Doors" effect ("Doorway" in Keynote, a 3D-effect that looks like entering through the door) might be appropriate, but keep in mind that this is a one-time opportunity. You cannot use it on every slide. People get tired very quickly. Please don't use the effects just because they are there.

WHERE TO GO NEXT?—VISUALIZATION RESOURCES

If you aren't sure how to visualize your data or idea, here are a few web resources to help you:

- ► **Many Eyes:** An experimental website by IBM Research and the IBM Cognos software group. Upload your data, choose a visualization, and then make a screenshot! There are currently 20 different types of visualizations to choose from.

  `http://www-958.ibm.com/software/data/cognos/manyeyes/`

  or

  `http://goo.gl/PQ2Zu`

- ► **Chart Chooser by Juice Analytics:** This is a web engine with the slogan "Your data meant for action." There are currently 17 different types of charts available. Unlike the previous engine, you choose the visualization type first and upload the data second. You can also download the results in PowerPoint!

  `http://www.chartchooser.com`

- ► **Periodic Table of Visualization Methods:** This site is a smorgasbord of 100 visualization methods in 6 categories. Not all of them are applicable to slides, but some are definitely fun. If you're bored and want something novel and groundbreaking, don't go here, because you will lose half of your day browsing.

  `http://www.visual-literacy.org/periodic_table/periodic_table.html`

  or

  `http://goo.gl/RdE86`

SUMMARY

The key points to remember from this chapter are as follows:

- **Show change.** If you want to explain or persuade your audience, if you want to change their thinking, you need to show change. The problem with most diagrams is that they don't have any juxtaposition within and thus don't go anywhere. Try drawing things the way they work, not the way they're structured. Replace organization charts with organigraphs.

- **Don't shy away from simple solutions.** Don't be afraid to use simple comparisons like Venn diagrams and 2×2 matrixes. They can be powerful, but the trick is to have a real (not an imaginary) opposition within. But avoid visualizations for the sake of visualizations.

- **Think!** Before designing a data visualization chart, ask yourself: "What am I trying to say exactly?" Let the chart demonstrate this and only this idea. Get rid of chartjunk: unnecessary labels, legends, backgrounds, and so on. Don't succumb to default settings; they are far from optimal!

- **Don't avoid the obvious.** The 20th century has seen a lot of tricks with data visualizations. Please don't try to fool your audience with fancy charts or uncommon comparisons. Always try obvious visualizations first. If there's an elephant in the room, deal with it.

CHAPTER 7

The Slides' Unity

IN THIS CHAPTER

▸ Trying to make your slides pretty
▸ Designing without becoming a designer
▸ Deleting the logo; using fonts and colors
▸ Combining pictures with text
▸ Making rules and capitulating to them

This is the last chapter in Part II, which deals with aesthetics of slides. This chapter talks about proportions (again), colors, fonts, and using pictures and text together. Applying the principles and methods you learn from this chapter will not only make your slides look better, it will also make them clearer and more accessible to your audience.

AVOIDING UGLY SLIDES

Aesthetics are very important; in fact, it is the second most important aspect of a slide, after basic functionality. Think for a moment about the first . . . well, the first anything, actually. Consider the first cars. They weren't too pretty. Look at the brass-era automobiles, Ford A and Ford C. With all their brass charm and even though most of them were luxury items, aesthetically they were nothing more than badly upgraded horse carriages. But then, they actually moved without a horse, which was a miracle at the time. People tend to forget about aesthetics when something is truly novel technologically.

The reason those cars didn't look good was because the design lacked unity. The carriage was designed for a horse, not a gasoline engine. Shiny brass parts didn't help that much. Only when designers started designing chassis for engines did cars start to look decent and even pretty. And it's not just cars. The first battle tanks looked like water tanks. The first airplanes looked like flying bookstands. The first personal computers . . . well, have you ever seen the Apple I? It looked like a huge typewriter in a wooden case made by someone who had no idea how to work with wood. Why did it sell? It was one of the first fully assembled computers for hobbyists, and they didn't care much about how it looked as long as it worked.

But now we don't see many ugly cars. We don't see ugly planes. Modern battle tanks look amazingly cool, even though aesthetics are not a prime concern there. There are almost no ugly computers. Most of the slides produced by non-designers (and most of the slides in this world *are* produced by non-designers) look like they've just appeared on Earth yesterday.

Why is that? I blame the software, or more specifically, its defaults and the amount of choice it is offering to the user. These are top two reasons why (despite enormous hassle with file formats) I prefer Keynote to PowerPoint: better defaults and fewer options. That's right, *fewer*. I am not a professional designer, and neither, I suppose, are you. We don't need to do anything and every-thing. We just need few things that work. Unfortunately, the authors of PowerPoint succumbed to a well-known illness called "featurism." They've added a lot of options but sacrificed the quality and overall usability of those options. As a result, most PowerPoint users live under impression that if they paid for all those options, they now have to use them all.

This phrase from one of the presentations by Steve Jobs precisely describes my feelings when I look at most of the slides I see: "So, we've taken a look at this market and it's a zoo! It's a zillion little Flash players and the market is incredibly fragmented; nobody has much market share . . ." It *is* a zoo when it comes to slide design! There are a million fonts, colors, and styles of pictures. Many slides look incredibly fragmented, and no single item on the slide has strong dominating position, not even a header. They look like somebody took a template, which wasn't great from the beginning, and then applied some "creativity," trying to really "improve" it with lots of borders, gradients, and logos. People are desperately trying to make things prettier, but the result is hodgepodge and lack of unity. Sometimes it's because their ideas aren't conceptually solid. Sometimes it's because they practice decoration, not design.

I've met lots of people (especially in "serious" fields) who were suspicious of aesthetics and design. "Beauty is deceptive," they say. They think presenters should be concerned solely with the substance and that spending any time trying to improve the form is just wasteful. And there is, of course, some truth in that. Beauty can be deceptive; after all, it's just an outward appearance. I am strongly against decoration for the sake of decoration. To me, aesthetics is not about making things prettier. It's about making things better, more efficient, and more competitive. This is why the chapter on aesthetics is the last chapter in the part of the book about slides. Conceptual design precedes aesthetic design, but the latter has its rightful place.

For one thing, there's a well-known connection between aesthetics and usability. Good-looking things can seem easier to comprehend; aesthetics aids learning. In 1995, Japanese researchers Kurosu and Kashimura found that cash machines with better-looking interfaces seemed easier to use to most people. They just felt more intuitive to the users. However, all the experiment tested was an a priori judgment—people weren't actually using those ATMs, they were just looking at the interface designs. But then in 2000, three Israeli scientists—Tractinsky, Katz, and Ikar—demonstrated that this effect holds true even after the actual use. People generally perceive aesthetics as an indicator of how understandable the system is. If the system's developer makes an additional investment to make the system better looking, users make an additional effort to study it. Aesthetics pays off.

▶ Aesthetics aren't just deception. Aesthetics and usability are connected. Good-looking slides can seem easier to understand and aid the audience in following your point.

Secondly and most importantly, aesthetics helps in selling. In the 20th Century, packagers came to the conclusion that good-looking products sell better. Now the packaging is so good it's hard to throw away. Is this good or bad? Is it wasteful? Arguments can be made either way, but right now that's the way it is, that's how human psyche works. We sometimes forget that presentations are mostly about selling, not necessarily products, but ideas. It doesn't matter whether a presentation is for a scientific concern, a not-for-profit, or a business. It doesn't matter whether your clients are internal or external, or whether you think about them as your clients at all. If you are in front of them, then they are your clients; they are your audience. So sell. Persuade. Make a difference. You can do it more or less aggressively, but you cannot avoid it. So what if you have to throw away your presentation's "packaging" afterward? It doesn't cost much to recycle slides, does it?

▶ Packaging is as important for selling ideas as it is for products.

SLIDE DESIGN FOR NON-DESIGNERS

What do you *really* want from your slides? You want them to improve your communication—make it clearer and more concise. Also, you want to produce an emotional impact. Coincidentally, this is precisely what the audience wants. They don't want decoration. They want clarity, and they

▶ Self-restraint is much more important in slide design than creativity

want to be alive during the process. So design is not about decoration; it's not about adding stuff. Rather, it's about following simple rules and ruthlessly deleting everything that doesn't fit.

SLIDE DESIGN—THE MINIMALIST APPROACH

There's a very effective solution to "the zoo" problem I mentioned earlier with presenters using a million fonts, colors, and styles of pictures: just use white background with black Arial font, a minimum amount of illustrations, and no other colors for your diagrams. This gives the slides a very strict look and produces a much-desired uniformity. By the way, if you don't want to know anything about design, it's best to stick to this approach. It works. It is certainly not the best approach, but it clearly says that you are concerned with substance. Some people appreciate that.

However, beautiful as it is, this approach fails on one important count—it doesn't invoke emotions. It doesn't take advantage of the aesthetics-usability effect. It misses the opportunity to differentiate your communication from the rest of the crowd. It says that although you care a lot about substance, you don't care about design. And nowadays if you don't care about design, it's perceived that you don't care about selling your ideas.

It is true that design became an important competitive advantage in the last couple of decades. Roger Martin, dean of the University of Toronto's Rotman School of Management, famously said: "Businesspeople don't just need to understand designers better—they need to become designers."

▶ Also, leaving some crudeness and naiveté in your communication makes it seem more hand-made, more real, and more authentic.

He didn't mean, of course, that you should become a professional graphic designer. He meant that you should study design and learn to think like a designer when you need it. There's a great book by the designer Robin Williams called *The Non-Designer's Design Book*. I love the title! This is precisely what I am suggesting you do about your slides. Study some design without becoming a designer. If you don't study at all you inevitably end up creating decoration and not design. If you study too much, people will think that you're a designer and start evaluating your work using different, much more stringent, criteria. I think that there's really no point to aspiring to heights reached only by the pros. It's much better to be a good amateur than a bad professional. So you need to find your own personal sweet spot on this S-curve (see Figure 7-1).

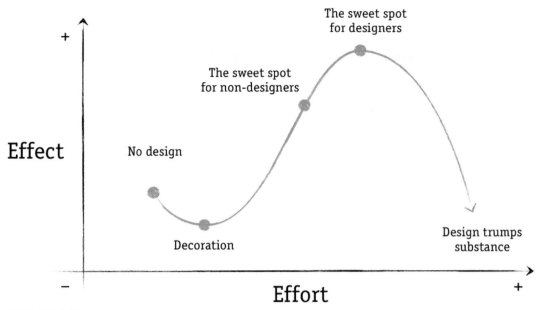

FIGURE 7-1: Finding the sweet spot.

As a non-designer, what do you really need to know? At the most basic level, there are three main design points to remember. You might find them familiar because these are the same principles that hold this book together: focus, contrast, and unity.

▶ **You need to have a strong focal point on your slides, something the slide is "about."** This is the most important thing. You need to understand what your goal is, what problem you're trying to solve. Matt Groening, the creative genius behind *The Simpsons*, said once: "I demystified the creative process. I saw it as an exercise in problem solving. I went at every job as a problem to be solved." So if you have troubles, keep asking, "What is the problem I am trying to solve? What am I trying to prove, explain or illustrate? What is the challenge in this?" If you think your design is too dull and simplistic this is most likely because the problem was too mundane to begin with. Interesting problems produce interesting solutions. Focus on the problem first.

▶ **Secondly, if you really want to emphasize anything, you need to create a sharp contrast.** You can accomplish it using visual elements of contrasting sizes, colors, forms, and so on.

▶ **And finally, you need to mercilessly delete anything that doesn't fit the overall concept.**

Of course, the devil is in details and there's much more to learn. But if you follow those three principles, you will be safe most of the time. No, *safe* isn't the right word. *Clear* is. You will be clear. Let me illustrate these principles with a case study.

> **WARNING** Some of the recommendations I'm giving here might contradict your company's presentation guides. But even if you already have a specially designed PowerPoint template, you can still read this chapter and learn some design tips. If you find that your template isn't perfect (most of them are outright bad), maybe you can modify it to better suit your needs.

Case Study: Kirov Oblast Healthcare Slide

Have a close look at Figure 7-2. This is an actual slide from a presentation on public healthcare reform in one of the Russian regions, Kirov Oblast. The logo in the upper-right corner says "Kirov Oblast Public Health." RF stands for "Russian Federation," and PFD stands for "Privolzhsky Federal District," one of seven major regions Kirov Oblast is part of. This is the second slide of the presentation; its goal is to give the audience some background facts before the real action begins.

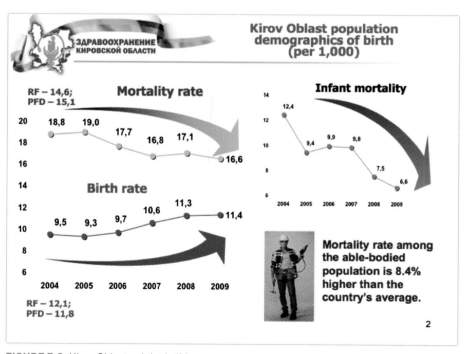

FIGURE 7-2: Kirov Oblast original slide.

I like this example because I know that people who did this presentation cared about the result; this wasn't just a formality for them. They really tried. I don't know if you've noticed, but despite their best efforts, the slide doesn't work. This is a typical "zoo" slide—too many colors, too much text, too many gradients, too many headers, too much of everything. Let's try to make this slide better by applying those three principles of design I just mentioned.

HAVING A STRONG FOCUS

The Kirov Oblast slide has at least five fairly independent headers. The logo text, the header text, and the chart titles are all approximately the same size. The brightest and the biggest visual elements on the slide are the flag and the arrows. Some point upward, some downward. What's it all about? Can we make it clearer?

Let's start with the logo. This is a rather typical problem: it occupies too much space. I'd love to make the header bigger, but I just can't; there's no space. Can we make the logo smaller? I doubt it; it has too many small details that will be illegible at a smaller size. Do we need the logo at all? Probably not. Do we need to remind the audience whom the speaker represents? Do we need the audience to remember the logo because it's new to them? The answer is no to both questions. (There's also a question as to whether the logo is particularly attractive, but let's leave that out of the equation for now.) So we don't need the logo. How do we brand the slides then? Take the logo's colors—blue, green, and red—and its font, which is Franklin Gothic.

Next, it's time to tackle the header. We can make it big now, but it's still too descriptive and lacks action. It's also a bit misleading; the slide is not really about births. So what's the point? What are we trying to say? It seems like the point is that although the stats are improving, the situation is still quite bad. Let's make sure the header reflects that thought.

CREATING A SHARP CONTRAST

Look again at Figure 7-2. How do we know the situation is improving? The mortality rate is falling while the birth rate is increasing. This is good although still not good enough; there are still more people dying. Also, the situation in other Russian regions (RF and PFD) is significantly better. Okay, here's the contrast. Ideally, you need to have two slides: one comparing birth rate and death rate and a second comparing rates with other regions. But let's assume that you are limited to just one slide for some reason.

How do you make a comparison? Line charts are fine; the only problem is with colors. Green doesn't quite represent mortality; it is traditionally associated with something positive. Let's swap the colors around: red will represent mortality and green will represent births. So, it's a life versus death slide. Nice idea. Not new but still quite powerful.

CREATING UNITY BY MERCILESS DELETING

Now we need to eliminate everything that doesn't fit. Do we need the infant mortality rate? No. We can have it on a different slide if it's necessary. This is a dramatic improvement, by the way. The infant mortality rate has gone down by almost half in 5 years; good job there. This could be the first slide in the presentation.

Do we need the text, "mortality among the able-bodied population"? I doubt that. First of all, picking a small-sized stock photograph of a guy with a hand drill to represent the able-bodied population is a bad idea. If we desperately need an illustration (we don't), a symbol would do much better. But secondly and most importantly, what are we trying to say? That we are 8.4 percent worse than the rest of the country? But look at the left chart—our overall mortality rate (16.6) is 12 percent higher than the country's average (14.6) anyway! Obviously, 12 percent is even more than 8.4 percent, so I guess we don't need this illustration and additional information in the lower right corner of the slide either.

Next, consider the chart. Do we need those big bright arrows? We probably did before when the slide was overcrowded, but now we don't. The trend is clear enough. Do we need both axis labels and value labels? No. Can we visualize figures for the country's average and regions' average on the same chart? I guess so. What colors should we pick? We should choose something as close to the original green and red as possible, but distinctive enough to differentiate. Figure 7-3 is a redesigned slide. Is it any clearer now?

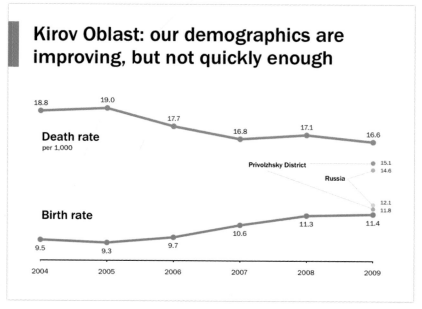

FIGURE 7-3: Kirov Oblast redesigned slide.

The new slide has a clear statement in the header, which is supported by the chart below (focus). We can see that the gap is closing but it is still wide and that we are still lagging behind other regions (contrast). Finally, by eliminating unnecessary detail we achieve clarity and consistency, now nothing looks like it doesn't belong here (unity). Not only this slide is easier to understand, but it also looks much more professional.

Now you can see how to apply the same principles in different situations by working with proportions, colors, fonts, and pictures. There are lots of important nuances to cover that cannot be explored within just one example.

Choosing the Right Proportions

Proportions have to do with focus, the topic of Chapter 5. You cannot work with proportions unless you've established a clear goal of the slide. Size signals importance. You need to make important points big and the rest of the stuff progressively smaller, but to do that you first need to decide what's important and what's not. Once you make those decisions about importance, you will be able to establish a clear visual hierarchy. Another way to communicate importance is to move an element up. The lower an element is in the layout, the less important it seems. A good place to observe this principle is on the front page of a newspaper. The most important element is the newspaper's title, probably big enough to be seen across the street. Then comes the lead news story. Its headline is set in the second biggest font size and it has a big photo. Under the headline is a quick summary of the article, which is set in even smaller size. The text of the article itself is even smaller size, making it a level four. There's probably level five text, too—really small letters well below everything else such as copyright notices, and so on.

As far as typical bulleted slides are concerned, level one is typically the header, level two are the bullets, and maybe there's a level three with page numbers which most of the time you don't need. Figure 7-4 shows a rather typical slide template, in which levels two (the sub-headline) and four (the page numbers) can probably be eliminated altogether. For a "non-thinking" slide, I recommend having just one or two levels, for a "thinking" presentation, you could add a couple more, but still four is an absolute maximum. Always ask yourself, "Do I really need another level?" Please don't be afraid of whitespace. Only when you have enough whitespace can you make the main message stand out. This makes the main message more vulnerable, but that's the whole point.

Resist the urge to utilize every inch of the slide. This approach produces nothing but clutter.

When it comes to proportion with photographs, the photograph will inevitably dominate your slide and it should, therefore, be large enough. By making your pictures small, you're diminishing their emotional impact. If you don't want emotional impact, just lose the pictures! The only exception is when you are illustrating your bullet points with either pictograms or photos; in this case remember to keep them equal in size and uniform in look.

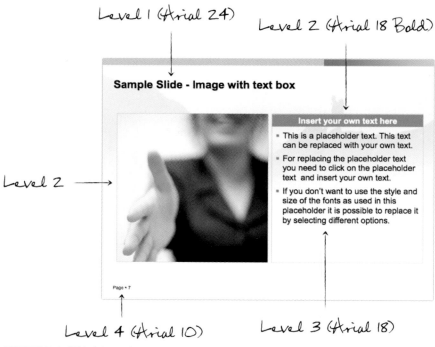

FIGURE 7-4: Slide hierarchy.

CROSSREF You can look back at Figures 5-15, 5-16, and 5-21 in Chapter 5 to see how the White House designers dealt with the issue of proportion for photos and pictograms.

Another important point is that the difference in sizes should be clear enough. Look back at the Figure 7-2 for example; the header is level one, the chart titles are level two, and everything else is level three. However, the main header's font size is 20, while the "Infant mortality" text is 18. The difference isn't visible enough; it looks more like a mistake. In the redesigned version, the header is 40 points, level two is 25 points, and level three is 14 points.

Choosing Colors

Your choice of color generates an emotional tone for your overall presentation. There's symbolism in colors. Most of them are associated with distinct psychological states, and those associations can be quite powerful and enduring. In Western culture, black symbolizes morbidity or death, white represents chastity, red symbolizes blood, pink symbolizes romance, and so on. A number of those associations differ across cultures. For example, white is a color of death in Japan, and the bride's dress in China is traditionally red. With presentations you have the added issue of typically including brand colors. But what if you don't have a corporate brand book or a style guide? What if all you have is a logo? Or maybe not even a logo?

The first color to choose is the background one. Is it going to be dark or light? The general rule is that if you are presenting in a large and darkened venue, a dark background is preferable. Also, a black background looks really cool if you are presenting on a white wall without any screen; this way people cannot see your slide's boundaries, and the pictures and text just float in space.

> **NOTE** However, if you are using a black background, you can kiss goodbye any attempt of printing your slides: too much wasted toner.

Another point to consider is that a lot of stock photography is isolated on white. If you have a white background for your slides, isolated photographs work seamlessly; otherwise, you probably need to spend time removing the background.

Suppose you've decided to have a colored background; if so, which color should you use? Look at your company's logo. Does it have a color dark enough or light enough that you can use as a background? If you don't have a logo, just pick your favorite color. The color of your eyes would probably work. Whichever colors you use, your dark color better be really dark and your light color better be really light. Avoid picking colors in the middle. Otherwise, you will have trouble finding a contrasting color for the font (see Figure 7-5). For the main font color, I suggest you chose black or white. Dark gray or light gray might work, but the further they are from black (or white), the more likely legibility can become as issue.

▶ *If the logo doesn't have an exactly appropriate color, remember you can lighten or darken any color which is already there.*

Ok   Not Ok   **Ok**

FIGURE 7-5: Background and font colors.

What other colors can you use? If your logo has any other colors, use them. If it doesn't, it's time to do some color matching. You probably know that some colors "match," which means they look like they belong together. What are those colors and how do you find them? Surprisingly, the author of the first theory to address this issue was none other than Johann Wolfgang von Goethe, a famous German poet, the author of *Faust*. In his 1810 book *Theory of Colours,* he was the first to propose a color wheel where red was in opposition to green, and blue was in opposition to yellow. The simplest color-matching techniques are based on these oppositions. This is pure math; you don't need to match anything manually. A computer program does it all. You can use an offline tool like ColorSchemer (www.colorschemer.com) or web sites like Adobe's Kuler (kuler.adobe.com) or Color-Blender (www.colorblender.com). On a Figure 7-6, you can see the most widely used principles.

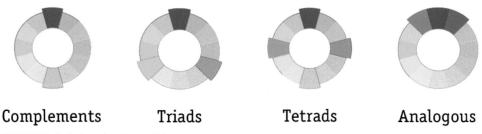

Complements   Triads   Tetrads   Analogous

FIGURE 7-6: Color wheel oppositions.

Some of those tools require you to enter an RGB code for your primary color. If you're on a Mac, you can easily identify a color using the DigitalColor Meter app or a system-wide magnifying glass tool (see Figure 7-7). If you're on Windows, it's trickier. You need to open your file in Paint (or make a print-screen if you don't have a file) and use the color picker to identify the color (see Figure 7-8).

Your next challenge is to use your primary and secondary colors and resist the urge of adding any more colors unless you really, really need them. Figure 7-9 shows the White House logo, along with the color wheel and the colors actually used in designing the slides for President Barrack's Obama's State of the Union address in 2011. Yellow, red, and green were used to highlight different aspects of the slides, and shades of blue were used for less important differences. Does it make sense to you now?

Figure 7-10 shows a final example of how you can create meaning with colors. The first slide uses random colors and looks plain. The second slide uses colors to communicate the message. There are two basic categories—patients and doctors/hospitals. Patients are red and doctors are blue. The darker the blue, the more difficult case this place can handle. There are no easy patients here, but if there were, they'd be light red. Is this visual language clear to you? To me it's pretty obvious, and you can really add meaning to your slide using color to help carry your message.

FIGURE 7-7: Mac color picker.

❶ Open the file   **❷ Pick the color**   **❸ Press "Edit colors"**

                                                                        ❹ Copy values

FIGURE 7-8: Using Windows Paint to identify colors.

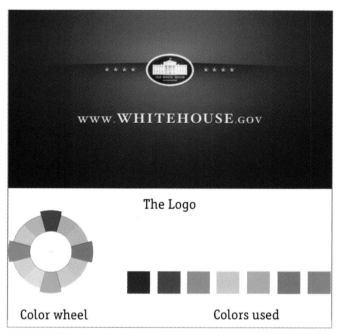

FIGURE 7-9: The White House palette.

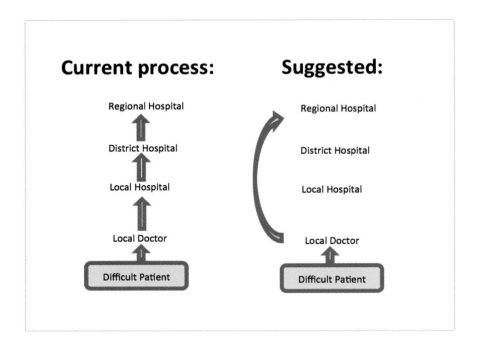

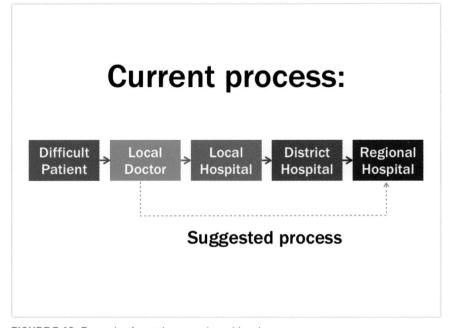

FIGURE 7-10: Example of creating meaning with color.

BASIC PRESENTATION COLOR GUIDELINES

If the preceding seems like information overload to you, then here are three basic rules to help you design your slides from scratch:

1. Start with a template where your background is white and your text is black. Seriously. Resist the urge to be different, readability is much more important.

2. Pick one bright color for highlights, preferably the dominant color of your logo. Red, green, or blue would do. Don't highlight more than one thing per slide. Use gray (the shade that's in the middle between black and white) for charts.

3. Don't add any more colors. (Maybe one, if you really, *really* need to.) *Voila.* At least as far as color is concerned, your slides will look professional.

Working with Fonts

"Which fonts do I use? Are there any rules?": Those are probably two of the most popular questions that people ask at my workshops. Lots of people are taken aback by the amount of fonts their operating system or office suite offers. We know that fonts are different, and we see some people use fonts masterfully. But how do they do it? I think that's a fair question for a non-designer.

NOTE Once again, if you have a particular font you should use according to your corporate style guidelines, by all means, find out what it is and use it. However, if you have certain freedom here, read on.

Typography is a highly interesting subject. I would argue that your choice of font is much more informative than your choice of color. The font really does say a lot about you. It also has a potential to greatly improve (or dampen) your communication. Fonts are like non-verbal expressions for written words. You can say the same word with many different expressions. Likewise, you can set the same word in different typefaces and produce vastly different responses. You can make your words look bold and confident or shaky and irresolute. You can make them look louder or quieter. You can produce deep and powerful impressions using fonts, and all without spending hours searching for pictures! Fonts are like your accent, like your handwriting style. Even if you use the default fonts like Arial, Times, or Calibri, the fonts you choose tell something about you. Maybe it is that you're very formal or very lazy or don't care about design at all. As I've reminded you before in this book, you cannot *not* communicate.

So, what are the rules about choosing fonts? First of all, you need to understand that there's one single most important parameter for a font—its readability. Is the font easy or difficult to read? The rule of the thumb here is to choose more readable fonts for your main text and less readable fonts for highlighting important points. No, seriously. Difficult-to-read fonts make text more memorable and the difference is fairly significant, up to 14 percent. However, as this requires additional effort on the part of the audience, you cannot use that indiscriminately, whenever you please. Use decorative fonts for headers, a few important words that you want the audience to remember, but never for the main body text. People cannot remember everything anyway and they hate when you try to force them to.

> **NOTE** According to a 2010 article in *Cognition* by Princeton scientists Connor Diemand-Yauman, Daniel Oppenheimer, and Erikka Vaughan, difficult-to-read fonts like Monotype Corsiva or Haettenschweiler produced up to a 14 percent better recall. Isn't that cool? Unfortunately, there's a dark side as well. A 2008 research by Hyunjin Song and Norbert Schwarz demonstrated that people may remember more but they are much less motivated to do anything about it. In this study, participants read instructions for physical exercises or cooking recipes in either easy-to-read font (Arial) or difficult-to-read font (Brush Script). After reading, the Brush Script group predicted that activities would be more difficult and require almost twice as more time in comparison to the Arial group. Looks like with fonts you can strive for either recall or impact, but you cannot have both.

Apart from readability, fonts produce different emotional responses because people attribute different characteristics to different shapes. Thick fonts are perceived as "heavy," thin as "light," geometric fonts are "cold," and fonts with rounded edges are "warmer" and "softer."

As many of you no doubt know, there are several different groups of fonts. There is no generally accepted classification for fonts, but Figure 7-11 shows five types of fonts that you might encounter in presentations: Serif, Sans Serif, Slab Serif, Script, and Decorative.

The most profound difference is between Serif and Sans Serif fonts. You probably know what "serifs" are—they are the tiny strokes at the ends of the letters. They produce invisible lines underneath and above words that lead the eye, with the purpose of improving readability. They actually do improve readability, especially in smaller sizes in print. However, if you look at your operating system's interface, you don't find many of them. Sans Serif fonts work better on computer screens, at least in smaller sizes. Since you are designing "for the last row" (a credit for this rule goes to Garr Reynolds), that is, for maximum legibility, fonts used in presentations are big enough to negate this difference. So, you can use both Serif and Sans Serif fonts (but not necessarily at once).

Fonts can be italicized. Here lies another distinction between Serif and Sans Serif fonts. If you look at the Figure 7-12, you'll see that Sans Serif italic isn't much different from a regular font; it is just slanted a bit. On the contrary, italicized Serif has an entirely different shape, very close to handwriting. Both italics, however, greatly reduce readability. It is customary to use italics for quotes (review Figure 5-15 in Chapter 5) and sometimes for the names of books. Other than that, I suggest you avoid italics. On no occasion should you use it for highlighting; use bold type instead. Don't use underlining either. It crosses out parts of words and generally is hard to read. Stick to bold.

▶ Can you use both italics and bold in cases where bold is already taken for something else? The rule is that if you need more than one highlighter, you don't know what you're trying to say.

Arial   Sans Serif

Times   Serif

Officina Serif   Slab Serif

Brush Script   Script

Dolores   Decorative

FIGURE 7-11: Types of fonts.

> **NOTE** Strictly speaking, the proper term for the whole collection of variations including bold, italics, and sometimes also condensed, expanded, and so on, is *typeface*, while the word *font* is reserved for a particular variation like Arial Condensed Bold. After some deliberation I decided to use the word *font* everywhere because this is what a non-specialist would do in everyday life.

Yes, fonts have different weights. There's bold and normal and sometimes even more than that; for instance, Helvetica Neue comes in six different weights on every Mac by default (see Figure 7-13). This is a great advantage as it allows you to apply different weights according to the "weight" of your message. Thin fonts look very elegant, refined, and subtle; bold fonts look very, well, bold and forthright. Bolder fonts are more difficult to read; it is not recommended that you use them for the body text, only for emphasis.

Arial Regular
Arial Italic

Times Regular
Times Italic

FIGURE 7-12: Regular text and italics in Serif and San Serif fonts

Slab Serif fonts are different from regular Serif fonts in one important aspect—contrast. If you look at Figure 7-11 again, you will notice that there is a lot of variation in thickness of strokes on the Times font. Look at the letter "e" in particular. Its tail is very thin but the middle is thick. This is called *contrast* in a font. Now look at the Arial font; its letters stay mostly the same. Serif fonts are typically high contrast, whereas Sans Serif fonts are low contrast. However, the Slab Serif fonts are low in contrast and lack serifs. Officina Serif used in this book is a characteristic representative of this group. Another font in this category you might have on your computer is called Rockwell. Slab Serifs were invented for printed ads and headlines; however, a very recent trend is to use them also for main body text, like in this book.

Helvetica Neue UltraLight
Helvetica Neue Light
Helvetica Neue Regular
Helvetica Neue Medium
Helvetica Neue Bold
Helvetica Neue Condensed Black

FIGURE 7-13: Helvetica Neue in different weights.

Are there any other high-contrast fonts like Arial? There are some (like Optima), but apparently not enough to justify the existence of a distinct category. Have a look at Figure 7-14 to appreciate the differences. Both Optima (high contrast) and Officina (low contrast) look quirky and unconventional. It takes skill and practice to use them, and I won't be covering them in this book.

The last two categories are script fonts and decorative fonts. They are both used for the same purposes—to create atmosphere. Scripts emulate handwriting; decorative fonts are either Serif or Sans Serif fonts but distorted in some quirky fashion to make the effect more interesting at the expense of readability. If you have a closer look at a sample decorative font on Figure 7-11, you will see that it is a modified Slab Serif. Under no circumstances should they be used for the main body text, but they work great for headers or short blocks of text. More on them later; for now, let's have a closer look at the two most widely used categories: Serifs and Sans Serifs.

	High contrast	Low contrast
Serif	Times	Officina
Sans Serif	Optima	Arial

FIGURE 7-14: Contrast and serifs.

MONOSPACED FONTS

There's also a group of fonts called monospaced fonts, and they use both Serif and Sans Serif characters. They are called monospaced or fixed-width because all of their characters occupy the identical amount of space; wide letters like "w" are the same size as thin letters like "i." Figure 7-15 shows examples of monospaced fonts that are probably installed on your computer. Even though Consolas and Monaco are generally Sans Serif fonts, they still use serifs for letters like "i" or "l". Unless you have computer code in your presentation, you should avoid those fonts.

Winter 138	Courier
Winter 138	Consolas
Winter 138	Monaco
Winter 138	Menlo

FIGURE 7-15: Monospaced fonts.

SERIF FONTS

Serif fonts are also sometimes called Antiqua because they are based on the letterforms of *capitalis monumentalis*—Roman square capitals. Those fonts are classy, stylish, and formal. The Serif fonts you most likely have on your computer are shown in Figure 7-16.

Rates 138   Times New Roman

Rates 138   Georgia

Rates 138   Constantia

Rates 138   Cambria

Rates 138   Garamond

Rates 138   Bodoni

FIGURE 7-16: Serif fonts.

▶ That can be an important consideration in your font choice. If you need to transfer your presentation to different machines and platforms, these fonts present on most computers are the safe fonts to use.

The Times font dates back to 1931. Since 1992, this font was distributed with every copy of Microsoft Windows, which made it one of the most widely used fonts around. Avoid it. I'm not saying it's a bad font, but it's grossly overused. If you like it, consider Georgia as a replacement. It is also a Microsoft font, but luckily it wasn't made the default of any popular application. It has somewhat wider serifs but the most notable difference is in its non-lining figures. Since many numerals look pretty much the same (say, Times' 3 and 8), attempts were made to distinguish them by height. The result looks a bit funny and somewhat less official, but keep in mind that this is not for decoration. Varying heights do improve legibility for numerals.

Constantia and Cambria are newer fonts, and they have a much more modern feel. Look at the forms of serifs. Which one do you think is more elegant and which one is heavier? These are excellent fonts and aren't widely used, yet are present on every computer with Microsoft Office.

The last two fonts—Garamond and Bodoni—may not come by default on Windows computers. These stand among the greatest fonts ever. Despite being produced in the 16th and late 18th centuries, respectively, they remain wildly popular. Garamond is a Renaissance-style font, its gentle stokes reminiscent of ancient handwriting. It is typically associated with all things Renaissance: education, science, research. A font closely related to Garamond is used in the Wikipedia logo. In contrast, Bodoni doesn't look like handwriting at all: each letter of this font was carefully engineered with precise instruments. Just look at the contrast between the thinnest parts (called *hairlines*) and the thickest parts! Use Bodoni if you want to give an impression of luxury and sophistication, although keep in mind that it might not be compatible with other Windows machines.

SANS SERIF FONTS

Figure 7-17 shows two different Sans Serif fonts. Can you guess their names? Yes, they are different. The biggest difference is in the letter "a," but every other letter is different too. If you're good in analyzing patterns you will soon realize the principle. The bottom font's letters end with a line, which is either strictly horizontal or vertical (a technical term for those lines is "terminals"). The top font's terminals are skewed a bit. This font is called Arial. The lower one is called Helvetica. The difference between Arial and Helvetica might seem subtle, but it is actually quite profound. Like Times New Roman, Arial suffers from overuse. Helvetica doesn't suffer from overuse; it enjoys overuse! Why is that?

Sales

Sales

FIGURE 7-17: Two Sans Serif fonts.

Are those terminals such a big deal? No they aren't (although some typographers might disagree). The difference is that Helvetica is overused by professional designers, whereas Arial is overused mostly by people who don't have a clue what they're doing. Russian typographer Yuri Gordon said once, "The only quality criterion for a decorative font is the amount of good design produced with this font." Judging by this standard, Arial is a very bad font. When you use Arial, you evoke unconscious associations with all those bad designs created with it. That isn't such a great idea.

Okay, so what if you don't have Arial and you're on Windows so you don't have Helvetica either? Maybe Tahoma or its sister font Verdana (created by the same designer with slightly different proportions) would suit better? Hardly. Neither fonts are bad; in fact, Verdana was even nominated for the Best Of British Design Award in 2006. Unfortunately, they both suffer from precisely the same problem Arial does. Swedish furniture retailer IKEA in 2009 changed its catalog font from Futura to Verdana, infuriating the design community and provoking a media storm, which became known as Verdanagate. Why? Because type matters.

Figure 7-18 shows several "safe" fonts that almost every computer has. The topmost is Tahoma and the next one is Trebuchet (another Microsoft font though much less geometric).

Franklin Gothic is one of the classic 20th Century American typefaces named after Ben Franklin. Calibri is one of the newer fonts from Microsoft Office 2007, which is starting to suffer from the same problem Arial does. It is now the default in Word and people are gradually beginning to loathe it. Finally, Corbel looks very much like Tahoma except it's fresher and has non-lining numerals. If I had to choose among these fonts, my preferences in descending order would be Corbel, Franklin Gothic, and then Trebuchet.

Rates 138　Tahoma

Rates 138　Trebuchet

Rates 138　Franklin Gothic

Rates 138　Calibri

Rates 138　Corbel

FIGURE 7-18: "Safe" Sans Serif fonts.

Figure 7-19 shows four other famous and widely used fonts. Gill Sans is a default font in Apple Keynote. Myriad is a default font in Adobe Illustrator and also the font used by Apple in presentations and elsewhere. The font Meta was designed as an antithesis to Helvetica and became so popular that it was dubbed the "Helvetica of the 90s." Futura was the font that IKEA used before switching to Verdana; it is one of those geometric German fonts that emerged in the 1920s. Notice the form of the letter "a." It's very strict and machine-like, just a circle and a stick. All the other fonts are known as humanistic fonts; they are much closer to handwriting and produce a much warmer in feeling. What font do you like better? What font are you?

SCRIPT AND DECORATIVE FONTS

Are decorative fonts ever good for presentations? Surprisingly, some of them are. Lawrence Lessig used a P22 Typewriter—a distressed typewriter font, which is free for personal use. Paying homage to Lessig, Dick Hardt used American Typewriter (comes with every Mac) in his Identity 2.0 presentation. Before Apple universally adopted Myriad, Steve Jobs used a font called One Stroke Script, a handwriting script that bears some resemblance to Comic Sans, but in my opinion is a much better font.

Rates 138   Gill Sans

Rates 138   Myriad

Rates 138   Meta

Rates 138   Futura

FIGURE 7-19: Famous Sans Serif fonts.

▶ If you see a font you like, you can later identify it. Take a snapshot with your cell phone and upload the picture to www.whatthefont.com. If the quality of your photo is sufficient and there are enough letters, it will identify the font for you.

Handwriting fonts are a distinctive subset of decorative fonts. Their readability is quite low, and under no circumstances should they be used for large blocks of text. However, they're great for callouts and notes. They are used to produce an atmosphere of all things informal, hand-made, and authentic.

Sadly, most of them look quite inauthentic. Their biggest problem is that the same letters in different words look precisely the same, which never happens in real handwriting. Every "b" in your handwriting is slightly different. Some recently designed fonts, however, include different variants of the same letters. Figure 7-20 shows different shapes of the letters

FIGURE 7-20: Letters in a quality handwriting font.

"b" and "d" from the Cezanne Pro font, which was created by the P22 foundry for the Philadelphia Museum of Art. Such thoughtfulness deserves much respect. Type several "b" letters in the handwriting font you like. Are they the same or different?

> **WARNING** As an aside, because of its gross overuse by amateurs, please don't use Comic Sans. There probably has never been a font hated as much by designers and non-designers alike. Other decorative fonts you should probably avoid are Brush Script, Curlz, and Impact, but none of them gets even remotely close to Comic Sans in terms of universally acclaimed loathing. There's even a website called **www.bancomicsans.com** which, as the name suggests, calls for universal ban of this font. Comic Sans might be appropriate for a lemonade stand, but not for a presentation.

So, should you ever use decorative fonts in presentations? Some people say "no." But I think there's nothing wrong with using decorative fonts per se. It's just difficult to resist the word *decorative* and use the font not merely for decoration but to communicate meaning. Why do you need that font? What are you really trying to say? Is it applicable to your context? These are important questions. Have a look again at the Dolores font at the Figure 7-11. It will work great in presentation about children. Will it look good in a presentation about a space shuttle? It might, but only as a joke. By picking a quirky font, you are committing yourself to a difficult task of matching it with the rest of the environment. This takes time, knowledge, and practice. This is how you start thinking like a real designer.

Three Important Notes on Typography

There are three very common typography mistakes that I see in presentations all the time:

- ► ALL CAPS for large blocks of text
- ► Justified alignment in narrow columns
- ► Mixing Arial with Tahoma or having three different handwriting fonts in one presentation

The first mistake comes out of a desire to be loud, the second out of a desire to be neat, and the last out of a desire to be entertaining. All those attempts fail: they come out not as loud, neat, or entertaining but as irritating and confusing. My intention here is to help you avoid those pitfalls and provide alternative ways for reaching the same goals.

ALL CAPS DECREASE READABILITY

In 2004 the U.S. Federal Highway Administration approved Clearview as a replacement for Highways Gothic, a font that was traditionally used for more than half a century. Even more importantly, the road signs were no longer set in all capital letters. Since 2004, new lowercase signs started to replace the old signs around the country. According to some motorists, looking at new the signs is like putting on a pair of reading glasses. They are crisper, cleaner, more legible, which is exactly what you need while driving.

Why is it that sentence case is much easier to read? Apparently, people don't actually read words letter by letter. Rather, they grasp the form of the word, which is consistent even among fonts. When you capitalize words in your presentation, you are certainly amplifying the emotional impact. You are making the word SHOUT. However, you are also breaking the form of the word, making it unrecognizable and forcing your readers to actually read the word letter by letter. This can waste milliseconds for one word, but seconds and minutes for large texts. Figure 7-21 illustrates this idea. So, use all capitals only when you really want to shout something and keep in mind that you cannot shout all the time. Your audience will go deaf pretty soon. Alternatively, just use bold or color highlight to emphasize whatever you need to emphasize.

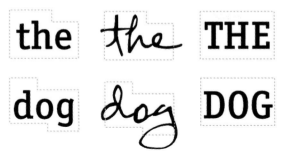

FIGURE 7-21: Using all caps breaks the forms of words.

AVOID FULLY JUSTIFIED TYPE

If you're setting something in all caps (say, a logo), you can increase the character spacing to make the word more distinct, more interesting. This won't kill readability too much as your audience already has to read it letter by letter. However, if you increase character spacing in a lowercase word you are actually inserting spaces between the letters, signaling the reader to stop after each letter. This is highly irritating (see Figure 7-22) and is the main reason why you need to avoid fully justified type. It is much better to align your text to the left (or to the right) than to try and make it fit ideally into a narrow space. Trust me, it won't make it look any prettier and it will mess up readability. If you want to achieve neatness, use hyphenation or play with a column width and font size. This requires some manual labor but produces far better results without sacrificing readability.

THIS WORKS

This doesn't

This works again

FIGURE 7-22: Choosing letter spacing that works.

USE CONTRASTING FONTS

The only reason to add another font to your presentation is to communicate something different. If you need it, use a distinctly different font. Use a font from another font group. Use a font with a clearly different weight. Match regular with bold, not bold with black (black is even bolder bold). Use Sans Serif Corbel with Serif Constantia or Georgia, not with Tahoma or Helvetica. Please don't use more than one handwriting font in any one presentation! Figure 7-23 illustrates this principle.

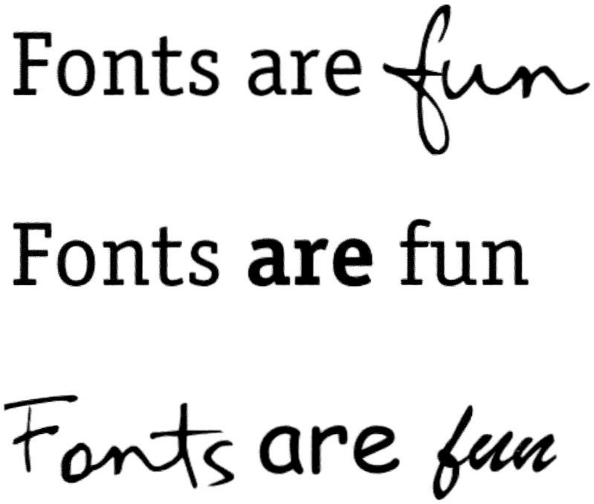

Fonts are *fun*

Fonts **are** fun

Fonts are *fun*

FIGURE 7-23: Contrasting fonts.

The first line works because the word "fun" doesn't just read "fun"—it is fun! It is fun in contrast to a much more official Officina. The second line works because the weight is clearly different and you know where the stress goes. The last line doesn't quite work, because I used three handwriting fonts. It looks like three different people wrote three different words; they don't even look like they belong to the same sentence. Why did they do it? What's the meaning? Avoid using different fonts if you don't have clear answer to these questions.

> **CROSSREF** Have a look at Figure 5-9 from Chapter 5 to see how the fonts were combined in President Obama's address.

WORKING WITH PICTURES

The biggest problem with pictures is the same as with fonts: People use them for decoration rather than for illustration. Suppose you have a lot of text about some topic (say, computers).

Why not add a tiny picture of a computer to the side? Here's a perfectly good reason why not; such an image introduces a distraction and accomplishes nothing. It can probably work in a children's book where the illustrator has time and skills to produce a beautiful illustration and the reader has time to appreciate it. It doesn't quite work for presentations, where neither condition is met. If you want to give the audience a quick hint about the slide, don't use photos or clipart. Instead, use simple pictograms without any backgrounds.

Sizing Your Pictures

Always remember that the key element of any slide that contains a picture is the picture, not the text. Thus, the picture should be sufficiently large. Making your picture small is like putting the most important information in small print in hopes that nobody will notice it. It's not what you are trying to accomplish, so make your pictures sufficiently big, preferably full screen. If your picture becomes pixilated, replace it.

▶ Use www.tineye .com to find the larger version or just find a similar image.

Pixilated images are painful to look at. They produce an emotional response which is directly opposite from what are you trying to accomplish. Remember this wisdom by Scott Adams: "Power-Point slides are like children; no matter how ugly they are you think they're beautiful if they're yours." Your audience will be looking at your slides much more critically than you. If you sense that the picture is slightly pixilated, it's probably way too much pixilated already. Replace it.

What if your picture isn't large enough to go full screen? Suppose you have a picture on a complex background, like Picture 1 in Figure 7-24, on the top left. At this point some people create blurry edges in attempt to blend the picture with the background (Picture 2, middle left in Figure 7-24). As you see, it doesn't work; the picture is too different. However, if you decide to make a picture even more different by adding shadow or a frame (Picture 3, bottom left in the figure), it will work! Of course, if your background is white you won't have these problems in the first place (see Picture 4, the right side of Figure 7-24). Few people would notice that the picture is slightly darker than the background. Adding shadow wouldn't work now (Picture 5, middle right in the figure); this time you don't need to separate the picture, you need to integrate it. Make the image slightly brighter and blur the edges (Picture 6, bottom right in the figure). This is where blurring really works.

Choosing the Right Format

Have you ever noticed visual "dirt" around letters and wondered where this comes from? There are different file formats for storing pictures. The most popular of them is called JPEG. It is a lossy format, which means it sacrifices quality for size. Due to the way that JPEG's compression algorithms work, the most visible damage to quality is done at the object's edges. It works fine for most pictures, but not for pictures that contain lettering. Since letters are mostly edges, they get distorted too much. There is another file format, PNG, allows compression without informa-tion loss. Figure 7-25 illustrates the difference. Have a closer look at the curves in the letters P and G, where distortions are most evident. With PNG images, you get a bigger file size (some-times way bigger), but in exchange letters and objects will be crisp and dirt-free.

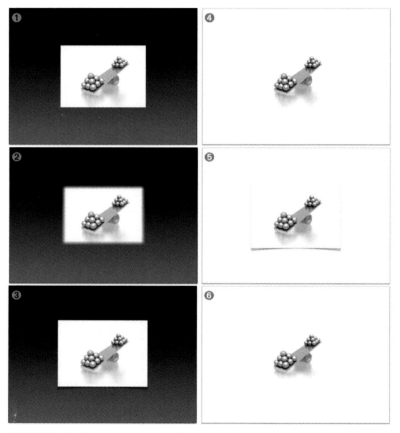

FIGURE 7-24: Matching pictures with backgrounds.

> **NOTE** There are also several formats for vector graphics, which allow your pictures to be freely resized and even recolored without any loss in quality. Vector formats don't support photographic images, but work great for simpler objects like drawings or pictograms. The most popular vector format is called SVG; many images you can find on Wikipedia are in this format. If you're on a Mac and use Keynote, you can import an SVG file via an applica-tion called EazyDraw, which exports into Keynote file format. For the more technically inclined, there's also a freeware command-line utility called svg2key.

Preserving Your Picture's Proportions

Please don't change the picture's proportions, the so-called aspect ratio of width to height. Such a change distorts your images. I don't know why but PowerPoint distorts the proportions almost automatically whenever you try to resize an image. To prevent it from doing it, make sure the checkbox "Lock Aspect Ratio" is checked (menu Format ➔ Picture ➔ Size, it is usually checked by default) and resize the image while dragging the picture by its corner, not by its edge. In a PC version you can also resize without distortion by holding the Shift key while dragging, but not on a Mac. There's no such problem with aspect ratio in Apple Keynote.

FIGURE 7-25: JPG versus PNG.

Combining Full-Screen Pictures and Text

Figure 7-26 illustrates different ways of combining full-screen pictures with text. If you write your text directly on a picture, chances are it won't be legible. This is what scares some people. Therefore, they reduce their pictures, diminishing the impact. Don't go this way. You have a contrast problem here; the text isn't separate enough. So solve the problem. How can you improve the contrast? The most obvious way is by adding a shadow. You can also add a background for the text. The color of the background should contrast enough both with the text and with the picture. In this example, the picture is mostly blue, so an orange, yellow, or red background will work. If you are concerned about losing part of your image, make the text box semi-transparent. Do you get the idea? Design is easy once you know what problem you're trying to solve. Knowing how to use your tools is also important, but if your problem is well defined, the tools will come. Focus on the problem.

UNITED WORLD IN A SLIDE DECK

Your slides are a separate reality. It's a different world with its own laws. You are the master of this world, its creator, and you are responsible for setting up those laws. What colors exist in this universe? Is it 3D or 2D? Is it hand-made or computer-generated? It is new or old? Is it classy or informal? One of the tests for truth, for believing in something, is consistency and coherence. Do the elements match one another or do they conflict? When you're adding a shadow to a text box, ask yourself if you have shadows in this world. If one box has a shadow, everything else must have a shadow, too. There are many questions to answer, and it will be actually easier for you to borrow most of the laws from the reality you see around yourself every day. We don't see many text boxes around us, do we? However, we see a lot of signs with frames. It could be a road sign made of tin or just a piece of paper affixed to a wall. What physical object does your text box represent? Is it paper? Is it glass? Is it stone? Is it metal?

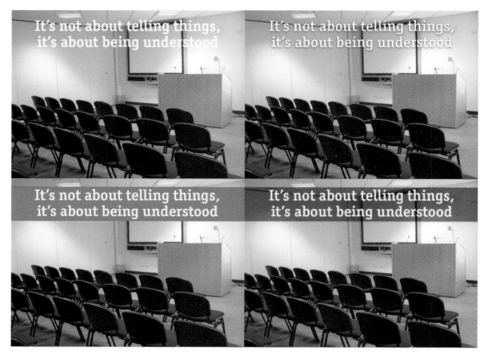

FIGURE 7-26: Combining pictures and text.

What about letters? In our reality letters could be printed, written, or drawn. If they are big enough they can also be physical and have depth, drop shadow, create a reflection. This could work just for a few letters, not for a large block of text. What about lines? A line could be drawn with a marker or with a pen. Can it possibly have shadow? No way. An arrow can exist as a drawing, in print, or as an object. Again, an object can have a realistic shadow, but the drawing can't. Here's an object that can never exist in reality: handwriting with a shadow or with a 3D effect applied. It's impossible and, therefore, unbelievable. In other words, whatever you do, try not to do it unless you really mean it.

NOTE   One thing that I really like about the Mac OS X interface is that I am always pretty sure where I am. I am in the world of metal and glass. The window border is metallic grey (probably aluminum alloy?), and the buttons are clearly glass. Now if I look at Windows 7 interface I don't know what I see. Aero? Yes, but what exactly is "Aero"?

Figure 7-27 shows a couple of examples of things that do and don't work. The first slide has a stylish 19th century border; you cannot use a modernist Futura font here. You also cannot use old-fashioned scrapbook-style picture frames with color photos. This background demands a formal font, sepia pictures, and frames that resemble actual old photographs. The next slide's background looks very industrial and modern. You can't really print on this surface so you have to pretend that your letters are physical, so give them a shadow. Also, if you give your picture some depth, make it 3D, it will work better. And, of course, you cannot have any handwriting here.

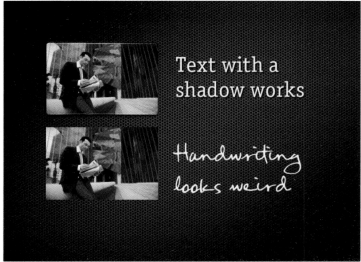

FIGURE 7-27: Consistency and inconsistency in your slides.

▶ The beauty of having a strong background (or anything strong) is that it makes most of your choices for you.

These two examples have one thing in common; they have very strong backgrounds that define most of the laws. What if your background is white? Then you have more freedom, which isn't necessarily good. You have fewer rules and have to make intelligent choices every time. So you have to make the white background stronger. A white background usually invokes a paper-like metaphor. Now you have to fully capitulate to the fact that your background is paper. This is a paper reality. You now cannot have text with shadows anymore because your letters are printed. Your boxes and arrows now should also be printed, hand-drawn, or made of something physical—plastic, glass, or metal. Make your next decision and then follow it. Remember that simple laws often produce very complex and interesting behavior, whereas complicated laws produce stupid behavior.

> **NOTE** Of course, laws are made to be broken. Sometimes you can create an interesting juxtaposition by adding a 3D object to an antique background, but then this becomes a law. This is what your new world is now about. You have to keep adding 3D objects.

Over the past couple of years, gradients become very popular. I now see people using gradients in every other presentation. However, it almost never occurs to them that gradients are not decoration. They have a purpose, which is to give an object depth. Gradients are how people see light bouncing from different surfaces under different angles. When you are adding gradients to your text box, you are creating a 3D object and now you have a 3D universe. You have to make sure that everything conforms to that rule.

Figure 7-28 shows a couple of gradient examples. The topmost example doesn't work. Unless this is a legend for heat map, it is absolutely impossible. How can you make red become blue and, more importantly, why would you want to? The middle one isn't good either. Supposedly, the

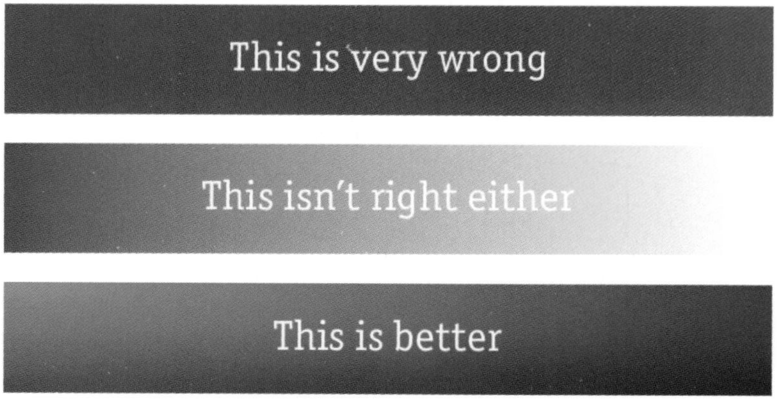

▶ One of the common design assumptions is that as a rule light comes from the upper left corner, so make sure your gradient is lighter on the left and darker on the right.

This is very wrong

This isn't right either

This is better

FIGURE 7-28: Using gradients.

light is so bright that the blue almost disappears. Why don't you just make something about that light? It makes your text fade. Gradients like this might work for arrows but this is the only exception I can come up with. The last example is better. The contrast is subtler, the text is visible, and it starts to resemble how things actually look in real life. (Go back to look at one of President Obama's slides in Chapters 5 or 6. See how gradient is applied there.)

One final thing. Don't try to make it look perfect. As Frank Roche (whom I already quoted elsewhere in this book) said once, "Leaving some raw edges in communication makes it real."

This is true; real things aren't perfect. There's a whole Japanese concept of aesthetics called *Wabi-sabi*, which is described "beauty of things that are imperfect, impermanent, and incomplete." We all understand that your slides were made by a person and not by a precision slide-making robot. It's the same thing as with handwriting. It is attractive because it is human. No two handwritten letters are the same because it's just impossible to make them the same, so we don't even expect them to be the same. If they are sufficiently alike, we trust the handwriting to be authentic. It isn't about being exceptionally strict with any of the rules; it is about keeping the tone of your communication consistent. And this is what the next chapter is mostly about.

SUMMARY

The key points to remember from this chapter are as follows:

- ▶ **Design is not decoration.** The purpose of aesthetic design is not just to make your slides prettier. The main purpose is to make your slides clearer, to reduce clutter, and to streamline your communication. The secondary purpose is to invoke appropriate emotions. By improving information aesthetics, you also make your message more accessible to your audience.

- ▶ **Slide space is precious.** A typical logo occupies too much of this space without adding much. Rather than branding your slides with a logo, use a coherent color palette and distinct fonts. This can achieve the same results without mechanical repetition of the same visual element.

- ▶ **The picture is key.** A picture is always the most important element of your slide. Make the image big; find an image with better quality if necessary. Combining text with pictures is easy once you know what problem you are trying to solve.

- ▶ **Make your reality consistent.** Establish ground rules and then practice self-restraint. Constraints are a blessing; now you don't have to make intelligent decisions every time. Don't try to make your design perfect. The goal is not to be slick; the goal is to be authentic.

PART III

DELIVERY

CHAPTER 8   Focus in Delivery
CHAPTER 9   Contrast in Delivery
CHAPTER 10   Unity in Delivery
CHAPTER 11   Where to Go Next

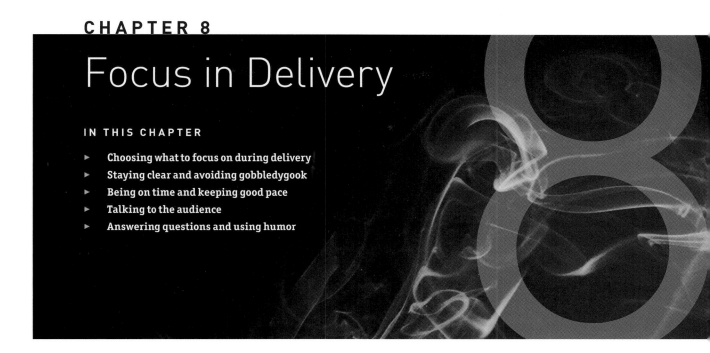

Focus in Delivery

IN THIS CHAPTER

- ► Choosing what to focus on during delivery
- ► Staying clear and avoiding gobbledygook
- ► Being on time and keeping good pace
- ► Talking to the audience
- ► Answering questions and using humor

This is the first chapter of the third part, which deals with delivery.

The key question for this chapter is, "What should you focus on while delivering your presentation?"

I assume here that your presentation is well prepared and that you don't need to improvise much.

Everything related to improvisation is covered in Chapter 10.

WHAT SHOULD YOU FOCUS ON DURING DELIVERY?

Although I personally regard polishing your delivery as far less important than working on your content, structure, and maybe even slides—your slides, to a great extent, determine your delivery—I still think delivery is a subject important enough for a separate part. This is simply because delivery is what your audience sees and hears in the end. In the end, they hear a voice that's either confident and strong or weak and crumbling. They see a person whose body language projects either passion or indifference.

It is certainly true that preparation matters a great deal, and I'm not going to take any of my earlier words back here. At the same time, on many occasions, I've witnessed speakers who went onstage unprepared and sometimes without any slides at all and yet gave very powerful talks. Certain people are able to speak with conviction without much preparation and can still shake the audience. How do they do it? It is said that they do it "by the power of their personality," that they have "charisma" or "chutzpah"—but what does that mean exactly? On the other hand, sometimes the talk seems well prepared and the speaker obviously knows what he or she needs to say. The only problem is that the talk still comes out pointless and boring. Again, the question is, "How do they do it?" (although this time with a slightly different intonation).

> **NOTE** By no means am I alone here in my focus on delivery. Public speaking is, perhaps, one of the oldest subjects of study on Earth. There are countless books, manuals, training programs, and even organizations whose sole purpose is to improve your delivery skills. And some of those books and seminars are actually quite good! Does the world need another one? My firm belief is that it does. First of all, there's still no definitive manual, which is a signal that despite ages of research, the problem is still unresolved. Public speaking is pretty much determined by culture. It is constantly evolving. The changes can be technological (PowerPoint), but they can also have to do with values. As society's values change, we start appreciating different things in life, and in public speaking. This is not a closed field, and there's still much to be studied.

There was interesting research published in *The American Journal of the Medical Sciences* in June 2005, called "The 10-Minute Oral Presentation: What Should I Focus On?" This is a question that strikes me as being very obvious yet largely unanswered. The article was written by medical doctors (Carlos Estrada et al.) and is one of the very few comprehensive scientific studies of the subject. By "comprehensive," I don't mean extensive, as the article is barely four pages long. What I mean is that most of the studies that I read before were dedicated to some particular aspect of delivery, like nonverbal communication or even use of swear words (more on this later). This one was about presentations in general. Over the period of four years, the authors observed

44 presenters from more than 20 academic institutions at various scientific meetings and analyzed feedback from the audience on three domains—content, slides, and presentation style.

As a result, they were able to identify key success factors for scientific presentations: things that the audience appreciated or thought could be improved. Are these factors different for business presentations? I doubt it. Just look at the chart shown in Figure 8-1. It makes total sense. There are no surprises as far as content and slides are concerned, which is the reason why I didn't quote this research earlier in the book. However, there are some surprises about the last domain.

▶ One big surprise is there's nothing about body language in the research.

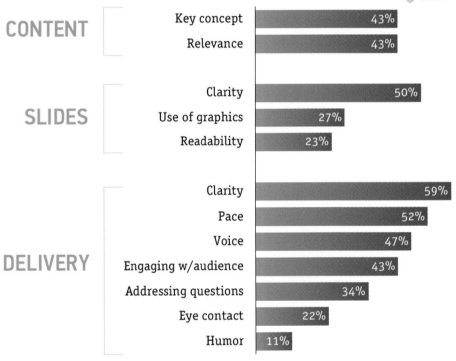

FIGURE 8-1: Key success factors according to Estrada et al.

You've probably heard that according to "scientific research," what matters most is how you look (55 percent), second is how you sound (38 percent), and a distant third is what you say (7 percent). This sounded a bit suspicious to me when I heard it, so I looked up the original research. The "7-38-55 rule" was derived from a 1967 article by UCLA professor Albert Mehrabian. The research was concerned with inconsistent communication, such as when the message "I love you" was delivered with a somber expression. In cases like this, the look, of course, overpowers the content. But we don't usually speak this way during presentations, so this finding is hardly of any significance in this context.

In the research by Estrada et al. there's nothing about body language. However, the authors mention other aspects like verbal clarity, pace, voice, engaging with the audience, addressing questions, eye contact, and, finally, humor. And this is what I think you should focus on. I want to deal with each of these subjects, one by one.

CLARITY

— *You can begin now.*

— *Ladies and gentlemen, I would like to present you a *** development program, which was devised by the Ministry of *** and approved by the resolution number ***. Among the key goals of this program are . . .*

— *Okay, stop here. Please talk to me. There's no one else here. Look me in the eye and talk to me. Don't talk to the audience; they are not here.*

— *The said program was developed . . .*

— *Yes, but explain it to me.*

— *Okay . . . Look, it's quite simple. There's a region called *** which has great difficulties with ***. We had a contract with the Ministry of *** and produced a program for them. According to the program, monitoring procedures should be implemented in the following . . .*

— *Hello! I'm here!*

— *Monitoring . . . Damn! Okay, our task here is to collect the data and make sure that the volumes of *** are equal to the volumes of ***; do you get it?*

— *Much better; please continue . . .*

This is an excerpt from a coaching session with a client. I've omitted some of the details to protect confidentiality, but I didn't add anything to this dialogue. This is how things sometimes are. While delivering and even while rehearsing a presentation, people often switch to "bureau-cratese" gobbledygook. They don't talk this way anywhere else. They don't think this way. At maximum, they sometimes write this way, but that's pretty much it. Since they don't have a lot of practice, speaking in gobbledygook during a presentation requires a lot of conscious effort. They have to make a real-time translation, which is difficult! As a result, they are constantly mumbling and fumbling, uttering outright nonsense and looking like dolts. About half of their sentences are pointless, so it takes them twice as much time to communicate the same idea.

> **NOTE** For some speakers, the use of gobbledygook speech is involuntary. They literally lose their ability to speak like a real person. Do you have this problem? If so, you're certainly not alone. I see this a lot, and as far as I understand, this tendency has to do with self-acceptance. We unconsciously try to hide our real personality, our real ideas, behind the fog of complex words because we fear that people won't like us as we are. We are afraid to be seen as "unprofessional" or "lacking in expert knowledge." This is a very broad problem of which gobbledygook is but one of many symptoms. I will be dealing with it more in this chapter.

On a number of occasions, I've seen seasoned bureaucrats who were able to achieve a certain fluency in gobbledygook—which leaves an even more awkward impression. It's not just that they are lying to us—they are lying to themselves, too! Luckily, almost no one can speak in this dialect in a real conversation with another person, at least not without smiling.

Gobbledygook is not exclusive to government officials or people working closely with the government. There are scientific or business equivalents. This is a language people use to protect their corporate interests, to avoid competition, and to shy away from truth. You can recognize it by an excessive use of passive voice, abstractions, verbs converted to nouns, and meaningless speech embellishments. This is an equivalent to decoration in design. It might sound pretty, but its true goal is to conceal the underlying mindlessness. When I hear that "the document will be submitted to the experts' meeting for endorsement," I know that this document is doomed. It will be in the process of endorsement for three years and will lose all its meaning. It will be further presented by a person who doesn't want to present it and heard by an audience who wants nothing to do with it.

In my previous consulting life, I spent a year and a half working on a project for the Russian Ministry of Economy. Here's a big surprise: even hardcore bureaucrats don't like presentations delivered in this manner! They absolutely want documents to be written in this dialect. But the presentation is more likely to succeed if delivered in a regular speaking language. Another big surprise: according to the research by Estrada et al., scientists hate scientific jargon, too! One of the key "don'ts" was "don't use jargon and difficult-to-pronounce words." The business environment seems to be the last stronghold of gobbledygook, where some people actually enjoy listening about "scalable advertising solutions" and "demand-driven business models." I would agree that some people actually look way smarter than they are when they talk like this. But really, is there any good reason to alienate your audience just to appear smart? If you recall the best presentations you've heard, chances are they weren't full of jargon and formal language.

NOTE In 2007, Todd Bishop at The Microsoft Blog (`http://blog.seattlepi.com/microsoft`) analyzed two keynote addresses with language-assessment tools from a website called `www.UsingEnglish.com`. One address was, quite predictably, from Bill Gates, another one from Steve Jobs. Both addresses were delivered to comparable audiences of computer specialists and journalists. The venues were International Consumer Electronics Show and Macworld Conference and Expo, respectively. In 2007, Jobs was already known as a master communicator while Gates was a mediocre presenter at best. It is easy to see why: Jobs's speech was much more accessible. On average, he used 10.5 words per sentence, whereas Bill Gates uses twice as many—21.6! About 2.9 percent of Steve's words were difficult (had three or more syllables), whereas Gates had 5.11 percent difficult words, again almost twice as much. It seems that one of the secrets of great communication is simplicity.

What's the matter? Are we afraid to seem like unprofessional simpletons? No sane person would accuse you of being unprofessional if your overall message makes sense. We think that complex words are more precise and speed up communication. They don't. Maybe they are sometimes easier to say, but they are harder to process. So, why do we keep doing this? Why do we keep hampering our communication for no real reason?

My only hypothesis is that it has to do with shifting cultural expectations. During the industrial revolution, we were trained to appreciate science and complex ideas in general. Speakers were trained to talk with elegance and sophistication, to use long sentences and complex words. This was a sign of being intellectual; complexity was desirable and admirable. It still is—just not in oral communication. Life is complex, and we don't need to complicate it even more for the purposes of decoration. We can go back to the basics now.

▶ Above everything else, concentrate on being understood. Speak in a clear voice and use simple language. Seriously, there's nothing more important than that.

I was once talking as a guest speaker at a business breakfast for a group of hoteliers (yes, they use PowerPoint, too). This was a good talk. I collected a record percentage of business cards from the audience, but the most pleasant surprise waited for me after it all was over. I went behind the stage to disconnect my laptop and stumbled upon a technician sitting there. I thanked him for the perfect functioning of equipment: my microphone, sound, and video output from my computer had all worked flawlessly. He thanked me back. I asked what for. He said that he sits behind the stage every day listening to all the presentations. My presentation was one that struck a chord with him. He never presents himself and never uses PowerPoint. He is not my target audience; my talk was not designed for him. Still, by using plain language and humor (discussed later in this chapter), I was able to connect with him even without seeing him. For some reason, this moment of sincere appreciation was worth more than all the business prospects I gained that day. So, my advice here is simple: talk to people. Don't design your presentations for scientists, businessmen, or bureaucrats. Design them for humans. If humans understand your talk, scientists will understand it, too. Your ideas might be complex, but your language doesn't have to be.

PACE

Pace has to do with how fast you talk and whether you keep within your allotted time limit. Both seem to be quite important, although in somewhat unexpected ways.

Speed

In the research by Estrada et al., people frequently complained when speakers were too fast. That part came as a bit of a shock to me. I am a fast talker. I also know lots of good communicators who speak quite fast. One example is Mark Kukushkin, one of the best known Russian business trainers with whom I had the privilege to study. He is well known for his rapid and almost unvarying pace. I personally don't mind when the speaker talks fast. To me, this is a sign of advanced verbal ability. I have observed presenters speaking slowly—apparently, some experts even recommend this because it is believed that the "words have more weight"—and they always come off as pompous jerks. At the same time, I have to admit that I do sometimes hear people complaining about Mark's speed. Some aren't that fast in processing. Maybe when you speak too fast, you just "blow them away" and not in a good way? This is certainly a possibility. I did some research myself and discovered that if you speak fast, you are sometimes perceived as anxious or formal. So, I can't deny that the problem exists. What exactly is too fast, though?

> **NOTE** Speaking speed is measured in words per minute (wpm). According to the National Center for Voice and Speech at the University of Utah, a friendly conversation is somewhere in the range of 110–150 wpm. Audio books are typically recorded between 150 and 160 wpm. This is probably what the optimal speaking speed is. If you have no idea what your wpm speed is, record a part of your presentation and count the words for a couple of minutes. This is a bit tedious but will give you a good idea whether or not you are speaking too fast. My own average speed is about 160 wpm—relatively fast but not too fast.

I also searched for scientific articles that deal with this subject. It turns out that although people do sometimes complain about fast speakers, for the most part, they like them. According to the article "Speed of Speech and Persuasion" by Norman Miller et al., published in 1976 in the *Journal of Personality and Social Psychology*, rapid speech facilitates agreement with nonobvious statements. Speakers with a faster pace were rated consistently higher than slower speakers. So, if you want to change people's minds, speak faster. However, for pro-attitudinal messages, a slower pace is more desirable. These findings were replicated and refined in a number of other experiments. Another interesting study called "Interviewers' Voices and Refusal Rates in Telephone Surveys" by Lois Oksenberg, Lerita Coleman, and Charles F. Cannell was published in 1986

▶ Speak faster when you're trying to persuade, and slower when you're affirming the obvious. Pause for commas; stop for full stops. I once timed Steve Jobs and his rate varied from 80 wpm to 200 wpm. Meaningful variability rules.

in *Public Opinion Quarterly*. This study attempted to uncover the voice characteristics of successful telephone interviewers. According to the study, better interviewers had greater ranges of variation in pitch, greater loudness, faster rates of speaking, and clearer and more distinct pronunciation.

So, yes, speaking at 250 wpm (or faster) would probably hurt, but otherwise, speaking fast isn't that bad. The problem is not with speed; the problem is with variability and distinctness. Obvious messages sound better when said slowly; nonobvious are better when said fast. If you don't vary your speed, you become monotonous and people fall asleep. And of course, if people cannot distinguish one word from another it doesn't matter much whether your pace is slow or fast.

Time Limit

▶ Don't worry too much about going over your allotted time. Do worry about being good. If your talk is good, you will be forgiven both by the audience as well as by the organizers.

If you've ever spoken at a conference, you know that there's always a time limit, which is almost never observed. I personally think that you should finish on time just as a sign of respect to the organizers—there's really no other reason—and it's not an issue you should be overly concerned about. The audience doesn't typically mind you going over your time if your performance is good. The public even demands encores from musicians and comedians, right? It's the same with presentations. If you really rock, your audience will demand more. One of the most flattering comments you can read in the feedback forms is that the presentation was too short.

The TED conference is famous for its strict 18-minute limit; however, there are exceptions even at TED. In 2006, Tony Robbins went over his time. Arguably, with his reputation as a master presenter, he shouldn't have done it, yet he did. He made no attempt to continue; he just acknowledged that the time was over and prepared to leave without finishing his talk. At this point, Chris Anderson, the host, intervened and asked him to continue, which Robbins did to the audience's delight. In 2005, the same thing happened with Janine Benyus, a natural sciences writer who isn't world-famous for her presentation skills. Once again, she made no attempt to stay on the stage but she was asked to finish. Why? Because she was good (as well as humble).

NOTE   According to TED curator Chris Anderson, the 18-minute limit was introduced after the organizers realized that the speakers too frequently understood "15 minutes" as "20–25 minutes." Setting the limit to exactly 18 minutes was an attempt to reach precision. It was further facilitated by installing a large countdown timer in front of the speaker and turning on loud music whenever somebody went over.

Guy Kawasaki isn't humble. His "Art of Start" lecture went 10 minutes over, and he was literally pulled off the stage by the organizers. He knew he was over his time, yet he wasted even more time by making jokes about being over his time. The audience loved him! One of the greatest presentations ever delivered! I once watched Russian governor Nikita Belykh speak for 40 minutes, when his time limit was 15. It was a good talk. He made both serious and humorous points, and his audience easily forgave him for taking more than twice his allotted time.

▶ You need to acknowledge that you're over your time as soon as you notice it. This is a great moment of truth. If they ask you to stay, they liked you. If they don't ask you to stay, chances are the issue isn't about you going over your time anyway.

VOICE

Voice is a big issue in public speaking. There's tons of advice about on how to speak, how to breathe, and how to resonate. Also, lots of people don't like the sound of their own voice. If you've ever tried to record your voice, you know it sounds a bit alien. We don't hear our voice the way other people do. When I first heard my voice recorded on an answering machine, I was enormously disappointed. That's not my voice! I wanted my voice to be lower and deeper. Later, when a career of professional public speaking appeared on the horizon, I decided to do something about it. I visited voice seminars for actors and public speakers, but none of them worked for me. They were too short; it seemed like voice requires longer practice. So, I decided to learn to sing.

> **NOTE** Just if you're really interested, this is why your voice sounds different to yourself. When you attempt to speak, you automatically trigger the so-called vocalization-induced stapedius reflex. One of the nerves in your cranium contracts the stapedius muscle in your middle ear. At the same time, another cranial nerve contracts a muscle in the auditory tube, called the tensor tympani. The result is suppression of the sound of your own voice by approximately 20 decibels. Earwax further decreases the sound intensity. All mammals have this reflex, and birds do, too. Otherwise, they'd go deaf from their own tweeting.

I always loved singing and was naturally good at it as a child. However, by adolescence, my voice had deteriorated, and I'd lost those few vocalizing skills that I had. So, at the age of 27 I got myself a teacher and spent three years learning how to sing in classical Italian fashion. I started with Russian folk songs, which (like most folk songs) require a very strong voice and breath. After about a year, I switched to romances and sentimental art songs, which were very popular in the early and mid-20th century in Russia. They require much less power and much more artistry. Compared to folk songs, romances are very complex; they are about love and pain and death and fate, all at the same time. You need to feel what you're singing.

So, I did this for a while. I was actually quite good and even gave a couple of concerts. But you know what—several years later, my voice wasn't any lower or deeper. I can make it deeper when I make a conscious effort, but when I let it go, it goes back to normal. Of course, when I need to be heard, I am heard. I was once giving a seminar for 150 participants in a forest without a microphone (please don't ask why). It did put considerable strain on my vocal cords, but they didn't even hurt next day and my voice was intact. So, what's the moral here? Do you need to train your voice if you're a professional public speaker? Maybe, but I don't think it's a strict requirement. Do you need to take lessons if you speak only on occasion? I seriously doubt it. Granted, if you have a speech impediment, it's good to have it corrected—but that's out of the scope of this book. You don't like how you sound? One way to get over this is to record yourself reading your favorite short story and then listen to the recording for some time. After a while, you'll get accustomed to your voice.

The research by Estrada et al. just says that your voice should be strong and that you should speak to the microphone if you have one. The emphasis is again on clarity. I honestly don't know whether Guy Kawasaki, Steve Jobs, or Larry Lessig took any voice lessons. My key finding from two years of singing Russian romances was that people just don't sing like this anymore. Early 20th century singing (as well as public speaking) borrowed a lot from theater. Theater implies a stage and a crowd sitting far away from the stage. They can't quite hear and see what's going on there. A good actor, then, was somebody who sounded louder and made vastly amplified gestures. Consequently, public speaking was full of theatrical mannerisms. It wasn't even speaking; it was declaiming. But look, we don't do this anymore. Contemporary speaking style is much more casual and conversational. You don't need to be a trained artist; you just need to be yourself. You need to be authentic.

▶ Don't worry too much about your voice. Relax and let yourself talk to the audience just like you talk to your friend. It will be all right; the audience doesn't expect a declamation anymore.

Professionally-made video presentations are typically voiced by paid actors. However, on one occasion when we were making a presentation about Virtual Private Networks (a specialized computer subject), we decided to use a real system administrator as a voice actor because the professional voice actor we tried before obviously had no idea what he was talking about. I think this is the future. Again, if you watch performances by contemporary professional speakers like Malcolm Gladwell or Merlin Mann, you see that they are not actors. You might call them quirky. They have edge and obviously have a passion for what they're doing. They are "interesting characters," but they aren't acting. They aren't expending any conscious effort to appear as somebody else. They are just being themselves.

ENGAGING WITH YOUR AUDIENCE

It was 10 a.m. on Saturday in Nakhabino, Moscow Oblast. I was booked for a private conference to deliver my standard one-hour talk about presentations. (Even though I did some research on the audience, you never know who you're going to face until you actually face them.) So, who was my audience now? I looked at the audience and I saw about 50 people of different regions from all over Russia, mostly men and mostly wearing business attire. Let me restate this: it was a Saturday morning at a country club and people were wearing suits and ties. This meant that I was doomed. This was not my audience.

They were the President's Program Alumni. The first Russian President, Boris Yeltsin, founded the program in 1997 with the goal to educate (or rather, to establish a then nonexistent class of) young Russian managers. Here I was 13 years later. Most of them were now in their late 30s and 40s, small business owners and executives and from regions far poorer than Moscow. Presentations? Storytelling? Slide design? They had other things to worry about. Like children and mortgages. They certainly knew much more about "real life" than I did—who was I to teach them? My typical audience was much more relaxed and hip. To make matters even worse, I was unable to position my laptop so I could see my next slide. The screen was very small, the projector was bleak, the cables didn't quite fit my laptop, and my slides looked greenish.

I introduced myself and included a Twitter hashtag. "Who uses Twitter here?" I asked. Nobody used Twitter. Not a single person! "Who knows what it is?" They all said they knew what it was, but I think they'd just heard of it from the news. "President Medvedev wrote in his Twitter...".

"They just don't have time for Twitter," I thought. "This is not my audience." But I started talking. Two Caucasian-looking guys kept having a lively conversation between themselves right in the first row. (By Caucasian, I mean Muslim people from the Caucasus region.) I jokingly told them to shut up. They said they were from Dagestan. (If you understand the context, this sounds like a mildly disguised physical threat. I do know the context.) It bumped my adrenaline level up, which is probably what I needed on this particular Saturday morning.

"This is a great test for my presentation," I said to myself. "If I can't connect to this audience, I am full of hot air." Luckily, this was a pretty standard talk, and I knew what I needed to say. But then I got the strangest feeling—the moment before I said a sentence, I knew it was not going to work. The phrase wasn't wrong; it was just empty. I didn't feel it. It was meaningless. However, by that time, it was too late; I couldn't abort it. It was on the tip of my tongue and I had to say it, but then I needed to also explain it. So, I explained. Quotes from foreign books didn't impress them at all. I had to tell a little story about every quote: "This is a guy from Silicon Valley, which, if you know, is American Skolkovo." They laughed.

In the end, I started talking about authenticity and honesty. This was where I started to lose eye contact. They didn't look away; I did. I couldn't talk about honesty to this audience. They knew life; I didn't. Who was I to tell them how hard honesty is? I forced the eye contact. Things got better. Ta da! I ended with applause. If anything, I learned how to end with applause. I was a bit over time and there was no time for questions. However, the moment I got off the stage, the audience rushed for my business card. The Dagestani guy came in to shake my hand. Not my best talk. But this handshake made me proud. Now, what did I learn from that experience?

Keeping Your Focus on the Audience

What makes the biggest difference is whether or not I am able to focus on the audience. The results differ dramatically. When you're a professional speaker, you always try to make your next talk your best talk. But you still have good talks and bad talks. It's just part of the job, like with any job. This is especially obvious when you're giving the same presentation many times, again and again. The content is almost identical, but sometimes it works and sometimes it doesn't. What's the difference? The difference is whether you are fully engaged or just somewhat engaged with this particular audience. Engaging requires caring. Do you really care about the people sitting in front of you? Is this "your" audience? Do you really want to talk to them? To challenge them and to contradict them? To persuade them and entertain them? If you do, you need to engage, to get closer, to get intimate. If you succeed at that engagement, it will be a good talk.

> **NOTE** If you're able to focus on the audience, you can have an actual conversation with them. As I said before, a presentation is just an attempt to have a conversation when there are too many people in front of you. And conversations are not just about who is speaking. Just as the speaker cannot *not* communicate, the audience can't help constantly talking back in their own (nonverbal) ways. You just have to notice it. Even if you are delivering a monologue, you still can have a conversation.

When you talk to a person one-on-one, you watch for feedback, mostly in the nonverbal form. You watch the facial expressions that your listener returns to you. This is their way of talking when the auditory channel is occupied by you. You see this feedback and you change (even if you aren't aware of it!) what are you saying according to the feedback you receive. Sometimes, you change nonverbal or paraverbal parameters of your speech, like intonations, pace, and volume. You can also change what you're saying, such as by using different words or adding examples when you feel you need them.

However, when you speak to multiple people, the amount of feedback is overwhelming and often contradictory. You simply cannot respond to everyone. At this point, many presenters enter what I call "broadcasting" mode. They start to speak as if they're on a radio, like the audience isn't there. This sends a message, too. The audience gets it almost immediately. They think, "Oh, you're not talking to me? Then I will just mind my own business." Then they communicate this by reaching for their BlackBerries and iPhones.

So, the key question is, "How do you focus on the audience even though there are so many of them?" To start, you can use a couple of key strategies:

▶ **First, you can focus on the audience only when you don't need to focus on your content as much.** This happens when you forget about the audience while preparing and really work on your message. If you know precisely what you want to say and you aren't too rigid about how to say it, you can customize your talk to the audience on the fly.

Of course, if you know what the audience will be like ahead of time and can customize your talk while you're preparing, good for you; do it. If this is a one-time presentation, you should absolutely do it. However, life is bigger than your plans. People are often unpredictable. They don't have an obligation to react the way you expect them to react. So, to a certain extent, you have to improvise in each and every talk. But the basis for every improvisation is routine.

▶ **Second, focus on particular people—one person at a time—and not on the "audience" in general.** You need to keep scanning the faces of the people sitting in front of you to understand what they feel and react appropriately. If you see that they are bored, do something! Bad presenters tend to ignore the audience. It seems like those presenters think they are better off not caring about the result. The problem is they are only going halfway. They are accepting the fact that the audience feels bad, but they try to suppress their own feelings about this fact. Accept it! A very obvious and helpful reaction is simply to say, "Okay, I see that you're bored; let's talk about the next topic" and watch for feedback. They might say, "No, it was all right. Please continue." When I just began doing this, I was frequently wrong. Some audiences just don't display their enthusiasm openly. Sometimes, you don't know until you ask.

▶ *During the talk, you need to be open to both verbal and nonverbal feedback from the audience. You can do this only when you are not preoccupied with yourself (and this is why preparation is especially important).*

Learning to Read Your Audience Better

There are two ways to get better at reading your audiences. The first is to learn to recognize facial expressions. It is a skill that can be improved. There are several excellent books and training manuals on the subject. American psychologist Paul Ekman is perhaps the most widely known expert in this field.

> **NOTE** On the first test that I took on the subject of facial expressions, I scored 8 out of 14 (it was in Ekman's book *Emotions Revealed: Recognizing Faces and Feelings to Improve Communication and Emotional Life*). I wasn't doing too well in the beginning. However, on my last online test, I scored 10 out of 10. I got to the point where people started asking, "Alexei, can you tell me how I feel about this?" because I was quicker at identifying their emotions than they were. Practice makes perfect.

Another way to read your audience—one that is slower but much more rewarding—involves using empathy and compassion. These are big words, but they simply mean feeling what other people are feeling. Humans do this automatically all the time; being social animals, we're hardwired for this. Did you ever notice that if you watch the same film with a different person sitting next to you, it feels different? You can even find some films enjoyable in some company and not enjoyable in others.

▶ Lack of compassion is the key reason for death by PowerPoint.

If you practice compassion, you get better at it. And you should be getting better at it if you want to become a good presenter. Most presenters aren't inherently callous. They don't really want to inflict suffering onto their audience. They just shield themselves from the ongoing feedback and think it's all going well as long as they are talking. They are not feeling what the audience is feeling. And this isn't right. This is one of the worst crimes a presenter can commit.

There are many ways to practice compassion. I will discuss one of the ways in the next chapter, which has to do with learning from other speakers. But the most direct way of getting to know what the audience feels is by asking. Conversations are about asking questions; so, whenever you suspect something is wrong, just ask.

Fist of all, if you keep asking meaningful rhetorical questions (seems like an oxymoron but it's not) and pausing after them, you can watch for the audience's reaction. If it's sluggish, this is a sign that you've lost contact. If the audience is relatively small, you should ask a question related to the contents of your presentation and see if anyone bothers to answer aloud (as I discussed in Chapter 3). Of course, you can't receive an answer from everyone. But that's not the goal; the goal is to engage them, to make them care. It could even be a simple yes or no question. Sometimes, nobody replies, verbally or nonverbally. Then, I just show them with my own head: "Look, this means yes and this means no, so what is it?" They smile and give me some feedback. But you can also ask direct questions about how your audience feels:

"I've been talking for quite a while; are you all right there?"

"Do we need a break?"

"Are you still with me?"

▶ If you are unsure about the audience's feelings, just ask. It really, really helps.

When you ask three of those questions in a row, it seems like you can overdo it. Sure, you can. Is this a reason not to do it? Most certainly not. You might think that asking questions like this is a sign of insecurity, and maybe it is, but again, one of the worst methods of dealing with insecurity is trying to suppress it. If you are insecure, just admit it. We all are. You can never get rid of speaking anxiety completely; even experienced speakers get nervous onstage. There's nothing to feel guilty about. "Do they like me?" is the question that never quite goes away. We all worry; but that's not a problem. The mistake is ignoring your audience.

MAKING EYE CONTACT

Eye contact is the single most obvious indicator that a conversation is happening. You can be silent and still have a conversation with a person when you look each other in the eye. Sometimes, keeping this conversation is difficult enough even with a single person. But it is very difficult with multiple people. Why does the audience love eye contact? Because it's an indication of honesty.

It's not a big secret that public speakers lie. I catch myself lying in almost every presentation. Of course, I try to minimize the amount of lies, but I can't predict everything in advance. Especially when I'm improvising, the desire to cut corners and say things that are easy to say is huge. But it's difficult to lie when you're looking other people in the eye.

According to Dr. Gwyneth Doherty-Sneddon of University of Northumbia at Newcastle,

> *Looking at faces is quite mentally demanding. We get useful information from the face when listening to someone, but human faces are very stimulating and all this takes processing. So when we are trying to concentrate and process something else that's mentally demanding, it's unhelpful to look at faces.*

Looking at human faces requires a tremendous amount of mental processing, and so does lying. It is hard to do both at the same time; that is why parents ask their kids to look them in the eye while they're being questioned. Your audience isn't much different. Most Westerners are suspicious of shifty-eyed people.

> **NOTE** In the East, this matter is treated a bit different. Averting one's eyes is a sign of polite submission. A friend of mine teaching in Japan tells me that sometimes the audience might avoid eye contact with the speaker entirely, which makes connecting with that audience very, very difficult.

Prolonged eye contact is challenging. Some people are uncomfortable with looking at the audience because they're afraid to seem aggressive. The verb "face" does indeed have some aggressive connotations. "To face fear, to face the enemy ...". Some presenters don't even talk to the audience when they deliver their presentation. They talk to their notes. They talk to their slides. They talk to their laptops. They talk to the space somewhere behind the audience. They talk to themselves.

You can be afraid of the audience; that's okay. Just admit it and start doing something about it. But you cannot change people without challenging them. The surprise comes when you actually start looking at them and find that there is nothing to be afraid of in the first place. This is a purely psychological limitation. But apart from the psychological, there are certain physiological limitations to consider. For one thing, sometimes you just can't see all of the people in the audience. The worst-case scenario is when you are presenting in a huge auditorium where the scene is so brightly lit that that the audience dissolves in the dark. This is when humor becomes very important because laughter is now the only feedback you can get from those you can't see. Applause is another possibility, but it's much more difficult to get. Happily, the idea of plunging the audience in the darkness is becoming less and less popular. Let's talk about more common situations.

CONFIDENCE MONITORS HELP ONLY THE CONFIDENT

At one of the TEDx conferences I was helping to organize, we installed a huge plasma TV right in front of the speakers so they could see the current and next slide, as well as the time left. This is called the "confidence monitor." You feel more confident seeing your next slide and knowing what you are going to say next, hence the name. Also, because presenters could see their current slide, they didn't need to turn their backs to the audience. In theory, this would prevent them from talking to their slides. Or, at least, so we hoped.

Unfortunately, what we discovered was quite different. If the speaker doesn't want to talk to the audience, no confidence monitors are going to help. Some speakers still talked to the slides and one ended up giving his entire talk looking at the plasma TV! As an added bonus, he had a habit of pointing at the TV screen with the remote we gave him. This remote wasn't infrared so it wasn't necessary to point at the screen while pressing the button, but you can't break habits that easily. TV + remote = pointing! He looked like a person talking to a TV while switching channels. For him, it was much easier to talk to the TV than to the actual people in front of him.

Figure 8-2 demonstrates an average person's field of view. This is how wide you can see without turning your head. The actual field is even smaller; most of it in any given moment is peripheral vision, which is good only for recognizing motion and well-known patterns. Figure 8-3 shows an overhead view of a presentation space with 20 people. If you stand like this, you will get very good contact with people right in front of you, some contact with people on the periphery, and very little contact with people sitting too far (depending on how well you see) and in the corners. This is no good.

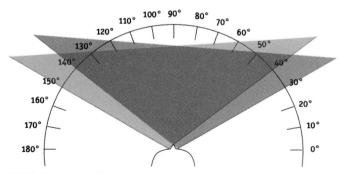

FIGURE 8-2: Average field of view.

If possible, ask people to move closer to each other in front of you, so you can see them all without turning your head. If you're in a large auditorium, ask them to sit close to each other;

trust me, it is much easier to talk to them when they are together. Otherwise, you need to constantly walk, turn, and scan the audience, keeping contact with all who are present. The corners will get less attention anyway, but on no occasion should you ignore them completely. Tunnel vision is dangerous because if you lose the corners, you get in trouble. The corners are where cell phones ring, papers rustle, and people cough and fidget, unconsciously asking for your attention. Give them your attention before they unconsciously ask for it.

▶ maintain eye contact with your audience. Apart from talking, this is your single most important job.

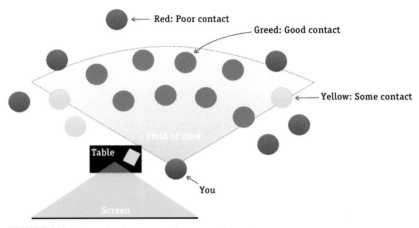

FIGURE 8-3: Example of presentation space layout.

Beware of the objects that obstruct your view: tables, laptops, and so on. I personally never speak from behind lecterns and try to get any tables out of my way. If there's a chance to get off the stage and speak on the same level with the audience, I do it. I know that it is unusual for professional speakers to avoid devices that supposedly help them by protecting them from prying eyes, harboring their notes, making them appear bigger. But I think this is all unfair and don't think I need this.

▶ In the 20th century, public speaking was top-down. In the 21st century, it's much more peer-to-peer. We should get used to it.

FREQUENTLY ASKED QUESTIONS ABOUT DELIVERY

Before I move on to the subject of answering audience questions, I want to answer a few frequently asked questions about delivery myself.

Question 1: "I am afraid that I'll forget my speech; can I use my notes or cue cards? Can I read my presentation?"

The short answer is no. I really don't recommend it. Being a big fan of authenticity, I am always suspicious of people who read their notes. However, I can also quote a longer answer from "the TED Commandments," which is the official recommendations for TED speakers: "If your choice is between reading or rambling, then read!"

(Continues)

FREQUENTLY ASKED QUESTIONS ABOUT DELIVERY *(CONTINUED)*

But if you have slides, you shouldn't be rambling, should you? They do work as cue cards and notes. Well, for some people they do, for some they don't. When death by PowerPoint was at full swing, people were putting text on their slides and reading it aloud, turning their backs to the audience. This was a disaster. This was even worse than reading prepared speeches from paper. But now, there isn't much text on our slides and people are forced to speak from their minds. Honesty, at last! Right? Wrong. People still can't speak from their minds; it's too risky. What do you do, then? In the best case, you rehearse so vigorously that you end up memorizing the words, and sound canned and unnatural. But look, there's another possibility: You can get back to the 20th century and read from your notes, showing your beautiful laconic slides as a nice prop. What a triumph of mind!

Mark Twain once said that if you tell the truth, you don't have to remember anything. If you just talk without notes and make eye contact, your audience will assume that you're honest. Suddenly, you become trustworthy and authentic. Sure, there's a risk of forgetting what to say, but that's a big subject I cover in detail in Chapter 10.

Question 2: "How do I set up a 'confidence monitor'?"

A confidence monitor shows your current slide on the laptop positioned in front of you (so you don't need to turn your back to the audience to look at the screen) and your next slide so you can confidently move along. It might also display the current time or a countdown timer. Figure 8-4 shows a screenshot from Apple Keynote's presenter screen. You can also get almost the exact same picture in PowerPoint. I am surprised that so few people use one because it is extremely helpful and activating it actually not that hard. Figure 8-5 explains how to do it in PowerPoint and Keynote.

FIGURE 8-4: Apple Keynote presenter screen (also called a confidence monitor).

If you use Keynote and for some reason are unable to position your laptop so you can see your next slide, you can set up a confidence monitor on your iPad or iPhone (I'm pretty sure you've got one) using a $1 application from Apple called Keynote Remote and a Wi-Fi connection.

And here's an even simpler trick that saved me on a number of occasions: When I present at an unfamiliar venue, I carry a 5-meter VGA extension cord. If the projector cord is too short, I can deal with that.

Question 3: "What's with the remote controllers I see some presenters have?"

Get yourself a remote controller. A clicker. A presenter. Call it whatever you want, but do it now. Seriously. I mean it, now. There are lots of infrared controllers; don't buy any of those. They aren't reliable enough. You can never be sure that it will actually turn the next slide after you press the Next button. It doesn't bring you much confidence. Get yourself a radio remote by Logitech, Keyspan, Kensington, or any other reputable company. They are not very expensive, and you'll save much more on anxiety pills. These remotes typically work within a 60– to 100-foot range with both Macs and PCs and they require no setup. Some advanced models have countdown timers with silent vibration alarms, volume controls, and many other immensely useful features like cool green laser pointers.

Please don't use radio mice to control your presentation. They look amateurish, and I mean that in a bad way.

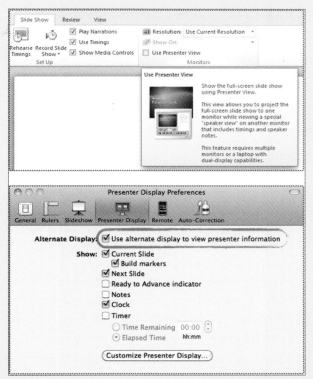

FIGURE 8-5: Turning on the presenter screen in PowerPoint and Keynote.

ADDRESSING ANY QUESTIONS

As far as questions are concerned, there are two separate topics, form and content: what you say and how you say it. From the content perspective, answering questions is no different from any other type of improvisation. In fact, it's simpler because you already have a topic. So, the most general advice is, "just say whatever you honestly think," which sometimes isn't easy. I'll discuss the challenges of being honest in this way in Chapter 10, which has to do with improvisation. This chapter deals with the form—how to say it. According to the research by Estrada et al., when addressing questions, it is highly desirable to follow these guidelines:

1. **Repeat the question.** Some people speak in a very low voice and the only reason you were able to hear them is because they spoke in your direction. Chances are you are the only person in the room who got it. Repeat the question louder. Don't look at the person who asked the question! This is not for them; this is for the rest of the audience. Make sure that everyone else heard it. Sometimes, you need to interpret the question because the person used jargon or some insider knowledge that nobody else has. You have to make sure everybody understands the question. Repeat it and watch for their reaction. Are they interested? Use their feedback to assess how detailed your answer should be. Again, the research by Estrada et al. states that people hate when you spend too much time answering a question no one really cares about.

2. **Thank the person who asked the question—but only if you mean it.** It is true that the phrase "thank you, this is a very good question" gives you some time to regroup. But if you say this phrase automatically, without thinking, people sense it. This is a bad cliché, and it undermines your credibility.

3. **You should be answering mostly to the audience and not to the person who asked.** This is a public meeting and not a private consultation. Look at the audience and see how they are reacting. When you finish your answer, look at the person who asked and see whether he or she is satisfied, too. If you're in doubt, it is perfectly okay to ask, "Did I answer your question?" They will appreciate it.

USING HUMOR (OR NOT?)

Humor isn't important. A 1998 study, "Making the Continuing Medical Education Lecture Effective" by H. Liesel Copeland et al. published in the *Journal of Continuing Education in the Health Professions* found that lecturers who identified important points, engaged the audience, were clear and organized, and used a case-based approach had better ratings. Use of humor was not associated with higher scores! Humor isn't big on the list Estrada and his coauthors came up with, either. Don't get me wrong; I love humor. I even took a course in standup at the American Comedy Institute in New York and improv comedy classes from the Upright Citizen's Brigade theater. I befriended a Russian standup comedian, Kolia Kulikov, and even have him on my client list because I sometimes give him feedback on his rehearsals while he pays me a symbolic ruble for doing so. I really love humor. I am also very keen to admit that for certain presentational styles, humor is entirely inappropriate and may even detract from the message.

My perception is that humor is immensely helpful when you have lot of improvisation. I think you just cannot improvise without laughing because you make so many mistakes in the process. It is no accident that we have lots of improv comedy and no improv drama. You don't need any more drama in improv theater. Things are already quite bad as they are. However, if you don't improvise a lot, if your presentation or lecture is about some highly specialized subject, if your audience is highly motivated, you don't need humor. You're not a professional comedian; you'll just screw things up. Leave it out.

Also, I don't think you should focus on being funny. If I learned anything from my improv practice, nothing kills laughter more effectively than deliberate attempts to induce it. I repeat: Do not try to be funny. Don't tell jokes; for most presenters, it's a total kiss of death. The problem is that when you expect your audience to laugh, they feel manipulated, and it is very natural for them to resist. So, they don't laugh, which you take as a sign of rejection. Things spiral downward from that point on.

▶ Don't try being funny on purpose; most of the time, it only hurts your speech.

> **NOTE** The truth is you don't really need to tell jokes. Just watch and the situation will become funny all by itself. Trust me, it will! You only need to notice it. The best humor is accidental. If your microphone works perfectly, great! But if it doesn't, it is funny. If your computer crashes, if you spill your glass of water on the first row, if you get a stammer you never had, this is funny. Every speaker's nightmare could be funny. It just might be hard to start laughing at yourself, but again, this is an acquired skill. I will deal with it in Chapter 10.

Let me finish with a couple of cases. In his 2006 TED talk, Al Gore spent 6 out of his precious 18 minutes doing standup comedy about losing presidential elections. Let me repeat: one third of his presentation was dedicated to just laughing at himself. And I think it was a good decision. It was an elephant in the room; nobody would listen to him and take him seriously if he didn't address this issue first. He screwed up big time; he needed to accept this publicly, which he did with grace and honesty quite unusual for a politician. Was he laughing a lot in *An Inconvenient Truth*? There are some jokes, but not that much. No reason.

In September 2010, Swiss finance minister Hans-Rudolf Merz burst into giggles while reading his speech on the subject of meat imports. Apparently, the speech written by his aides was full of "bureaucratese" and was entirely incomprehensible to anyone, including himself. The video of him laughing uncontrollably has collected more than a million views. He could have assumed a serious attitude and produced yet another parliamentary speech nobody cared about except maybe for a few interested parties. He chose to be human and became an Internet sensation. Congratulations there; great job.

SUMMARY

The key points to remember from this chapter are as follows:

▶ **Clarity first.** The most important thing in delivery is verbal clarity. This is what the audience overwhelmingly wants: to simply understand you. As much as possible, try to avoid "bureaucratese" and industry jargon. Instead, use everyday words and keep your sentences short. Talk like you're speaking to a friend, not to a whole room of people.

▶ **Don't worry about the time too much.** Try to finish on time, but don't worry too much if you don't. It is largely the organizer's responsibility. Your job is to be good; it is much more important. Of course, you should not forget about the time entirely. If your time is up, be the first to admit it. If the audience likes you and is interested in what you still have to say, you will be allowed to finish.

▶ **Whatever happens, keep talking to the audience.** Ask questions, look them in the eye, challenge them, and engage them. Watch for their feedback, both verbal and nonverbal. When you're in doubt about how they feel, just ask. The moment you stop talking to them, they reach for their cell phones. Don't talk to your laptop or your screen; there's no one there. Talk to the audience. A confidence monitor and remote controller will set you free.

▶ **Don't try to be funny.** Humor isn't all that important and it's risky. However, while improvising, you cannot survive without laughing at yourself. Get ready to do just that.

CHAPTER 9

Contrast in Delivery

IN THIS CHAPTER

▶ **Delivering passionate presentations**
▶ **Letting out your inner conflicts**
▶ **Confronting the audience**
▶ **Finding your hero**
▶ **Learning through imitation**

This chapter covers passionate presenting. There are two approaches to honing these skills. The first approach involves creating an active and heated discussion with the audience during your presentation. This requires both courage and the skills to handle the discussion. The second approach is about copying other passionate presenters in order to discover what you can and cannot do, to find your own style by contrast.

THE OPPOSITE OF MONOTONY

The New Oxford American Dictionary defines *monotony* as "lack of variety and interest; tedious repetition and routine." I don't know if you've noticed, but the connotations here aren't exactly positive. Monotony is on every list of public speaking "sins" and "don'ts." I am not even sure whether I should be writing about why monotony is bad. Why am I? I do so because I want to point out a contrast, of course. What's the opposite of monotony? It's being variable, emotional, and passionate. Now, *passion* is an interesting word, too. It comes from the Latin *pati,* originally meaning "to suffer," but now stands for "strong and barely controllable emotion." This resonates with what I was saying about going outside your comfort zone. Passionate speakers sometimes look disconcerted to the point of losing control. It has been said about Tom Peters (who is probably the most passionate speaker I've seen) that he is not happy unless he is angry. I find that the same is also true of me. And I cannot inspire other people unless I feel inspired myself.

The 20th century saw (and what's even better, recorded on tape) lots of great speakers. They were all speaking with passion, even if some of them had nefarious motives. In reaction to this passion, monotony became somewhat fashionable in academic circles as a way of differentiation; monotonous speakers were, in essence, saying, "Look, I'm not trying to play on your emotions." But again, there's no point in public speaking that doesn't play on people's emotions. Great public speakers of the 20th century—Kennedy, Churchill, even Hitler—were playing roles. The way they talked in public was very different from how they talked and behaved elsewhere. The public speaking tone was very ceremonial and solemn. They "acted out" the speech (which had often been written by their speechwriters) like professional actors act their roles. But that approach doesn't work anymore. We don't believe speakers when they use this approach. We've had enough, already.

> **NOTE** British comedian Eddie Izzard says that with the ascent of television, we developed a keen sensibility for insincere speeches. Politicians have to speak from their hearts—which is not an easy job for a politician.

The funny thing is the same thing happened with comedy. Once there was this cabaret, vaudeville culture, where you had professional performers with a repertoire of jokes written by professional writers. Jokes were interchangeable between comedians and so were writers. There was a problem with some comedians "stealing" other comedians' material. Essentially, the material was the same. The only difference was how well acted the show was.

In the 1960s, a number of comedians emerged who were writing for themselves and working in their own, distinct personal style. They had material that was tied to their comic persona, and nobody could steal that because it just wouldn't fit anyone else. They switched from third-person jokes ("Three men walk into a pub...") to the first person ("I walked into a pub the other day

▶ *The importance of acting has diminished; the importance of authenticity has surged.*

and…"). It wasn't just original; it was authentic. Even when it was made up, it was still very true. One classic example is Woody Allen, whose trademark is the topic of neurosis. Nobody can joke on this topic like Woody Allen because nobody is as convincingly neurotic as he is. Nervous people onstage weren't funny before Allen. They were pathetic. But now, thanks to Allen, they are funny. And it isn't just because of his brilliant acting skills. It is because of his honesty and openness. Today most of comedy is like this. An interesting question is, why did this happen? One answer is competition, but the second and much more interesting answer is that canned jokes have very limited power. They can only make people laugh. For some comedians, this just isn't enough; they are after much more than that. They are, in fact, politicians. They want change.

Today's public speaker is not a professional actor, either. He or she is an academic, a manager, or an industry expert. Consequently, today's public speaker doesn't have time to practice displaying passion, nor is one expected to. It's about being openly in love with whatever you're in love with. I'm not saying that acting is totally irrelevant in public speaking. If you have a chance, take an acting class, as it will improve your public speaking. However, this would most likely happen not because you acquired some new skills, but rather, because you let go of something that you shouldn't have been doing in the first place. Contemporary acting is a lot about relaxation and release.

> **NOTE** One of the best scientific presentations I ever saw was about nanoparticles! It was full of industry jargon and references to complex concepts from chemistry, physics, and medicine. Frankly, I didn't get most of it. But it didn't matter. The scientist delivering it, Russian physicist Yuri Raikher, was so obviously obsessed with nanoparticles that it was a pleasure to watch. For him, everything in his field was alive. Every little molecule had its character, behavior, and motivations. I know it sounds entirely unscientific. But apparently, this was the way he worked. He animated things to make sense of them. He was genuinely interested, which made him interesting to watch and listen. He wasn't playing. He was just alive.

BEING PERFECT VERSUS BEING PASSIONATE

The first secret of passionate public speaking isn't about speaking at all. Presenting is a projection of your everyday life. If your everyday job is colorless and boring to you, it's extremely hard to look passionate onstage.

You have to love what you do. I know this sounds banal, and I know you cannot force yourself into loving your job. So, if you don't love what you do and you want to be a good speaker, change jobs. We all understand this isn't easy, and I'm not suggesting you do it right away. But plan to do it. Keep your day job and start spending time analyzing the most interesting moments in your life. Go to a self-discovery seminar. Write an autobiography. Finding your passion in life is a quest and you have to embark on it—better sooner than later.

Passion is all about energy and this energy comes from an inner conflict. Why am I so passionate about presentation? Because I hate being bored and I know I can be a bore myself. In fact, I was quite a bore when I first started and I still sometimes become one, when I get caught in the small details nobody really cares about. I am passionate about improvisation because I hate routine, but at the same time, I know perfectly well that routine is the basis for all the improvisation there is. I am passionate about comedy because I don't like aggressive people—but I understand that the energy is there and that comedy is one of the socially accepted ways of channeling aggression. Comedy is an angry genre. I am passionate about communication because I was dramatically bad at it during my school years and still sometimes screw up big time—but then again, who doesn't?

> **NOTE** Everybody has inner conflicts. The problem is that not everybody is okay with publicly disclosing them. But if you think of it, interesting characters display their inner conflict, and if they don't, we start wondering why they are here at all. What's their interest in all this? Money? Guy Kawasaki, in his presentation about startups and bozos (*Don't Let the Bozos Grind you Down!*), admits that he was a bozo himself. I guess he still probably is sometimes. But he also speaks about it, and this is what makes him interesting. Steve Jobs is the CEO of one of the world's largest corporations, yet he comes onstage in jeans and sneakers. This is controversial; you're not supposed to present dressed like this. Why does he do it? I think he does this because he feels comfortable that way. And this is probably a reflection of his inner philosophy—yes, I want to be successful but I also want to do what I enjoy.

People tend to get anxious in front of an audience. There are many reasons for that, but mostly they are afraid to be exposed as incompetent or unqualified. When you admit (to yourself, for starters) that you are, in fact, incompetent and unqualified, you stop worrying about your public image and start worrying about your knowledge. This is far more productive. When I was beginning to speak about presentations, I used to open with the phrase, "Let me say that I didn't have any formal training in this. I've just decided to study a bit and this is what I've learned. This is good news because if I can do it, you probably can do it, too...".

Public speakers of the 20th century were impeccable. They were all-knowing. They were polished and sleek. They rehearsed their speeches until everything was perfectly articulated. Twenty-first century speakers, by contrast, are mere humans. They may not know everything. It is now acceptable and probably even fashionable to be imperfect. Widely publicized political scandals have at least one positive side; they taught us that even high-functioning individuals have dark sides. They also have things they don't quite like about themselves. They have their idiosyncrasies, too.

▶ *Twentieth century speakers were impeccable and all-knowing. Twenty-first century speakers have to accept and admit their imperfections, be honest that they may not know everything.*

NOTE The word *idiosyncrasy* is an interesting one. It stems from Greek idios, which means "own, personal" and krasis, which means "mixture." We are a mixture of different things. We can either deny it or admit it.

One of the speakers who had a profound influence on my speaking style was Andrei Lapin, a Russian raja yoga guru, who was once described as "a yogi, a bodybuilder, and a person of encyclopedic knowledge." This is a paradoxical, even bizarre combination. You see, if you're a bodybuilder, you're not supposed to be particularly well-read, are you? Very few bodybuilders have encyclopedic knowledge. If you're a "professor," you're not supposed to practice yoga, much less teach it. And if you're practicing yoga, why do bodybuilding? All his traits seem desirable and attractive, but the problem is that they seem to contradict each other. When I first met him, he seemed like a typical bodybuilder. His manner of speaking wasn't very intellectual. Frankly, most of the time he looked like either a village idiot or a slightly mad New Age guru. That was until he'd start talking about physics (he was a physicist by training) or quoting ancient Greek philosophers. His audiences loved him.

When we admit that we have inner conflicts and contradictions, we start working on solving them, and inevitably, this work of solving them becomes productive. It's like being an addict; you cannot start the treatment unless you accept that the problem exists. So, what is your problem? Accepting the problem gives you passion to work and to present. It also gives you courage to confront the audience. Comedians often laugh at themselves before they laugh at other people. This is also true during a presentation. If your goal is to change the audience, to make them better, you have to show them that they have certain deficiencies. You have to challenge them, maybe attack them. The easiest way to do this is to demonstrate that you have (or had in the past) the exact same deficiencies. Then, you hope that they will be compassionate enough to identify with you.

In the previous chapter, I mentioned Al Gore's self-deprecating standup during a speech at TED. Only after he spent those six minutes laughing at himself did he have the grounds to ask people to change their lives. During his vice presidency, he was a rather ordinary, monotonous speaker. Nothing special, really. Then, he lost an election and the world as he knew it changed. He became "that guy who lost to George W." He had nothing else to do. So, he went to travel on his boat in search of his passion. He grew a beard and decided that what really interests him in life is saving the environment. He entered the global warming debate with his "slideshow." In a couple of years, Eric de Place, a research fellow in one of Seattle's sustainability think tanks, wrote after seeing Gore's presentation:

> *Al Gore's slideshow was easily the best slideshow I've ever seen on this, or any other, subject, but Gore himself was a study in mastery, at once funny and earnest, erudite and thundering. (Where was this guy during the 2000 campaign?)*

▶ If you don't display any deficiencies, they have nothing to identify with! I think this is absolutely crucial.

Exactly my question. Where? And the answer is, "Well, he was busy playing the role of the nation's vice president." It wasn't him speaking during the election campaign; it was some other guy, a supposedly ideal Democratic candidate. Once Gore found his own passion, he became a great speaker. He found something he was ready to fight for, and so he did.

DON'T AVOID CONFRONTATION

After doing a workshop, I am always happy if somebody in the audience was objecting. I would love to say that I become happy *the moment* someone objects, but I can't because this would be a lie. In fact, I'm quite scared when people start to object. However, when the workshop is over, I am inevitably happy that it turned out that way. And so is the audience. This is very much like in storytelling: confrontation makes things interesting. Discussion is much more engaging than a monologue. For longer talks, I actually set it as a goal to myself: I have to provoke somebody in the first 10 minutes of the speech. Otherwise, it will be boring.

> **NOTE** Experienced performers can handle a very high level of aggression and get tremendous effects. George Carlin was one of those comic geniuses able to deliver routines called simply "the list of people who ought to be killed" and get standing ovations in the end. "Yes, so was Hitler," I hear you saying, but unlike Hitler's fans, Carlin's fans never started a world war.

It is true that most speakers tend to avoid confrontation and for good reasons. One of the problems of our civilization (at least from a presentation perspective) is that we've spent centuries trying to minimize conflicts and are still far from succeeding. We know that people get hurt in conflicts. So, when you're presenting alone, and the audience is large, you don't feel like challenging them because of this instinct you have to minimize conflict. But the context of a presentation is different from the context of a whole civilization. You don't have to worry about having a conflict with your audience; they won't kill you! The word "conflict" is not really a synonym with "violence." They might fire you, but that sometimes is a good thing, too.

You might say that challenging the audience as an invited speaker is much easier than doing the same thing as an insider. As an invited speaker, you are already in a position of authority; you're up on the stage—even if there's no actual stage. Also, there are many fewer consequences; even if you fail miserably, nobody would come to you tomorrow at the water cooler saying, "That presentation you gave yesterday was a disaster, wasn't it?"

However, for an insider, it is much easier to talk in terms of "we," rather than in terms of "you." As an insider, you are at a much better position to say, "*we*'ve been doing it all wrong"—as opposed to "*you*'ve been doing it all wrong." The latter phrase is difficult to accept for most people. When you make yourself a subject of your own criticism, it is easier for the people to think something like, "You know, maybe he's right" and lean toward your side. On the other hand, if you are not including yourself as a target, people are much more likely to adopt a defensive stance.

Either way, if you want change, you must have a discussion. Otherwise, why present?

Handling a Discussion

Starting a discussion with the audience is really easy. All you need to do is to cease censoring yourself. You see, the conflict is already there; all you need is to stop pretending that everything is perfectly okay with all the people in front of you. You need to get moderately angry at something that relates to them, maybe with somebody else who closely resembles your audience, maybe with some particular person in the group. I don't have enough courage to confront the whole group, although I have seen this done successfully. And then, you just express this dissatisfaction. This is where the dance begins. They recognize that this is about them; some of them get defensive and counterattack.

HANDLING THE EXPERT IN THE CROWD

Sometimes, I encounter an expert in my audience. Presentations are a very broad field so I often encounter somebody with much more experience in scriptwriting or graphic design, for example. I tend to avoid discussions with experts. Yes, I am concerned about my reputation, but this is not the main reason. The problem with experts in a group setting is that they speak in their own language, which is often incomprehensible to the rest of the group. Pretty soon, it becomes a discussion just between the two parties. Believe me, I've tried to have those discussions, but terms and names start flying around that nobody else knows or cares about. So, when I hear the second very specific question or objection from the same person, I just say, "Apart from you and me, nobody else understands this question, right?" I look at the audience. They nod. "I am very sorry, but your questions are overly specific. We cannot afford a private discussion at the expense of everybody else; do you agree? Could you please write your questions down so we can discuss them later?" If the question is well formulated and the audience really cares, I am keen to answer. Sometimes I can reformulate the question for the audience if I think the question is worthwhile. But most times, taking the conversation with the expert audience member to the side after the presentation is over is the best approach.

For a discussion to be interesting, opponents should match each other. I typically choose a heavyweight, somebody in a position of authority. The company's CEO will do. Most of the time I start my workshops by criticizing the company's own presentations. I request such presentations beforehand so I have a chance to prepare. And my job is really easy; most presentations aren't very good, anyway. So, I start telling them what I think, trying to be humorous and not too vitriolic. Even when the CEO or a marketing manager isn't present, somebody starts defending the presentation, and it is never a low-level employee. It's typically another manager, which makes the competition fair. Of course, I am more knowledgeable in presentations (which is the reason why they invited me in the first place), but they know their field, which inevitably has some very important "specifics." Now, I have to prove that those "specifics" don't undermine my argument. The trick is to let them lose in a graceful and respectable manner, or win in a manner that is satisfying and edifying to both of us. I'm really trying to be committed to my field and not to myself. It is okay for them to win, too. This is my chance to learn.

Again, the goal is not to have a monologue but a dialogue, an exchange. It's not an exchange when you're closed off to receiving new information. One recipe for failure is to silence your opponents with forceful arguments without really addressing their concerns. Let them speak and—even more important—hear what they are saying.

Using Humor

▶ Successful speakers don't mind good questions, even if those questions challenge their assumptions or conclusions. Even though you are in a teaching position, be willing to learn. If you're not learning, nobody else is.

A 1992 movie *Glengarry Glen Ross* contains an iconic sales meeting scene in which a successful salesman Blake (played by Alec Baldwin) "motivates the team" by parading around his gold watch and verbally abusing everyone else in the room. The apparent intention was to make people angry at themselves and try harder at their work, but the end result wasn't exactly what Blake was aiming for. Still, despite ultimate failure, Blake's approach contains some prerequisites for success. If you want people to stop doing something they are doing and start doing something else, you can't play nice all the time.

One way to confront people without making too many enemies is comedy. Comedy is all about conflict and anger and calling names. If you watch even the friendliest comedians in slow motion, you notice anger being flashed at the audience very frequently. They just know how to release this emotion as laughter. How do they do it? Two tricks are useful: context shifts and exaggeration.

For example, if you want to criticize some particular behavior of your audience, you might jokingly attribute this behavior to some other group and not to the people you're talking about. "Let me tell you a story about my previous job . . ." or "A friend of mine told me that at their company . . ." The tone should be playful enough for the audience to recognize that you are not really telling a true story but instead talking about them in a mild disguise. You can even jokingly compliment your audience by making them dramatically better than that "other company": "I know in our company, we've already gotten over this mistake. It's even difficult for me to understand how they could keep doing it, but still, this is what they do . . ." Don't expect the audience to laugh. Again, you are not a comedian. But for your purposes, even a humble smile would be enough.

The second trick is to criticize in very exaggerated words, so the audience understands that you are kidding but at the same time sees the seed of truth in your words. For example, since I'm not a priest or a minister, I can get away with calling my audience sinners when I'm speaking about "seven deadly sins of presentations." They realize that I don't really mean that they are "heading for eternal damnation" if they continue doing this—although there is a certain truth in what I'm saying. Next, they either accept it or fight it. I am comfortable with both of those choices. In either way, it will be difficult for them to continue doing what they were doing and still enjoy it.

Don't Be Afraid to Offend Them

There is no point in saying stuff everybody agrees with. Furthermore, there is no point in softening your language. Just say what you have to say. I am not suggesting that intentionally offending people is a good idea. But if you want to make a difference, I do think that avoiding offense at all cost is an exceptionally bad idea. If your speech didn't offend anyone in a group of 30+ people, that probably means it was either badly scripted or badly delivered.

▶ New ideas that do not risk offense aren't really new ideas.

> **NOTE** There's also a chance that you've acquired the Holy Grail of public speaking: changing people without making them uncomfortable. But the chances of this are slim. Even the Dalai Lama hasn't gotten there yet. So, the rule is that in a group sufficiently large, a couple of people will be seriously disappointed by your talk. This is perfectly normal and even desirable. You cannot make a lot of friends without making a few enemies.

Of course, some people find it difficult to become confrontational. If you're a polite person who shies away from conflict, this is my message for you: Please don't be afraid to offend people while speaking. Please don't shy away from strong, articulated positions and strong language. (If it's not difficult for you, you probably don't have any problems displaying your passion anyway.)

> **NOTE** By the way, scientific research is on your side here again. In 2005, Cory Scherer and Brad Sagarin from Northern Illinois University divided 88 students into three groups and showed them a videotaped speech. The speech was mostly the same for all the groups, except for one small detail: one version contained the word "damn" in the beginning, one version contained the word at the end, and the last one was clean. The scientists were trying to measure whether the impact of this four-letter word would be positive, negative, or nil. Would light swearing improve communication or undermine it? It turned out that the speeches with "damn" in them were more persuasive, the speakers were rated as more passionate, and the credibility did not change.

And by saying you should use "strong language" I don't mean to say that you should swear just for the sake of it. First, using swearing to fake passion when you have none won't work. Also, the use of swear words depends a lot on the audience, on what is considered "mild" swearing, and so on. I also have to warn you that other research (Mark Hamilton, "Reactions To Obscene Language" in *Communication Research Reports*, 1989) has demonstrated that for counter-attitudinal topics, listeners might use swearing as an excuse to reject the message. The point is that swearing can be persuasive because it shows passion and a loss of control on the part of the speaker. You may seem rude, but at least when you swear, you care. Such language deriving out of passion might just be a cure for all the pointless formal speeches we encounter throughout life. I was once presenting to a group of 250 people, and the first applause I got coincided with me uttering a four-letter word after some hesitation. The audience wasn't happy about the word. They just welcomed me having the guts to tell the truth.

However, "strong language" doesn't just refer to swear words. It means different things in different contexts. For example, one of the most popular scientific lectures on YouTube is a 1.5 hour–long speech on nutrition and sugar by Robert H. Lustig, a UCSF Professor of Pediatrics. As of April 2011, it was viewed more than 800,000 times. Nutrition is a hot topic, but that's still great for a lecture full of words like "metabolic" and "ingestion." How does Lustig sustain the audience's attention for 1.5 hours? He uses some strong, polarizing language. By "strong," I mean strong for a scientist, of course. For example, in the 20th minute of his speech, he says:

> *High fructose syrup and sugar are exactly the same; they are equally bad. They are both dangerous, they are both poison. Okay? I said it.* Poison.

He calls sugar "alcohol without a buzz" and talks about "the Coca-Cola conspiracy." Did this offend somebody? I bet it did. Did some scientists think at this moment that he was going too far? Maybe. But he was honest and passionate. What he does obviously matters to him. He goes to great lengths to prove his point.

Don't be afraid to polarize the audience. Sure, it is dangerous. Maybe you'll even lose this particular presentation. But you will maintain your integrity, which is far more important in the long run. Stand for what you believe in. If what you believe is wrong, the world will let you know.

Dealing with Hostility

With an approach like this, it is no surprise that I happen to offend people. This alone is not a problem. If the person is open to discuss the offense, we just discuss it. Sometimes, I apologize. Other times, people don't know precisely why they are offended. It's just a feeling on their part. I have this feeling sometimes and you're probably familiar with that feeling, too: a person walks onstage and you already know by the way he or she walks that you hate this person. What they say is not important any longer. Whatever it is, it is wrong. When I am in the audience and I get this feeling, I prefer to keep my mouth shut unless the speaker says something really outrageous. But some people don't have this barrier. And this is bad because as a speaker, I have no chance to apologize for something I didn't do the first place.

An equally bad situation is when people know exactly what they are offended with, but they are uncomfortable discussing it. So, they choose instead to nitpick about other issues. Because this is a speech and not a scientific article, I cannot entirely avoid faulty language (overgeneralizations, and so on) so they have a lot of material to feed on. Pretty soon, this becomes a drag. The good news is that the rest of the audience hates those guys. Most of their questions are important only in the moment and are dangerous only because they interrupt your train of thought. They carry no real meaning; there's nothing to learn from them. This gives you a perfect excuse to shut them down. There are a couple of good approaches to do this:

▶ One approach to handling this sort of hostility is to ask the audience politely to raise their hands before speaking. When they do it, and if you know certain people are going to be trouble, just point at them with your hand or give them a nod so they know you've noticed them. Don't get back to them for another minute or so. Finish talking about your current slide, get to your next logical step, and then ask them what their question was. By that time, it is obvious even to them that the question was pointless to begin with. After a couple of failed attempts, they will start thinking before asking—which might make their questions dramatically better. More dangerous, too, but also more productive.

▶ Another way of dealing with this situation is to expose the game. This is not an easy task; it does require a lot of courage but could lead to a very fruitful discussion. What are they really trying to say? What is the discussion really about? What is the conflict on the level of beliefs and values? Ultimately, this is what your talk is all about. It's not about details; it's about philosophy, it's about approach. What's the difference in your attitudes toward life, business, or science? Pretty soon, you will either have an agreement with the dissenters, or you'll realize that you cannot resolve the issue here and thus agree to disagree for now. The tension will disappear immediately, and you will be able to carry on.

> ▶ I'll repeat this: sometimes, you will get an angry, hostile opponent, and it's not a nice experience. The fear of offending your audience and getting an angry "client" is big. This fear is what makes your presentations monotonous. Don't succumb to it.

A Word on Written Feedback

Sometimes, when you're presenting at a conference, the organizers provide you with written feedback about your presentation from the audience. You've probably filled out those feedback forms yourself, rating content, delivery, practical value, and stuff like that. As a rule, such feedback will be pretty much useless. In my whole career, I never received positive written feedback when I thought the presentation was bad, and vice versa. Overall, it is very predictable. A surprise may arise when somebody who was silent during your talk decides to tell you how much he or she really hated whatever you had to say. It's usually just one person but this could ruin everything for you.

> **WARNING** This happened to me on at least one occasion, and it took me a couple of days to bounce back. I know some presenters who were devastated for weeks after receiving criticism from just one person in the audience. Don't let this happen to you. You don't even know this person; don't let them suddenly become so important.

I think written feedback is overrated. In the end, people vote with their wallets and feet. They either come or don't come next time; they either buy or don't buy from you. According to my own experience, written feedback is a bad predictor of anything. On the other hand, the visual feedback an audience gives you with their faces is an excellent predictor. This is truth. If you see a person in the front row obviously very unhappy with your talk, you know you've got a problem here. He will rate your nonverbal communication as "poor" and write some nasty stuff about your choice of topic on the feedback form. Should you trust his opinion? Nonsense. Nobody can write anything useful with a face like that. For you, it might be much more productive to ask him or her "Is there anything wrong?" at the appropriate moment of your presentation and have an open discussion.

Also, they don't write this feedback for you in most cases. They write it for themselves. They were the ones out of luck today. They happened to come to the wrong presentation and spent hours waiting for the feedback form to release their anger. I don't think you should be disappointed because of their feedback; you should be compassionate towards them.

> **TIP** Listening to Tim Minchin's "Song for Phil Daoust" helps. It is a song by an Australian comedian who once received a very bad review from the *Guardian* while on tour in the United Kingdom. Search for it; it's brilliant. It includes some great advice on mature ways of dealing with negative feedback.

LEARNING FROM OTHER PEOPLE

Several years ago, I discovered an amazing way of becoming a passionate presenter. It is really quite simple. It's been around for ages. But we've managed to use it better most recently, as video cameras have became widespread. The method is to watch other great presenters.

> *If you want to write like Shakespeare the first thing you can do is read Shakespeare. Once you have read it all, you will realize that, while you can never write like him, you are now infinitely better read.*

writes Lea Carpenter, a literary expert. I suggest you go even further. Don't just read Shakespeare, write Shakespeare. Become Shakespeare. Don't just watch great presentations; you are probably doing this already, anyway. Copy them. Imitate them. Clone them. Become them.

I know what you are thinking: "What's the point of becoming Steve Jobs; the spot is already taken! I will be laughable! Also, the key is not to clone anyone but to discover my own style, right?" Right. In fact, that is precisely the reason to try this approach. You can't really understand who you are in isolation.

You can, however, copy other people and discover who you are by contrast, by discovering who you are not.

We typically don't know who we want to become—that is, until we meet another person who is doing precisely what we think we should be doing. We believe that by becoming that person, we will become our "ideal self." We are wrong at this point, but it doesn't matter. The motivation is so strong that it is foolish to ignore it. It's a useful energy. We need at least to try. So we spend years trying to become this person and then even more time trying to get rid of their patterns. But when (and if) we succeed, we become ourselves.

Another consideration is that you don't just need to discover your personal style, you also need to create it. Great people are great because they stand on the shoulders of other giants. Everybody was influenced by somebody else. Beethoven would have been impossible without Mozart. Impressionists would have been impossible without the Old Masters. I've heard many stories by comedians claiming that they've watched performances of their favorite comedians hundreds of times and tried to emulate them. It looked awkward and unnatural. But in the process of trying, they discovered something else about themselves and their own approach. It really works. Just go ahead and pick your giant.

> **NOTE** I copied talks from Malcolm Gladwell and performances from Russian actor and writer Evgeny Grishkovets to understand the art of storytelling. I was so excited about how simple it seemed from the inside that I even wrote and delivered my own hour-long storytelling monologue for the audience of 40 friends and acquaintances. I didn't get any reviews in the press, but it was a fun thing to do. And I learned a great deal from it. I also copied a TED presentation by the extremely energetic Harvard professor Daniel Gilbert to understand how to talk about complicated scientific subjects. I copied "lectures" by the Russian guru Andrei Lapin to get better at answering questions from the audience. I copied Steve Jobs, well, because he is Steve Jobs. Now, I am a unique mix of all those people. Did I become myself? I don't know. But I'm certainly unlike anyone I know. Did I become better? You bet. I saw many students of mine do this exercise, many of them with dramatic, almost unbelievable success. So, I invite you to repeat the journey, in your own unique way, of course.

We have lots of beliefs about what's possible and what's not in presentations, what one can and cannot do. We call a genius somebody who defies and transcends those rules. Do you want to experience this from the inside? To get into other person's body, to see what they see and to act the way they act? Copying them is the closest you can get to this experience, and sometimes it is close enough. People in the arts do it all the time. It is customary for young painters to copy classical painters to understand composition. I know this sounds funny but I copied slides by Steve Jobs in an attempt to understand how they work and made some surprising discoveries. Why not copy Jobs's speaking? Why not copy his gestures, his tone of voice, his tempo, and his timing? It's fun and it's also an excellent way of discovering what really works for you. It certainly works much better than simply reading about Steve Jobs.

> **NOTE** The process I am describing to you is in part based on the works of American linguist Dr. John Grinder, who, in the 1970s and 1980s, developed a similar process. The most important difference between my approach and the one Dr. Grinder describes is that video recording wasn't widely available at the time he developed his ideas.

Become More Passionate Using Compassion

The neurological basis for all this work is surprisingly well grounded in science. Humans are equipped to learn in precisely this way. In fact, this is probably how our civilization started to develop; we copied complex motor skills like hunting or working with tools from each other. How do we do it? Well, have you ever heard of mirror neurons? Discovered in 1992 in macaque monkeys, they made a spectacular journey from relative obscurity to being one of the most widely discussed recent discoveries in neuroscience.

Italian researchers at the University of Parma—Giacomo Rizzolatti, Vittorio Gallese, and Marco Iacoboni—were studying the motor cortex, the part of the brain controlling movements. In one of their experiments, they showed different objects to monkeys and observed what happened in the monkeys' brains with implanted electrodes. First, they discovered that there were a large amount of neurons in the motor cortex firing when the monkey simply observed an object. These are now known as canonical neurons; sometimes it is enough to observe an object in order to have a feeling about how to grasp and use it.

But then, they noticed that in some cases it wasn't enough to show the object to the monkey. The researchers had to use the object themselves (while the monkeys watched) in order for the neurons in the motor part of the monkey's brain to fire. The human uses the object and the hand area of the monkey's brain lights up. What's the connection? Apparently, macaques have an innate ability to simulate experience without having the actual experience. Monkeys are able to replicate the researcher's experience! (This works only when the researcher is doing something a monkey is capable of.)

Monkeys don't really learn by imitation; being social animals, they use mirror neurons to simply understand what other members of the group are doing. Humans, on the other hand, have developed much larger brains and have acquired an ability beyond understanding the experience. We are able to replicate the actual behavior. Many leading neuroscientists today, including Vilayanur Ramachandran of the University of California San Diego, believe that mirror neurons play a crucial role in the acquisition of motor skills and language. Ramachandran calls mirror neurons "Gandhi neurons" because they facilitate compassion. When we see fellow humans experiencing intense emotions, we can experience the same emotion by just looking at them. And this is a way of becoming a more passionate presenter; you practice compassion with other passionate presenters. You'll have the experience and understand how it's done from the inside.

> **NOTE** If you are interested in learning more about mirror neurons, watch Ramachandran's presentation at TED: `www.ted.com/talks/vs_ramachandran_the_neurons_that_shaped_civilization.html` or `http://goo.gl/JcZf`.

Choosing the Right Person

The first step is to choose the person you are going to imitate. This is probably the most difficult and important part of the whole process. Choosing the right person will provide you with enough motivation to study them thoroughly and get results. An ideal candidate is someone you deeply admire. If you pick the right person, you will get enough confidence in the process and continue practicing it with other people. On the other hand, choosing the wrong person will undermine the whole idea of studying by imitation. So, choose wisely. Who is your favorite presenter? Whom do you admire as a speaker? Which properties as a speaker would you like to acquire? Who has these properties? Who is your hero?

There are two roads to take here. The first has more to do with improving yourself, the second with fixing yourself:

- ▸ You can choose somebody who is the same gender, the same age or not much older than you are, and the same temperament. Your job will then be easier. You will get the quickest results this way. This is what most people do. We prefer people who are like us.

- ▸ There's also an alternative route, which is to choose a person who is like you but also very different in some important aspect. Somebody who has something you're missing. I have to warn you that this gap could be too wide and you might not be able to close it. But if you make enough effort, you can get some really fantastic results.

A student of mine, a young female working for a technology company, decided to copy Britney Spears. Let me tell you, she was nothing like Britney Spears. She was a blond female, that's it. That was the only thing they had in common. She was very quiet and sober-minded.

She looked hesitant while presenting and got easily confused. She didn't really like Britney as a singer but she had respect for her energy. So she picked several interviews by Britney and tried to copy her speaking style. It wasn't good at first. But she persisted. For weeks, she worked on Britney's trademark "Amazing!" exclamation. In about three months, she was a totally different person onstage. She became much more energetic, spontaneous, and passionate.

Working with Video

▶ Videos of better quality work better for this type of scrutiny, so if you have a choice of downloading a 50MB file or a 150MB one, choose the latter.

Next, you have to acquire a recording of this person. The Internet age makes this task relatively easy. Pick a fragment that is not too long, about 10 to 20 minutes. The 18-minute TED presentations are ideal.

One important thing to remember as you select: Some presenters rely heavily on feedback from the audience. If you want to emulate them, you need to see how their actions are, in fact, reactions to the audience. Also, when you emulate them, you won't be getting the same feedback, which might make you look awkward. However, most conference presentations happen in very large rooms where the stage is brightly lit and the rest is in the dark. Presenters mostly don't see the audience and don't have much interaction. The only feedback they get is laughter and applause (or sometimes no laughter and no applause). I've noticed that experienced speakers like Billy Graham are still able to somehow feel the audience. This probably comes from delivering many presentations in smaller venues; their timing and emotional charge are still perfect.

NOTE Check out these websites for great presentations:

▶ http://www.TED.com
▶ http://PopTech.org
▶ http://FORA.tv
▶ http://GelConference.com
▶ Apple Keynotes podcast at the iTunes store

It makes sense to choose a presentation that you actually have a chance to deliver somewhere, at least in part. As a presentation coach, I sometimes need to explain how Jobs's presentations are constructed. Given that his presentations are quite long and I don't have enough time to show the actual video, I just assume his role, deliver his presentation in Russian, and fast-forward whenever I need it. It's not an impersonation; I am not making a caricature of Steve. I am *becoming* Steve as best I can.

If you deliver lectures, you can include a short excerpt from somebody else's presentation with an appropriate notice. If you're imitating a standup comedian, you can entertain your friends. I don't recommend doing this at conferences, but I've seen it done in less formal settings by some professional speakers. Don't worry that you will look unnatural. Just warn your audience that this is not your material.

> **NOTE** Be sure to disclose that it's not your material and give credit to the originator. Don't make this the central part of your presentation. I like the TED's motto: "Ideas worth spreading." So, if you have a chance, why not spread an idea? Remember, you're not doing this to earn money or to get famous. This is just an exercise. And it is important to have something like a goal for this project. When is the show time? What's the deadline?

After you pick your piece, watch the presentation a couple of times. Don't do anything, just sit back and relax. Relax your focus slightly—not to the point where the picture becomes a blur, but to the point where your eyes travel freely after the speaker's movements, which is what happens during most speeches. Notice your breathing. Try not to move unless you really need to. Don't try to understand and analyze what the speaker is doing. Rather, feel it.

Your goal is to learn implicitly, unconsciously. You can pick up their feelings from their facial expression and breathing patterns, from their gestures, and from the way they move onstage. All you need to do is to stop paying attention to your own movements. Apart from mirror neurons, we have receptors all over our body that go back to our brain and tell us what is really happening. According to Ramachandran, if we prevent those receptors from working properly, if, for example, you anesthetize your hand, you will be able to feel another person's hand exactly like your own. When the receptors are working, you're able to distinguish your hand from other person's hand—which I suppose is a very useful thing in the long run but not what you need for this exercise.

> ▶ You need to feel what the other person is feeling, to have his or her experience.

Now, I am not suggesting you anesthetize yourself. Our brains are highly sensitive to change. If you stop moving, if you don't change your own sensations, if you release your tensions, you will feel like nothing is happening. Your own feelings and sensations then go into the background, leaving space for the other person's feelings and sensations. So, just watch the video, relax, and imagine that you are the person onstage. Put yourself in this person's place. What do you see? What do you hear? What do you feel? If you are really relaxed, you might even notice small involuntary movements of your own muscles in sync with what you see onscreen. That's your mirror neurons at work.

You won't be able to do this for very long. It's a bit tedious, watching the same talk over and over again. The good news is you don't need to. Our unconscious is very quick at picking up behaviors. At a certain point, you'll have a feeling that you've got it. You can then proceed to the next stage.

Creating a Transcript

Many talks at TED have been transcribed and subtitled. I still invite you to create your own transcript from scratch. There's a lot of evidence that people who write down information remember more. There's also some evidence (Anne Mangen and Jean-Luc Velay, "Digitizing Literacy: Reflections on the Haptics of Writing," InTech, 2010) that writing by hand is more beneficial than typing on a computer keyboard. This way, the information is stored not only from eyesight or vision but also from complex motions of the hand, so it can be later accessed via many different pathways, rather than only one.

> **TIP** Creating a transcript forces you to watch the talk in slower motion (it's a good idea to slow down the video speed so you won't need to stop it too often). You'll inadvertently notice many small details you weren't noticing before. It forces you to repeat the words in your internal dialogue many times as you hear them and write them down. This way, you also assume the position of a speechwriter. This is immensely useful.

I first read about this effect 15 years or so ago. However, I was reluctant to try it; it seemed extremely boring. But then, about seven years later, I was offered a freelance assignment to transcribe and translate recordings of a British hypnotist, Paul McKenna. Although I sometimes work as an interpreter at seminars and presentations, I rarely translate text in writing. I took this job because I had some interest in hypnosis, and coincidently I also needed money at the time.

I transcribed about two hours of McKenna's hypnotic inductions. I can't say it was the most exciting job I ever did. But later, one day, the topic of hypnosis came up during a conversation with a friend of mine. He asked me what hypnosis was all about. I tried to explain it to him and put him in a mild trance. I didn't do this on purpose, it just happened. Apparently, I'd unconsciously assimilated some hypnotic patterns from McKenna. I didn't become a hypnotist, and I still can't cure phobias and make people do funny things publicly, but I can put people in trances. (Not a very useful skill for a public speaker....) The point is that it worked. Try to create a transcript yourself. Yes, it can be tedious, but 18 minutes isn't all that much time. Total, it shouldn't take you more than a couple of hours. You'll notice the change the next time you're speaking publicly.

Reading a Transcript

The next exercise is to read your transcript aloud and try to imitate the speaker. What's even better, record your reading and then compare it to the original. If you don't like the results, try again. Don't walk and make gestures yet. Just read the text. Imagine that this is a radio broadcast and that the audience can't see you. Use your voice; copy the rhythm and intonation.

That will be challenging enough for now. Observe the pauses. Imagine that you *are* the speaker you're copying.

If the result is far from the original, try this—play the video of the original speech and turn on the subtitles while turning off the sound or making it barely audible. Now, try to speak at the exact same time the person's lips move. This will give you the sense of their pace, timing, and manner of speaking. Fast speakers like Ken Robinson will be tricky. With other folks, it will be easier.

> **TIP** Most TED talks come with subtitles, but if you don't have subtitles, you can create them. Several online services like Overstream.net can create subtitles for you. YouTube also offers automated creation of subtitles, although the results will be far from ideal. I invite you to try it, though.

When I was learning from stage performer Evgeny Grishkovets, I once read aloud a transcript from his 1.5 hour–long show. I had never seen that show before. It wasn't released on tape and I didn't see it live. All I had was the transcript published by the author. I saw his other shows, both live and on tape, so I had a pretty solid idea (or so I thought) about his performing style. So I read his show according to the notion that I had. I then listened to my own recording several times, like I did with the original recordings. It was good! I actually liked myself being Grishkovets. Several years later, when his show was officially released on tape, I bought it. Guess what—I thought it wasn't as good as my version! I thought he was doing it all wrong! It took me a while to get accustomed to his interpretation of his text.

Working with a Video Camera

When you're comfortable speaking aloud with a transcript, try to do it more realistically. Make screenshots of the slides from the video and put them together in PowerPoint or Keynote. If the slides are exceptionally good and you want to improve your slide-building skills, re-create them. Otherwise, screenshots will do just fine. By this time, you probably can remember the speech almost by heart. You don't need to know the original text word for word, anyway. Just ad lib if you forget.

> **TIP** If you have a lot of trouble remembering the text, don't worry about re-creating the original slides. Instead, convert the transcript into slides. Make sure the text is large enough so you can comfortably read it from several feet away. This becomes your tele-prompter. Place the monitor in front of you and use your remote to advance the slides.

Now, try giving the presentation while looking mostly at your imaginary audience and sometimes glancing at the teleprompter. If that works, turn on your webcam and record yourself. Compare your recording to the original. Is it close? Chances are, it isn't. Try again. At this stage, some analysis might help. What's the difference? What can you change in your performance so you become closer to the original?

By this time, you will start noticing certain changes. You will notice that you're perfectly comfortable delivering somebody else's text even though you wouldn't even dream of saying things like this as yourself. You will realize that you really don't know who you are and what you're capable of onstage. You will realize that you have much more plasticity than you previously thought. You will realize that you can do big gestures, pronounce bold and powerful phrases, and be perfectly comfortable with it.

I think I first noticed this when I was hired to do live translation of a presentation by Erick van Egeraat, a world-famous architect. As I mentioned, sometimes I work as an English-Russian interpreter. I translate seminars and presentations, and most of the speakers I translate are actually worth imitating. Erick was one of them. I remember him having a very powerful presence. He was tall and majestic, and when he spoke, he did it in a very proud tone of voice. I almost never spoke like this. Not until I suddenly had to.

As an interpreter, my goal is to be invisible. When I speak, I use the first person as if these were my own words. I also try to replicate the person's tone of voice and posture; I try to attach the same emotions to the same words. I try to become the Russian-language shadow of the person speaking. Essentially, it's the same job as learning by imitation, just better paid and with more responsibility. I remember myself thinking, "Wow, I cannot say words like this in the first person. I will look ridiculous." But I didn't. I just said it in Erick's tone of voice and it sounded good. I wasn't able to shake off his majestic posture until several hours after the presentation was over. That very moment, my life changed.

So try it. It's fun. It's even more fun if you do it with your friends or colleagues. That way, you have a real audience. The downside is that this audience gives you some very real feedback, but you'll get used to it. Within weeks, you'll see patterns of the speaker crawl into your own presentations. They might look awkward in the beginning. This is normal. Within months, you will make them your own; you'll modify them according to your own needs. You will also notice how patterns collide, interact, and give birth to new patterns, which will integrate into your own original style. (You will read about integration in the next chapter.)

I want to wrap it up with a quote from Steve Jobs:

> *It comes down to exposing yourself to the best things that humans have done and then try to bring those things into what you're doing.*

▶ Don't limit yourself to copying other presenters! Borrow from all kinds of performers: musicians, jugglers, mimes, dancers, comedians. Imitate, adapt, and mix. I did it and can attest that this is certainly one way to become a passionate presenter.

SUMMARY

The key points to remember from this chapter are as follows:

- ► **Passion is very difficult to fake.** Today's public speakers are not professional actors. They are managers, scientists, and experts. It is very difficult to show passion onstage when you have no passion for your job. If you don't like your job, you will never look believable as a presenter. Get yourself the job you like.

- ► **Don't be afraid to get into a discussion.** Discussions are much more interesting than monologues, and you will look much more passionate when there's something important at stake. Don't be afraid to confront, polarize, or offend the audience. Don't do it deliberately, but don't avoid it, either. Sometimes, this is what needs to be done.

- ► **Controversy is interesting.** If nobody's objecting, that means that you're not saying anything particularly interesting. Occasionally, you will lose the argument. This is a good thing, too. That's motivation to improve your knowledge and argumentation.

- ► **Imitate to find your own style.** Whenever you encounter a presentation you like, try imitating it. This is a great way of discovering your personal style, finding out what you can and cannot do onstage. Record your imitations and compare them to the originals. What's the difference? What might suit you better? Borrow not just from presenters but also from stage performers in other fields.

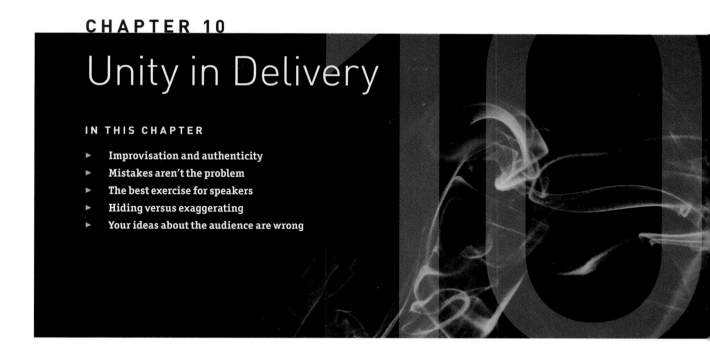

CHAPTER 10

Unity in Delivery

IN THIS CHAPTER

▶ Improvisation and authenticity
▶ Mistakes aren't the problem
▶ The best exercise for speakers
▶ Hiding versus exaggerating
▶ Your ideas about the audience are wrong

This chapter is concerned with what I believe are the two most challenging goals in public speaking: authenticity and improvisation. These two are intimately related. Speakers who don't improvise look canned. You cannot look authentic unless your speech is, to a certain extent, improvised. The reverse is also true. You cannot improvise unless you become authentic, coming in contact with your true self. So, how do you unify the two? How do you become authentic and start improvising? Read on to find out.

GOING WITH THE FLOW

There's great demand for authenticity today. The discussion about authenticity was probably started by existentialist philosophers, and then was echoed by the fringe self-help movement of the 1960s and 1970s, and gradually drifted to the mainstream. Positive psychologists are now designing authenticity questionnaires, Oprah is dedicating her shows to the topic, and there's even a book called *Authenticity: What Consumers Really Want*, which has sold well. There are many reasons for the interest in authenticity and most of them were beautifully summed by a game designer Jesse Schell exclaiming emotionally in one of his presentations:

> *We're living in a bubble of fake bullsh*t!*

Consumers and audiences want more authentic stuff. It is true that *authenticity* is becoming a new buzzword in business, much like *excellence* or *passion* before. But I think this one goes deeper. Once a purely marketing gizmo ("authentic leather trim"), authenticity is now more about the overall strategy, about the values and mission, about doing what we love, about hiring the right people and working with the right clients. This affects marketing, PR, and HR communications, both internal and external. This affects presentations. The audience now demands for the speaker to be "authentic." But what on Earth does that mean?

Authenticity in presentations is mostly about being true to yourself, looking natural and, in the end, practicing what you preach. It is about believing in what you're saying. Heavily scripted talk might look good on paper, but it doesn't look good onstage. You can see when the speaker just says words without really feeling them. Good speakers live through their speeches. Actors are trained to live through words that might have nothing to do with their true personality. Speakers are not actors, but they achieve the same effect by saying things they really deeply care about, when they live through the word, through the sentence, through the speech.

This is achieved by a certain degree of improvisation, by letting your unconscious mind make some decisions, by letting go, by allowing yourself to not know what you're about to say next. Sure, you have the overall flow of your talk, the sequence of slides that you have to show, the messages to deliver, your Twitter-worthy phrases to pronounce, and such. "One thousand songs in your pocket." Sure, maybe it was written by the marketing department. But the exact way you say it, your tone of voice, your breathing pattern, timing, and the emotions you attach to this phrase should be different every time you say it. They should be improvised. This is why good talks seem so authentic and real. To some degree, they are being made up on a spot.

Planning and rehearsing are still essential. But with the business environment getting more and more dynamic and unpredictable, improvisation becomes extremely important in every business domain that has to do with creativity: communications, design, and even client service. Businesses all over the world are learning to improvise. Even when I plan my pitch, I sometimes

▶ Authenticity is also (albeit to a smaller extent) affected by the factual accuracy of your speech. You must have the intellectual honesty to check your facts and the courage to mention that there might be other opinions on the subject.

find that my plans are woefully inadequate. At this point I can either bite the bullet and do the prepared talk (and I've seen many people take this approach with poor results) or follow my instinct in the moment. You have to improvise. The word itself, *im-pro-visus,* means "unforesee-able." And while you're doing this, you have no choice but to be authentic. This is your last hope.

Improvisation in Public Speaking

Properly executed improvisation is the best part in any performance. If you release yourself in the process of free speaking, you become a demiurge. You own the place; you own the audience. Slides still give you structure, and you can get back on track whenever you like. But sometimes you won't even want to. You start juggling your slides, showing them in a different order, showing slides from different presentations, and making up new concepts on a flipchart or whiteboard. You become expressive and driven. You get carried away. You look a bit like a crazy scientist, but your passion in undeniable and so is your impact.

Your language becomes unpredictable. When most speakers start a sentence, it's very obvious how they are going to end it. Not for you, not anymore. You'll become creative without much conscious effort. Your speech will become a bit like Yoda's. You can start defying the rules of grammar; not like a child who doesn't know any better, but like a poet. You'll become a master of language. You'll start creating interesting and meaningful words whenever you need them.

CREATIVE PHRASES EXCITE THE AUDIENCE

According to Professor Philip Davis from the University of Liverpool's School of English, this is more or less what Shakespeare did in his plays. He calls it *functional shifts*. Deliberate "errors" give wonderful unpredictability to his language. Expressions like "thick my blood," "the cruelest she alive," or "He childed as I fathered" aren't grammatically correct but they make perfect sense. What's more important, they touch readers in a very deep way. Interestingly, Davis' experiments demonstrate that our brains react to those peculiar phrases in a very peculiar way. It takes the brain about 400 milliseconds to show a peak response to a regular English expression. With Shakespearean phrases such as these, however, the brain needs about 600 milliseconds, which puts it in "a state of hesitating consciousness." Davis says this is how the "wow" effect works. Sentences like this excite the audience, activating emotional parts of the brain. In a normal state of consciousness, you'd never say anything like this because your "censor" won't let it through. Shakespeare made up his creative phrases beforehand, but since most improvisations are best when they're fresh, since their beauty is that they are a reaction to a unique moment, you want to let yourself get comfortable with being more unpredictable with your speaking language.

I observed that phenomena many times both as a speaker and as a listener. It is especially fascinating to observe at a workshop exercise, when the presentation's content isn't very important to you. As you are sitting in the audience and listen to other participants, there's really no reason for you to pay attention other than as a common courtesy. But as they speak, they are stunningly interesting to listen to. They aren't saying anything particularly profound. They are just sharing their recollections and thoughts. Most of the time it's not even funny (although it could be just hysterical). They are not very confident. There is really no reason why they should be interesting. No reason at all. Yet they are.

Perhaps it's precisely because the speakers don't do much at all. They aren't trying to come off as somebody they are not. They aren't mindlessly quoting anyone, including themselves, either explicitly or implicitly. They aren't posturing. They aren't protecting themselves. They are just being themselves, being honest and transparent human beings.

Being Believable

I was watching a presentation by Nokia's executive VP Anssi Vanjoki at the Nokia World 2010 conference and noticed that something wasn't right. He was angry. I mean very angry, to the point where he was almost spitting words out of his mouth. He was saying, "I am happy to report . . .," but it sounded more like "I am very irritated to report, but nevertheless . . . ." He wasn't boring. But he was passionate in a wrong way. He was struggling with the flow. He clearly didn't mean what he was saying. I later learned that at that time he had already resigned from Nokia because after his 20 years of service he wasn't chosen as the company's new CEO. The position instead went to an outsider, Stephen Elop from Microsoft.

▶ Yes, conflicts give us passion, but if you're angry with your own company, it is hardly productive. It comes across as bitter.

Being angry in a situation like this is perfectly understandable. However, no one should present with such a serious and unresolved conflict. It's hard to be persuasive that way. I don't know why he agreed to present (perhaps because he was scheduled to?), but I don't think he should have. It's really hard to give a good presentation when you don't mean what you say.

Consistency is persuasive. Inconsistency is not. If what we say is inconsistent with how we look, people tend to believe what they see. According to James Stiff, the author of two books—*Deceptive Communication* and *Persuasive Communication*—nonverbal cues are more important than verbal or social cues in evaluating honesty. Nonverbal signals can either confirm or negate whatever we say verbally. Our nonverbal expressions are largely subconscious. Yes, we can control them to a certain extent, but in moments of stress, we are very likely to lose this control.

NOTE   For more details on verbal versus nonverbal cues, see Stiff, J. B., Hale, J. L., Garlick, R., and Rogan, R. (1990), "Effect of cue incongruence and social normative influences on individual judgments of honesty and deceit," *Southern Communication Journal*, 55(2), 206–229.

Many presenters fail at this point because it is difficult to come up with great solutions for real problems. So people just say what they think the audience wants to hear, because all of us have the desire to please the audience and be liked. This behavior is normal. Speakers who don't have a desire to please risk polarizing their audience too much. But trying to be liked no matter what and going against your beliefs are two very different things. No matter how hard you try to be liked, if you come across looking inconsistent, like you don't believe what you are saying, your presentation will fail.

THE PROS AND CONS OF IMPROVISATION

Letting yourself go into the flow of improvisation and saying whatever is on your mind has many advantages and disadvantages. Let's start with the advantages, because they are easy to name.

For one thing, saying what you think solves the problem of remembering what to say. In the words of Mark Twain, "If you tell the truth, you don't have to remember anything." That's what some comedians do when they forget their routine. They just ad-lib, producing a stream of consciousness until the routine comes back to them. These can be the funniest moments of the show, when we see a genuine struggle of a comedian against his own memory.

The second advantage of telling the truth: it is liberating. As ancient Chinese philosopher Han Xiang wrote, "When you say what you don't mean and do what you don't want, you're not the one who's living." In the 1998 movie *Bulworth,* an aging politician decided to end his career with a series of improvised and honest talks about the true state of the Union. He inconvenienced many people, but his popularity took a sudden spike. The voters liked a bit of honesty for a change. According to Jim Kouzes and Barry Posner, the authors of an evidence-based model of leadership (and the bestselling book *The Leadership Challenge*), honesty is the number one trait that people cherish in their leaders. Number one. This research included thousands of people from all over the world. What's even more surprising, according to Kouzes and Posner, is that leaders who are more honest also are more effective.

This leads to the third advantage of truth telling: honest speakers are more persuasive and more attractive. There's a clear scientific consensus on this matter. You cannot help but look good when you tell the truth. Scott Berkun, the author of the great book *Confessions of a Public Speaker,* beautifully put it: "The feedback most speakers need is 'Be more honest'. Stop hiding and posturing, and just tell the truth."

Sadly, most contemporary public speaking is built on lies, pretense, and restraint that keeps you from being yourself. According to Kouzes and Posner, only 38 percent of business leaders are perceived as honest and just 13 percent of politicians are. I have to say that restraint and self-control aren't necessarily a bad thing. I know lots of people who could benefit from more restraint and self-control. As Russian archbishop Ambrosius, the author of a manual on improvised sermons, wrote in 1892, certain types of people are very willing to give improvised speeches, and they are precisely the ones who shouldn't be allowed to. Or, in the words of La Rochefoucauld, "Most young people think they are being natural when really they are just ill-mannered and crude."

So I'm not advocating radical honesty. I'm advocating relaxation of control when certain circumstances are met. I know you can't let go of all control. This is not an on/off switch; it's more like a slider.

The Right Context for Improvisation

Honesty and improvisation are two different things. There's calculated honesty and there are improvised lies. I think that authenticity is somewhere at the intersection of the two (see Figure 10-1). I don't think there's any context in which honesty is inappropriate. Seriously, I don't. There are many ways to tell the truth, and it is always possible to find one. It all depends on your creativity and compassion. That doesn't mean that I always follow my own advice. But honesty is the best policy, always. Yes, there are certain dangers; I do realize that. You can hurt others and of course you can hurt yourself. But as Mother Theresa said, "Honesty and transparency make you vulnerable. Be honest and transparent anyway."

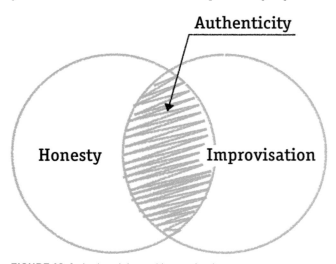

FIGURE 10-1: Authenticity and improvisation.

Let me give you one example. You might think that speaking the truth in a totalitarian state is not always the greatest idea. It's dangerous; you might lose your freedoms (although if you're living in a totalitarian state your freedom is already lost to a large extent), your family, or even your life. People who are not afraid to speak the truth are called *dissidents*. The Soviet Union was known for routinely jailing dissidents, so one of them by the name of Vladimir Albrekht wrote a little booklet called "How to be a witness."

The cornerstone principle of this manual was "always tell the truth." This wasn't only because lying under oath made you vulnerable from a legal standpoint. The dissidents took great pride in being honest and decent people, and many of them felt no obligation to abandon their principles under the scrutiny of the KGB. The goal of the manual was to allow the person to tell the truth and nothing but truth without incriminating either themselves or other people. According to many prominent figures in the dissident movement, it saved a lot of people from being jailed. The only move deemed more effective was to remain silent—which wasn't always an option.

Now, this method has nothing to do with free-flowing improvisation. On the contrary, the idea was to delay the answer as much as possible, buying the dissidents time to think. If you don't have enough time, if the stakes are high, or if you're under stress, don't improvise. Please don't improvise in court. This is generally a bad idea.

▶ Nothing reduces the quality of your improvisation more than high stress.

A good place to start improvising is during a more routine presentation, where small mistakes and imperfections are acceptable. Actually, small mistakes and imperfections are almost always acceptable. Even Steve Jobs' presentations are not perfect. In the end, it all boils down to your own willingness to accept mistakes.

British comedian Eddie Izzard and Russian guru Andrei Lapin probably had the greatest influence on me as a speaker. They are both known for their stream-of-consciousness style of delivery. I never really doubted that this was a good idea and I practiced it at every occasion. However, when I was giving my first seminar on this topic, one of the participants who was really struggling with the exercises finally uttered, "I cannot imagine Vladimir Putin answering questions at a press conference in this style!" I could only say *touché*. This style is hardly appropriate for presenters who are not willing to admit their mistakes. If you know anything about Putin, you know that he is very unwilling to admit his mistakes.

I would agree that both the standup comedian and the mad New Age guru have much more license than a business presenter or a politician. But as you read in Chapter 8 with the example of Swiss finance minister who laughed as his own incomprehensible language, admitting your faults isn't always a bad idea. Sadly, politicians for the most part don't seem to agree, but I hope this is slowly changing.

▶ Admitting your faults demonstrates much more responsibility and courage than keeping a straight face

Perhaps the most serious mistake you can make while in free-flow is to offend people. This happens mostly when your opinion about them isn't the highest already. Then you stop holding, and it just slips out. You let the cat out of the bag. A Russian proverb says, "A word is not a sparrow; once released you cannot catch it back." But can't we, really?

THE CASE OF THE NATIONAL THEATRE

In August 2010, there was some debate in London whether the Southbank Centre, one of the Britain's National Theatre sites, should be listed as a building of historical significance. The debate became particularly heated when Steve Norris, a London Mayoral advisor, gave this comment to the *Evening Standard*: "Not only do I not want the Southbank Centre to be listed—I think the National Theatre should have a Compulsory Demolition Order!"

Apparently some people at the National Theatre got upset. The theatre had a Twitter account set up for purely PR purposes. As with most accounts set up for PR purposes, it was rather boring and self-aggrandizing. I don't know what happened exactly, but their reply to the *Standard* commentary was surprisingly blunt: "Well, Steve Norris is clearly a giant ****" with asterisks representing one of the most offensive words in English language. Some 50 minutes later an apology was issued stating that the account has been compromised and that the tweet did not come from the Theatre staff.

We don't know whether the account was really hacked or not, but the point is that nobody believed it. The most popular hypothesis the public formed was that somebody from the PR staff forgot to log off from the official account before tweeting to their personal one. It's an understandable mistake. It's like sending a text message to the wrong person or mistakenly pressing the Reply All button. Everybody does that once or twice. And the reaction from most Twitter users was surprisingly positive:

> *@DisAgg – And to think I'd thought about unfollowing @NationalTheatre for them being bland. Best. Tweet. Ever.*

> *@johnfoley – Have to say I found that errant @NationalTheatre tweet to be refreshingly human.*

> *@jmc_fire – To be honest, I thought the @nationaltheatre c-word tweet was less offensive than their selective tweeting of good feedback on their shows.*

> *@NJMiller – This is the only interesting thing @nationaltheatre has ever tweeted.*

> *@LozKaye – For the first time ever I feel tempted to follow @NationalTheatre.*

One blogger by the name of Megan Vaughn wrote later: "For a moment there, you were my hero. The previously lackluster self-promotion that littered your feed was briefly enlivened . . . . You, our National Theatre . . ., were human after all. . . . Hooray for the National Theatre! Hooray for passionate tweets about relevant issues!"

Hooray to passionate presentations about relevant issues!

The real mistake here wasn't the tweet. The real mistake was taking it back in such a manner. Instead of simply apologizing in a straightforward way and perhaps gaining more credibility, the National Theatre tried to deflect criticism with an excuse that almost no one believed (whether or not it was really true). The reaction of the various Twitter users shows how much more the public valued the reaction, the language that seemed authentic over that which seemed canned and constructed.

RELAXING CONTROL

Figure 10-2 outlines how I think the process of speech works for most people. We know what to say slightly before we actually say it. The process of generating words runs before the process that controls words for appropriateness. We are able to censor anything we deem inappropriate before it is said. This is when we need to either generate something else very quickly or abstain from saying anything. This is when the awkward pauses happen.

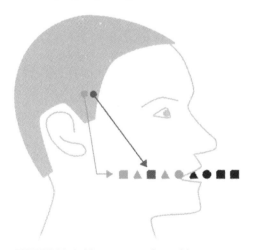

●→ **Generating text**
●▸ **Censoring text**
▪   **Raw words/thoughts**
▪   **Words said out loud**
▪   **Inappropriate words**

FIGURE 10-2: The process of speaking.

It's best to relax your quality control and instead rely on how the words sound when you actually say them and on the feedback from the audience. Here are my top three reasons for avoiding the approach outlined in Figure 10-2:

> ▶ **We look like we're lying all the time, even when we are not.** Those awkward pauses that come from censoring ourselves too much can make us look like we're being more

▶ The awkward pauses that can result from overthinking and overcensoring your own speech can make you appear you're lying (or not telling the whole truth) even when you are.

inauthentic than we actually are. Isn't the price of that sort of control a bit too high, then? If you are too afraid to offend your audience by letting the truth slip out, chances are you're presenting to the wrong audience.

▶ **Too much control destroys creativity.** In fact, nothing destroys creativity more efficiently. It makes the speech very calculated and, therefore, predictable and boring.

▶ **It makes us focus on what's inside.** During public speaking, it makes much more sense to focus on the outside. Whenever you hear a speaker who seems as if they are talking to themselves, this is often because they are controlling their speech too much. Do they really need the audience? Aren't they comfortable enough talking to themselves?

I think that, as speakers, we achieve the best results when we speak to the audience the way we speak to our friends. We're open and honest, and we still control our speech to a certain extent. We don't say whatever we think. However, we allow ourselves to have slips, pauses, and "umms."

WHAT KIND OF "UMMS" DO YOU HAVE?

You probably think that we don't need any more "umms" in public speaking. But "umms" are not the problem. It's what's behind the "umm" that's important. Some "umms" indicate a speaker is thinking on spot, and that's the kind of "umm" to encourage. There's nothing to hate about people thinking in front of us I personally find, watching a speaker think exciting. This is perhaps because thinking is such an intimate event, and watching a person think creates interesting suspense about what that person will say next.

Unfortunately, most people don't think when they say "umm." They just try to return behind the shield of safe content. We hate these "umms" because we are watching people suffering from the inability to just say what they think. They know what they want to say, but the "right" word or phrase eludes them and they think what they have on their mind isn't suitable for saying. This isn't a creative search; this is a bitter struggle against limitations they don't really accept. This is why it is so unpleasant for them to experience and for us to watch. Should they have picked the right words beforehand? No! They should just say what they think and move on!

▶ Our problem is that we micromanage our minds, controlling every word that is about to come out of our mouths. This slows down the speaking process, kills creativity, kills the flow, destroys enjoyment, and ultimately hampers the result.

The relationship between your conscious and unconscious mind resembles the relationship between a horse and its rider. The rider sets the general direction and then lets the horse do the job. He doesn't control every step of the horse; he trusts the horse to make decisions.

So, what should we do? Here's my plan:

1. Learn to say what you really think and how you think it, without much filtering. Learn to do it in private first, and then rehearse with a friendly audience. The goal is to be able to do it everywhere.

2. Listen to what you say (this is a skill too), watch for feedback from the audience, and notice when you make mistakes.

3. Accept, admit, and correct your mistakes. Watch the audience appreciating this with their nodding and laughing.

This is it. At this point your fear will be gone, and you can just watch yourself being creative. This is perhaps the single most rewarding and pleasant feeling I ever had—just watching my unconscious mind making smart decisions without much intervention from my conscious mind. You've probably had this experience; it's pure bliss. At times my internal "censor" comes back. But what's surprising is that it doesn't censor out strange or "inappropriate" words anymore. Instead, it censors out boring, ordinary, cliché words and phrases, replacing them with lively, interesting, and unpredictable language. I have no idea how this happens. This state is known in positive psychology as "the flow," a term popularized by professor Mihaly Csikszentmihalyi (pronounced "Chicks-send-me-high"). You may know this state from a sports or meditation experience as being "in the moment," "present," "in the zone," or "in the groove." Presenters have this state, too.

Rehearsing

Routine is the basis for every improvisation. I attended a couple of workshops on improvisational storytelling that were all about going with the flow, but my best results are always achieved when I know how the story is basically constructed. My best improvisational speeches happen when I make elaborate plans and ditch them at the last minute. Having a plan gives me backup and makes me confident. Mark Twain famously said, "Never could I make a good impromptu speech without several hours to prepare it." I totally agree with him.

▶ Preparation is an essential part of improvisation.

I want to speak about rehearsing first. The biggest secret with rehearsing is that it really works. Good speakers rehearse; great speakers rehearse even more. The reason why the TED conference is such a great show is because the organizers rehearse presentations with their speakers. I once rehearsed a 10-minute pitch for 2 hours until I got it right. And I mean rehearsed for 2 hours *after* the structure and the slides were ready. The effect produced became known locally as "the Kapterev effect." My subsequent workshops became overcrowded. I felt like I had some very unfair advantage over the other guys.

Finish your slides, turn on your projector (if you have one) or press Rehearse Slideshow (if you don't), and try delivering your presentation to an imaginary audience. Actually say the words aloud; this is the key. You would think it's pretty obvious what are you going to say, but believe me, often times it is just an illusion. When you try to say the words, you realize that it doesn't sound right. Sometimes you need to go back and redesign your slides. Sometimes you need to change the sequence. Occasionally you'll scrap the entire thing. This is also a great place to catch any glitches with the animation that you might have accidentally produced.

People tend to pay great attention to how the presentation starts. "Hello, my name is . . . ; today I will be talking about . . ." Now, when you rehearse for the second time (the first never goes right), you'll notice that the beginning doesn't sound too good. If you repeat it word by word, it becomes canned and mechanistic. This is when it's time to start rehearsing improvisation.

▶ Don't try to memorize your speech while rehearsing. If you repeat your presentation word-for-word exactly as you rehearsed it, it is guaranteed to sound awful.

Try to say something else, something different. Find another way of saying the same thing. Play. You're alone; no big risk here. Keep your eyes on your imaginary audience and just say whatever you think about the subject. Keep advancing your slides. Sure, you might start to ramble sometimes, but your slides should instill enough structure to keep you on track. The biggest advantage of rehearsing isn't in hitting something exactly right. The biggest advantage is in gaining confidence that you can find the way out even if you don't remember the words exactly. You have this capacity. This is when you relax and let it flow.

Next, tape yourself and watch the recording. You will probably notice that there are bumpy parts, where you stumble and don't know exactly what to say. When you watch these parts, you'll feel uncomfortable. There are also parts where you know what to say. They are better; you don't really feel any discomfort. On the other hand, they aren't very interesting to watch either. You know what are you going to say; you have a feeling "this part is okay." But inevitably, you'll find the best parts are when you didn't know what to say but you found a way to say something. The task was challenging so the solution turns out interesting. This sort of "rehearsed improvisation" is what you should ultimately be going for.

NOTE Did you ever see yourself on tape? I don't know about you, but when I fist saw myself it was a disaster. Who is this guy? Why does he speak in this manner? Why does he make those gestures! No, I can't watch this. Okay, it's me. I have to live with it somehow. This is a fairly typical reaction. I once polled about 100 people on my blog and only about 15 percent liked themselves on tape for the first time. Another 50 percent didn't like themselves and about 35 percent said that it was a disaster. The good news is that it gets better over time. Watching actually helps. You just get accustomed to what you see, whatever it is.

Letting Go

It will be harder with the real audience. Speaking your mind alone is one thing. It's easy, and most people can handle it. But speaking your mind, even to an encouraging and empathic psychoanalyst, is a very different experience. Speaking to a (presumably) judgmental audience can be a real challenge. The rule is that under stress we fall back to the previous level. If we've rehearsed specific words, we start mumbling. If we've rehearsed improvising, we start sounding uptight (which is still better than mumbling). If you want to be great, you need to learn to lower your stress level. There are many stress-relieving techniques, the trouble is most of them are so elaborate that you forget to apply them properly (or at all) when necessary. Consider using these simple ones:

► **Repetitive self-talk:** There's a well-known effect called Benson's relaxation response, after Dr. Herbert Benson who came up with it. In short, if you repeat anything, any word or phrase, in your internal monologue, you will relax. That's it, nothing else. Whether you are religious, spiritual, philosophical, or not, praying helps, mantras help. Try them.

► **Body awareness:** Without any attempt to change anything, just notice your breathing, your heartbeat, or the weight of your body. If you notice that your heart rate is too fast, that's fine. Congratulate yourself for noticing it. Don't try to slow it down. Just observe it. It will slow down all by itself. Don't expect it to slow down either; just watch it slow down. Trust me, it will.

► **Ask the audience for help:** But you have to be specific about the help you need. Many people start their presentation with the phrase, "I am sorry; I feel very nervous," which is the moment you in the audience know it is going to be bad. However, the reason it sounds bad is because what they are saying is entirely irrelevant. All who present become nervous; what makes this case so special? The audience wants to know, "What do you want from me? How can I help?"

I once watched a presentation by game designer Jesse Schell (whom I mentioned earlier in this book), who started by asking the audience to clap rhythmically and then proceeded with playing a harmonica! What's even more shocking was that his playing was really bad! He finally stopped, thanked everybody, and explained that he was very nervous and this calms him down. Wow! What courage! This was the point he got applause. So go ahead and ask. If there's something the audience can do to make you less nervous, ask for it. They want to see a good show, and they are willing to help. Just be clear with your request. Thank them and show them an improvement. Look at your hands and see if they are shaking. If they don't shake, announce it! If they *almost* don't shake, announce it! The audience wants to know the results.

▶ You are who you are, and the best way to change is to stay wherever you are really well. The best thing you can do is to assume that you have the right to be in front of those people and let go of the desire to be good at any cost.

The reason we get nervous is because we want to look our best. This is perfectly normal. However, we all have our limits. It's important to prepare your structure and slides, to rehearse, to work on your voice, or to go to public speaking seminars and acting or improv classes. But the moment you step onstage you are who you are. You cannot magically become someone else. The only thing you can do is to accept yourself with all your limitations and play within those limitations. This is the real chance to make your performance more authentic and thus dramatically better.

People onstage frequently get defensive. They cross their arms or feet or get behind a table or a lectern. They are trying to protect themselves, or are they? More likely they are protecting their cherished image of themselves and the goal (at least at that point) is not to get rid of that image entirely. Garr Reynolds advocates presenting "naked," in the sense of letting go of your image. However, I don't think you can really present "naked;" it's not about letting go of your image entirely. The audience needs to see something. To me it's about having the right "clothing." The goal is to get clothing that suits you and the occasion. This is the mistake most presenters (myself included) make. Metaphorically speaking, we try to dress in fake Gucci and hope that nobody will notice. Or, rather, we fear that somebody will notice. We try to exaggerate our credentials, the importance of our message, and our own contributions to the topic. Likewise, we try to exaggerate our charisma, our friendliness, and our spontaneity. But we can't! We can surely improve them by practicing, but once we're onstage there's very little we can do. We can only accept that for now this is who we are.

One of the best exercises for public speakers is standing, just standing in front of the audience doing nothing for a minute or two. Not saying anything, not moving, not shifting the gaze, and not even smiling. Maintain gentle eye contact with one person or just watch the imaginary horizon. Just stand. When people do this exercise for the first time, they have a compulsive desire to move, to produce something, to shrug, to grimace, to rock on their feet. It's uncomfortable to just be in front of the audience without any real reason. So people try to make something up, to have some interaction. However, it's futile and unnecessary.

It's a subconscious reflex, and if you don't fight it or support it, after a while it goes away. This is when you realize that you don't have to do anything to be interesting. You want to be liked, but you really have nothing to do to be liked. They will like you as you are. You notice it twice: first as the one standing and second as the one watching other people stand. It is really interesting to watch. A minute-long pause is quite exciting for the audience, even though it might seem like eternity for the speaker. This experience stays with you forever. You can now speak not because you are trying to fill an uncomfortable pause, not out of fear, but because you have something important to say.

Listening to What You Say

When you say what you think, listen to what you say. This skill is a hard one because of the way your brain works. Broca's area, responsible for speech production, is competing for resources with the neighboring Wernicke's area, which is responsible for understanding. It's the same mechanism that makes it hard to speak when somebody else's speaking. You are forced to listen, and it's difficult to speak and listen at the same time. However, if you redistribute the resources used to censor yourself to monitor your speech instead, you will be able to accomplish it.

If you don't listen to yourself, you have no chance to reflect on things you say. This is when you stop being an intelligent human being and become an unconscious generator of verbal garbage, not terribly entertaining or useful. When you listen to what you say, you are actually able to notice your mistakes and correct them. What's even better, you can also notice clichés and parts of your speech that don't sound natural. You now have an option to rephrase or reaffirm them. Here's an excerpt from a 2010 presentation by Peter Chow, the CEO of THC, the Taiwan-based manufacturer of smartphones:

> I am very excited today. You know, I say this every year... even eight years ago
> when we launched our first phone [...] But you know, it continues to be true! It's
> such an exciting time for the mobile industry!

Notice that he didn't avoid the obvious. He said, "I'm very excited," which is not the best phrase you can use to start a presentation. But then he reflected on what he just said, acknowledged that he was saying a cliché, and then reassured the audience that this is in fact what he meant. What a great idea! I was really impressed. In hindsight I think it was probably scripted, but it was still a great idea that came across as authentic.

I learned to listen to myself while being an interpreter. Interpreting is largely an unconscious process. Most of the words you say you don't actually say. That sounds paradoxical. What I mean is you don't make a conscious effort to say them; rather, you just listen to yourself saying them. This happens because you largely give up any responsibility for the content; the meaning is produced by somebody else. You just have to interpret it correctly. If you've never had this experience, try putting an earpiece in one of your ears and turning on an audio book on your computer or MP3 player. Repeat everything you hear out loud. As one of your ears will be open, you will inevitably find yourself in a split conscious mode. One ear is listening to the audio book and another one is listening to your own voice. You may close your eyes to direct more of your attention to the sounds. Notice your mistakes, your slips, but don't bother to correct them. Just notice them. If you stop noticing them, you will stop even trying to sound correctly, which isn't the goal.

Hearing what you say without thinking first gets you closer to the experience of having your mind in the flow.

> ▶ Listening to yourself is one of the most important skills for public speakers.

Integrating Mistakes

I have a little hobby; I dance. I'm into a rather peculiar form of dancing called *contact improvisation*. It was invented about 40 years ago by people practicing contemporary dance, Aikido, and gymnastics. There are no set movements or gender roles; dancers move in unpredictable trajectories, and the dance is very acrobatic. It involves lifts, handstands, leaning onto each other, and jumping. All this frequently happens at high speeds, and mistakes are quite costly. Do you know what contact improvisers do to let themselves dance freely without a fear of injury (and without much actual injuries for that matter)? They learn to fall safely to the point where they start enjoying it. This is precisely the point where falling itself becomes dance.

Fortunately, mistakes in public speaking don't typically involve falling. They are mostly about forgetting your words, fidgeting, crossing your arms, saying something stupid, spilling water, or dropping your remote. As an example, suppose you caught yourself crossing your arms, a common defensive gesture. You have several choices:

▶ Uncross them before anyone else notices and pretend that nothing happened. This is what most people do. This method is easy and quick. Unfortunately, even if people didn't notice that you were standing in a closed posture, they will notice you are rectifying it.

▶ Uncross them so quickly that everyone will notice and comment ironically, "I've been told not to cross arms on my chest. Apparently, some people think I'm hiding a weasel there or something."

▶ Determine why you've crossed your arms in the first place. This probably happened when you were talking about something you weren't entirely sure about. Cross your arms even tighter, to the point that everyone notices, make a defensive face, and continue discussing the topic. You will get laughs.

Mistakes present huge opportunities for laughter, and you can either hide them or make them as visible as possible. I prefer the latter approach; I think it is more honest and fun. Comedy is all about truth. You might think that hiding mistakes is safer, but actually it is much more dangerous because when you hide something, you can no longer control it. And the more you hide it, the harder it is to deal with when you ultimately need to correct it.

This is what I call a *mistake squared*. I was once giving an hour-long presentation (more like a lecture actually) at a nightclub. I came well before the beginning and had plenty of time to prepare. I connected my laptop to the projector, checked my remote, and tested a couple of slides to see whether they look good. Unfortunately, some guys were already sitting in the audience and I was reluctant to show the slides I that was actually going to use. Instead I tested some other slides; as you might imagine, I have plenty. They looked fine. So I thought I was prepared. That was my first mistake.

▶ This is one of the core rules of any improvisation: mistakes are inevitable. Learn to handle them. Make them part of the show. It could be fun. Falling is also an art.

People wandered in and eventually the show started. The host introduced me. I came onstage, pressed Play Slideshow, and looked at the screen. My heart sank into my stomach. The projector turned the "cardboard" background of my slides into a dark brown mess. The black font I used became almost invisible, almost but not entirely. It was somewhat visible. Then I made my second mistake—I decided to continue with barely visible text.

It wasn't a complete catastrophe. But it was pretty close to it. Fortunately, about half of my slides were photos. But when it came to my diagrams and the text, because the chamber I was presenting in was narrow and long, the people in front could still see something, but the people in the back saw mostly a brown background. So much for a presentation expert's presentation.

WARNING Please always check your equipment beforehand. Please.

But really the problem wasn't in the equipment. I mean, it was bad in this case, but could have been easily corrected. I could have excused myself, pressed Esc, opened my template, and changed the background to plain white, all in 3 seconds. Then I could have said "And this is the first lesson: always check your equipment . . ." But I didn't! The problem was that I made a mistake and did not accept the fact that I made a mistake. This was the real mistake. Instead of accepting the mistake, I chose to suffer for an hour and made my audience suffer with me. Why did I do it? In the previous chapter, I ranted about how not being perfect is supposed to make your presentation dramatically better. Why didn't I follow my own advice?

The first reason is that for many people in many situations (myself included), accepting a mistake isn't an automatic response. An automatic response is to hide the mistake, to pretend that this is how things are supposed to be. I know consciously that this is a bad idea, but I was not conscious enough. The whole kerfuffle happened in the very beginning, which is the most nervous part of any presentation. When you come onstage, the world changes so rapidly and the struggle to keep control of your emotions is so desperate that making a slip is very easy.

Accepting the mistake is the first step, but not the last one. After you've accepted it, you have to deal with it. This is a frightening part. Now it is obvious to me what I should have done. It wasn't so obvious then. I needed to improvise the solution, and we all know how risky improvisation can be. This is probably the reason why we try to hide mistakes. So you can plan to accept your mistakes, but mistakes are not about planning. They just happen. You have to retrain your subconscious responses; you have to plan to make mistakes. As always with improvisation, planning really helps.

Many professional performers have special routines for handling mistakes. When Eddie Izzard's jokes are met with silence, he pretends to write on his hand, "I shall never do this again," thus unleashing roaring laughter. Juggling champions Raspyni Brothers comically pretend to lose fingers in tricks with "razor-sharp" sickles whenever they drop one. One of my friends, a professional street juggler, claims that when he makes mistakes, he gets more money! He says that as an artist his job is not to toss objects but to create an emotional connection with the audience. Making mistakes is very human and makes it easier for the public to empathize with him. His routines are indeed hilarious. If he drops one of his flaming torches, he quickly puts the remaining ones on the floor and starts moving them around, crying "Floor juggling, ladies and gentlemen, floor juggling!"

The most frequent mistake improvisers make is to lose their train of thought. The most common reaction to this on the part of the speaker is "What was I saying?" I'm pretty sure you heard this phrase before. Again, the phrase is not a problem. Losing your train of thought is perfectly natural. There's nothing to be ashamed of. It's only painful to watch if the speaker gets disappointed and scared. Just get over it. There seems to be at least three easy ways to deal with this issue:

▶ **Pause:** Archbishop Ambrosius, whom I mentioned earlier in this chapter, writes about taking out his handkerchief and wiping the sweat off his forehead. By the time he does that, everything goes back to normal. I don't know about you, but most of the time I don't even have a handkerchief, and I hate pretending. To me, taking a long pause even without any handkerchiefs is okay. But I like the next method better.

▶ **Play with it:** Whatever you feel like doing automatically, do it but in a slightly exaggerated way. Give the audience a hint that this isn't really automatic, that know what you're doing. Eddie Izzard does his trademark "so . . . yeah . . ." and bounces on his feet. He does it very deliberately, and it looks like he is expecting something, not from himself but from the audience. By the time the audience realizes that they don't owe him anything, he's back on track. Andrei Lapin used to say simply "What was the question?", and it was hilarious because it confirmed his comic "mad New Age guru" image. He also used to promise to take memory-improving medicine but kept forgetting it. It doesn't matter what you do. The secret seems to be to overdo it, to exaggerate. Here are some more examples:

▶ *Situation*: You make a joke and only one person is laughing. *Response:* "Yes, thank you very much, sir; now, for the rest of you . . ."

▶ *Situation*: You say something that scares or disgusts the audience. *Response:* In a tone of a concerned parent, "It's better if you learn this from me rather than from the boys on the street!" (This is Andrei Lapin's approach.)

▶ *Situation*: The audience stares at you like they didn't get your last comment at all. *Response:* Say, "Lost you, lost you . . .," close your eyes, and pretend like you're trying to find your audience with your hands. Proceed with a different explanation.

Seriously, try anything. It's not about the words; it's about demonstrating that you're aware that something unexpected has happened. Just exaggerate it.

▶ The best thing about mistakes is that they are frequently funny. What an opportunity! Comedy is about mistakes. If you are ready to laugh at yourself, recovering from your mistakes can be great.

▶ **Ask for help from the audience:** This can actually work better than everything else. Comedians do it all the time. Sometimes the audience not only helps you to get on track, they also suggest new ideas that are quite good! All you need is to be open enough to accept the help. Unprofessional? It's only unprofessional if you are playing the "I'm an expert, and you're the fools" game.

Here are some more examples of integrating mistakes. These are from Steve Jobs:

"Clicker is not working . . ." (Loudly, apparently to the personnel behind the stage). "Clicker is not working!" (To the audience). "They're scrambling back-stage right now." (Laughter.)

(The software doesn't act like it should.) "Oh, give me a break!" (To the audience). "Anyway, you know what it's supposed to do!" (Laughter.)

"Mac OS X is gonna recognize the camera, which I guess I didn't turn on . . . I need some help here; it's technical!" (Laughter.) "My camera is not turning on. What's that? I did slide and let go. Not turning on . . . Here!" (Takes the camera and throws it to somebody in the audience.)

Please ask for help; they are willing to help and everybody wins! I was once interpreting at a very formal conference and forgot the Russian word for "virtue." This happens with interpreters all the time; we forget words. It is usually recommended to avoid the pause and use a close synonym. However, I was interpreting for a former German pastor, and the word had such wonderful religious connotations that I wanted to say it correctly. I just asked for help. Interpreters aren't supposed to do that; it's considered unprofessional. But immediately somebody gave me the proper Russian word (*dobrodetel*, in case you're interested) and it all went on quite well.

> **NOTE** You might think, "Ah, you just got lucky." The thing is that I always get lucky. Somebody always knows. And if they don't, well, it's not so horrible for me to not know it either then.

After I finished translating the speech, a woman approached me. She thanked me for a good job and stated that she was an interpreter herself and she always suffers when translations are imprecise. She agreed that it was a good idea to ask for help and not to compromise on the quality. I thanked her and asked her to give her opinion to the organizers, whom I suspected weren't quite happy with this episode of "dire unprofessionalism." She gladly talked to the organizers and praised my job, specifically mentioning my commitment to the accuracy of the speech. It turned out that she wasn't just any interpreter, but a former Russian interpreter for the Queen of England.

▶ The secret is to be committed to the cause, not to your public image.

When you care mostly about how you look, people will sense it and dislike it. If whatever you are doing you are doing for the greater good, people will appreciate it. You can still make stupid decisions, but if you are sensitive to feedback and willing to correct your mistakes, your mistakes don't really matter. The audience will forgive you.

> **NOTE** I find this to be true everywhere, even in a contact dance. If you are only committed to yourself, you tend to disregard your partner. If you're committed only to your partner, you might let them abuse the relationship. However, if you're committed to the dance itself, to the art, to the idea of dancing, nothing bad is going to happen. You will be dancing to the best of your abilities, keeping both you and your partner happy.

A Journey in Search of Truth

When you prepare your presentation, you have your goals. You also have some ideas about what the audience expects and needs from you. These ideas are wrong. You can never be 100 percent right; real people aren't the same as your ideas about them. So if you start a presentation hoping that it will go without a hitch, you are in for disappointment. If it does go without a hitch, you're either a genius capable of predicting complex human behavior or, the far more likely truth, there was no real connection between you and the audience. Maybe they just didn't understand what you were saying but chose not to ask questions to avoid looking stupid. Maybe they did understand but preferred to discuss it behind your back rather than talking to you. Some speakers are successful in creating a "reality distortion field" during their presentation (Steve Jobs is often accused of that). In this field everything seems to be logical and working, but once people get to their workplaces they realize that reality is more complex. This is when they start getting angry with the presenter.

> **NOTE** It's like with startups. The sooner you start prototyping, the sooner you realize that your ideas are wrong and figure out how to make them better. It has been said that if you are not ashamed of your product the first time you build it, you should have built it much sooner.

The sooner you start talking to the audience, the sooner you realize what's working and what's not with your ideas. This is your chance to learn, and if you are not learning, nobody else does. Don't be afraid to get messy. Your presentation is not a circus performance; it's not an act. It is a dialogue; it's a conversation; it's an exchange of opinions. It is a two-way street. If you want people to change, go ahead and change yourself. If you want people to accept their mistakes, go ahead and accept yours. Stop hiding and posturing. When you do, the audience shows you what your mistakes are. And then you both have to work together to fix them.

It won't work if you don't have any goals, or if your goal it "to inform." It won't work if you don't talk to the audience. It won't work if you don't challenge them. It won't work if you pretend to be a superman in a shining impenetrable armor. It won't work if you don't relax and allow yourself to be creative. It does require a lot of focus, courage, flexibility, and motivation. But so does every journey in search of truth. On the bright side, if you do all this, you'll be rewarded with not only much better presentations, but also much better ideas. Isn't that worth it?

SUMMARY

The key points to remember from this chapter are as follows:

- ► **Improvisation rules.** Authentic speakers improvise, honestly responding to whatever feedback they get from the audience. Improvisation is what makes speakers believable and separates them from a recorded broadcast. Improvisation is not magic but is a set of skills that you can practice.

- ► **The basis for improvisation is rehearsal.** Improvisation requires a quick and an agile mind, which you get when you stop worrying about things that you might have rehearsed. Rehearse more—but don't memorize your speech word-for-word. Otherwise, it will sound canned.

- ► **Speak your mind.** The most basic and important skill is just saying what's on your mind without much censorship. You give your unconscious mind a general direction, a basic topic, and then trust it to make decisions for you. Relax control of your speech; switch from censoring mode to monitoring mode. Listen to what you say as it's being said.

- ► **Mistakes are fun.** If you notice yourself making mistakes, admit them. Whenever you say something inappropriate, erroneous, or just stupid, correct yourself. Mistakes create tension that is best released in laughter. The easiest way to make your mistake funny is to exaggerate it. Not admitting mistakes creates a downward spiral.

- ► **Worry about the cause.** If your concern is about the cause and not about yourself, the audience will forgive you almost anything. Search for truth and don't be afraid to do it publicly whenever you need to.

CHAPTER 11

Where to Go Next

IN THIS CHAPTER

▶ **Checklist of presentation points**
▶ **The best books, blogs, and workshops**

Here you are, reading the last chapter. In conclusion I'd like to give you a checklist of the key points from this book and some references for your further improvement. This chapter can serve as a place you can go for a quick reminder of the important presentation points the book has covered. I will be repeating myself some, but for purely practical reasons. When you re-read information, synaptic connections in your brain get stronger. Or, as Russians say, repetition is the mother of all learning.

PRESENTATION CHECKLIST

Figure 11-1 contains the list of the most important points I made in this book. The checklist that follows covers these points in somewhat greater detail. Please read them carefully and make sure they are clear to you. If you are in doubt, go back to the corresponding chapter and review it. Every point in this list is crucial to the success of your presentation.

	Focus	Contrast	Unity
Story	Focus on the goal	What's the conflict?	Organize the flow
Slides	Focus on the message	What's the comparison?	Delete the unnecessary
Delivery	Focus on the audience	What's the challenge?	Admit the mistakes

FIGURE 11-1: *Presentation Secrets* key points.

Story

Focus on the goal

Ask yourself the following questions:

1. What is the goal? What am I trying to achieve?

2. What does the audience need?

3. Find the intersection between what you want and what the audience needs. This is the end of your presentation; this is where you need to lead your listeners.

What's the conflict?

Ask yourself the following questions:

1. What does the audience want?

2. What prevents them from getting what they want?

3. Who will be fighting whom for what?

This is the second part of your presentation.

Organize the flow

1. Design the introduction. What does the audience need to know beforehand in order to understand and appreciate your presentation? This might include the ground rules, the personal story, and the good news.

2. State the goal and the problem.

3. Present the solution. If your solution is multi-step, unify it using L.A.T.C.H.: location (visual metaphor), acronym (alphabet), time-based narrative, categorization, or hierarchy. Remember that each step is a mini-story!

4. Conclude. Present a quick summary and a call for action, and talk about values.

Slides

Focus on the message

Ask yourself the following questions:

1. What is the goal of this slide?

2. Do I need to remind, impress, explain, or prove? Depending on the answer, choose the slide type: text, photograph, concept visualization, or data visualization.

3. What is the hierarchy of this slide? What's the key message and what are the supporting messages?

What's the comparison?

1. Make sure your text and figures are visible against the background.

2. Most effective slides compare. Ask yourself the following questions: What's the change? Where's the difference? Is it highlighted with size or color changes?

3. Make sure different hierarchical levels of information are clearly different in size or color.

Delete the unnecessary

1. Re-read your text and re-scan your visuals for anything you can safely remove. Make sure your text is concise. Don't use five colors if you need two. Watch out for chartjunk.

2. Is the visual metaphor of the slide consistent? If your slides were a physical object, what would it be made of? Paper? Plastic? Stone? Do they obey to the laws of physics?

3. Imagine yourself seeing the slide for the first time. How does your eye travel? Does it go from the most important point to the least important? From the beginning of the diagram to its end? If not, redesign accordingly.

Delivery

Focus on the audience

1. Practice your delivery so you can focus on the audience while you're presenting—don't focus on what to say next. Don't repeat the same words while practicing; you will sound canned.

2. Maintain eye contact. Scan the audience from one side to another, making sure you look in the eye everyone who is in the room.

3. Talk to the people, not just in their general direction.

What's the challenge?

1. Ask questions even if you don't expect an answer. Challenge them. Give them difficult choices.

2. Don't shy away from conflict, embrace it. If nobody's objecting that means you're not saying anything particularly interesting. Fear and resistance to change are perfectly natural. You need to address these concerns.

3. If somebody asks a question, make sure you still talk to the whole audience, not just to one person.

Admit mistakes

1. Switch from censoring to monitoring. Say what you think but listen to what you say.

2. When things go wrong, don't try to hide it. Mistakes create tension, which is best released with laughter.

3. Be your hero. Improvise.

TAKING FURTHER STEPS

Failing sucks. Perhaps this is the single most important motivation for improving in anything. After "Death by PowerPoint" became a hit, for a while it felt like I didn't need to know anything else about presentations. Also, it felt like the field itself was small and well researched. My honeymoon with presentations ended when I started to work with one of Russia's largest production companies and to deal with many real-life situations involving many different clients. Pretty soon I discovered that my knowledge and skills were inadequate. I had to learn more.

So I ordered some books from Amazon, visited some workshops, subscribed to even more blogs, and bought some software. Predictably, this made things much more complicated and therefore worse—although at that moment I didn't notice. What I did notice is that the field is in fact extremely rich in content, and the possibilities for learning are almost limitless. The same thing will happen to you. You need some time to assimilate the knowledge from this book, to try things, and to see what works for you and what doesn't. After a while, your progress will slow and you'll hit a plateau, where you will live comfortably until you suddenly realize that, at least as far as presentations are concerned, you still have a lot to learn. Then you get your motivation to dig deeper, to go on to the next resource, the next learning experience. It's a slow process going from resource to resource like this, really assimilating what each has to offer, but unless you proceed carefully you risk being overwhelmed by the amount of resources available to you.

Too many books end with a recommended reading list that contains dozens and sometimes even hundreds of books in alphabetical order. This approach doesn't strike me as particularly helpful (although it probably does work as a display of the author's erudition). You can't read all of those books, and you are unsure how to prioritize so you end up ditching the entire list. So I came up with an alternative "only the essentials" approach, doing some prioritization for you. In the sections that follow I cover only the most essential books, blogs, or areas of practice for presentations in general and for the three areas of presentations (story, slides, and delivery) I have covered in this book.

GENERAL PRESENTATION RESOURCES

There are a number of competing approaches to presentations that are worth mentioning.

- ▶ Perhaps the most influential figure in presentations is Garr Reynolds. His blog is at www.prezentationzen.com. In 2006, I started to learn about presentations from this blog. "Death by PowerPoint" was mostly a compilation of Garr's ideas put in a sequence and visualized. Since I started reading his blog, Garr has written three books: *Presentation Zen: Simple Ideas on Presentation Design and Delivery* (storytelling and slides), *Presentation Zen Design: Simple Design Principles and Techniques to Enhance Your Presentations* (slide design), and *The Naked Presenter: Delivering Powerful Presentations With or Without Slides* (delivery). If you don't have any of the Garr's books, get the first one. It's the industry's bible.

▶ Next comes *Beyond Bullet Points: Using Microsoft Office PowerPoint 2007 to Create Presentations That Inform, Motivate, and Inspire* by Cliff Atkinson. This was the first book on presentations that I ever read. It was first published in 2005 and later updated; make sure you get the latest edition. As the name suggests, the best part of the book is about slides, but it also covers some basic aspects of storytelling and delivery. At the time I first read this the main advantage of this book for me was the abundance of useful PowerPoint tips; Microsoft Press published this book.

▶ Finally, another approach is Dr. Andrew Abela's 10-step extreme presentation method. His book is called *Advanced Presentations by Design: Creating Communication that Drives Action*. It doesn't cover delivery, only slides and structure. It is extremely thorough, detailed, and step-by-step; it contains worksheets, sample layouts, and more.

Next, I deal specifically with storytelling, slides, and delivery, one by one.

STORYTELLING RESOURCES

Storytelling is perhaps the easiest subject to practice. We do a lot of storytelling in our everyday life. We tell stories about our work at home, stories about our home at work, stories about our children, about traffic mishaps, pets—you name it. The problem is that we don't pay much attention to how we do it. The moment we are telling a story we are much more concerned with what to say rather than how to say it—because we never prepare properly. We never try to craft the story unless we need to lie. Who has time? We don't even have time for storytelling in business communications!

As Nancy Duarte said once, we've become a culture of first drafts. We just write things and click Send. We have precious moments in our lives, really unique situations probably good enough for Hollywood, and we just let them go without stopping to turn them into something really worth telling. This is unfortunate, and we can improve our ability to turn moments into stories, thus ultimately improving our presentation skills. So, how can you improve your storytelling ability? Consider the following resources.

Books

Robert McKee's *Story: Substance, Structure, Style and The Principles of Screenwriting* was the first book about Hollywood scriptwriting I attempted to read but I never managed to finish it. As a matter of fact, going to McKee's live seminar was my solution for not reading this book. I later learned that the book was never meant to be read linearly. Rather, it was conceived as a reference manual. It still sits on my shelf, and I now use it as a reference manual. So I still recommend you buy it.

▶ Surprisingly, I found the audio version of the same book very lively, entertaining, and maybe even a good replacement for the seminar itself.

The second book is John Truby's *The Anatomy of Story: 22 Steps to Becoming a Master Storyteller.* I heard about this book during a seminar by Arif Aliev, a Russian screenwriter and an expert on the subject. Although Aliev's seminar was excellent, the book is even better. By far this is the best book on storytelling I ever read, hands down. My greatest breakthroughs in understanding goals, motives, and structure came with this book. Truby's building blocks approach is the one that I use in my work. I cannot be too overzealous in recommending this book.

The last item on my list is Nancy Duarte's *Resonate: Present Visual Stories that Transform Audiences*. This book has one major advantage over all the other books; it actually covers storytelling as it applies specially to presentations. Although I didn't find much new information in it for myself, that doesn't mean you won't. Nancy takes her inspiration from the hero's journey structure made popular by anthropologist David Campbell and later by screenwriter Chris Vogler. The book is beautifully designed and full of insights from the industry's leading figure. I think this is an excellent investment, both in terms of money and time.

▶ This is probably the best book for beginners, especially if they don't have much intention of going really, really deep.

Workshops

There are many workshops on scriptwriting. I attended just one of them, perhaps the most well known: Robert McKee's *Story* seminar in New York. As the seminar's website (www.mckeestory.com) states, it was attended by 26 Academy Award winners, 125 Emmy Award winners, 19 Writers Guild of America Award winners, and 16 DGA Directors Guild of America Award winners. Peter Jackson and John Cleese attended this seminar. Despite all this I had a lot of doubts before going, but the seminar turned out to be fantastic.

McKee is one of the most passionate and charismatic speakers that I have personally met. He is a renegade; he is a cowboy. He wears a black hat and a leather jacket. His eyebrows are so thick they look like somebody cut two strips from a floor carpet and glued them to his forehead. He also jokes a lot, through borrowing sometimes from the late George Carlin. He swears, he isn't politically correct, and he fines the attendees for not switching their mobile phones off.

He calls what he does "lecturing" and he is right. For three days, from 9 a.m. to 8:30 p.m., he talks to 500 people who mostly just sit and listen. Of course, they also fidget, fall asleep, and sometimes walk away to have some coffee. This doesn't sound all that exciting and frankly most of the time it's not—except when it is. Because apart from all that, people also take notes, think, feel, applaud, and experience revelations of a lifetime.

McKee is one of the best storytellers I ever met. He can tell fantastic stories from ordinary life and make you feel like you were there. He is also uniquely capable of summarizing 1.5-hour long movies in 10 short sentences. Granted, parts of the seminar are inapplicable for the context of presentations, like those related to writing a dialogue or selling your screenplay, but the bits on structure and meaning are priceless. The biggest surprise was that his seminar wasn't about scriptwriting. It was about life, about truth, and about psychology. I've read a lot of psychology books, yet it sometimes seems that I learned more about psychology from McKee than from any other source.

Apart from McKee there are many good instructors on screenwriting, including John Truby (www.truby.com) and Christopher Vogler (www.thewritersjourney.com). Although I've never had a chance to attend their workshops in person, I did listen to the tapes and I can attest that they are very useful too.

Practice

Books and seminars are great for getting new ideas, but after you've acquired the idea you have to apply it. So, what to do? Try these practice points:

▶ **Retell every interesting story you encounter.** Try retelling your favorite TV show's episode to somebody who has no intention of watching this show. In a couple of attempts you will start to understand how TV scriptwriters think. The general rule is that by retelling other people's stories consciously you improve your own ability. The key word is, of course, *consciously*. This also makes watching TV a much more productive experience.

▶ **Start blogging in stories.** Now that it's all about Facebook and Twitter, "traditional" long-format blogs are losing popularity. However, I don't suggest you use your blog as a marketing tool. I mean if it works as a marketing tool that would be fantastic, but that's not the main goal. The main goal is to practice. Writing isn't live; here you can save your work and edit it later. Practice restructuring your thoughts. Try different schemas and scenarios. What if you start with a question? What if you end with a question? What if you make the problem part longer and the solution part shorter? What's best about blogs is that they give you feedback. You get comments, "likes," and hits. You can see what works and what doesn't. You don't need to do it every day; aim for one story per week.

▶ **Practice telling your own stories.** Every time somebody asks you why you did this or that, try not only to explain it logically, but also to come up with a story from your experience to validate your judgment. For example, when people ask me why I switched to a

Mac, I tell the story about my first computer, a Commodore 64, which I used mostly for games and my subsequent PC computers, which I used mostly for work. I explain how, on a Mac, work became play for me. You'll be amazed how well that works. Once your decision makes perfect sense to you, you will project that non-verbally in a very powerful and unique way. Try it.

▶ What's even more important, **practice your own Story.** I use a capital letter here because this is the Story that defines you, that explains who you are once and for all. Again, I am not suggesting that you make your story up. I suggest you invest time in constructing a proper story from the details of your biography. It should have a hero, a problem, a need, an opponent, and a transformation. Practice telling it and see what happens. Notice which parts excite you the most. If one day your story comes back to you from a stranger—"Oh, I've heard of you; you are the one who was . . .", you know you're on the right track.

SLIDE RESOURCES

As far as slides are concerned, there are two different (although closely connected) fields you can draw upon: graphic design and information visualization. Both fields are on the rise, with new names, books, blogs, and concepts popping up all the time. Unlike storytelling, which is all about structure and deeper meanings, design is visible; it's inherently outward-oriented. You can see it.

Books

I was totally blown away Robin Williams' *The Non-Designer's Design Book.* This book really changed my life. Read it. The three principles formulated in this book largely came from several design principles Williams formulates. This book changes your everyday perception of things. Suddenly, you can tell good visual communication from bad visual communication.

As far as visualization methods are concerned, after reviewing a number of books, I am still convinced that the best book for beginners is Gene Zelazny's *Say It With Charts: The Executive's Guide to Visual Communication.* The book is quite old, so the word "executive" could be safely ignored. Now it is a guide for everyone. When I was researching material, I re-read it from cover to cover, and it is still an excellent read. Gene really got it: "Think what you want to say, say it, and then remove everything superfluous."

▶ Surprisingly, a book by the same author about presentation design isn't good. It is pretty obvious that she doesn't design a lot of presentations herself and doesn't really understand the specifics of the genre.

Edward Tufte remains the unquestioned authority on the subject of advanced visualization methods. I have all of his books:

- ▶ *Beautiful Evidence*
- ▶ *Visual Explanations: Images and Quantities, Evidence and Narrative*
- ▶ *Envisioning Information*
- ▶ *The Visual Display of Quantitative Information*

I don't know which one to recommend; they are all fantastic. Just pick the one that appeals to you most. They all have wonderful illustrations. They look good on a coffee table, and make great conversation topics for guests. That is, apart from their purely practical value, of course.

Feeds

There are a couple of RSS feeds and mailing lists you can subscribe to if you want to improve your design skills. The first obvious candidate is SlideShare's slideshow of the day. This feed features the best presentations from all over the world selected by the websites' staff. The address is www.slideshare.net/ssod, and the idea is to change your standards rather than teach you anything directly. This feed makes you want more. When you see all those beautiful slides (mostly made by professional designers), you just can no longer put up with the 12-point Times New Roman template.

The second website I wholeheartedly recommend is *Before & After Magazine* (www.bamagazine.com), which specializes in showing things before and after. The subtitle "How to design cool stuff" is both very telling and true. You need a subscription to see all of it, but some of the cool stuff they have is free on the mailing list. Check them out.

There are lots of blogs on data visualization; it's a really hip subject at the moment. This is what I am currently subscribed to:

- ▶ www.coolinfographics.com
- ▶ infographicsnews.blogspot.com
- ▶ www.informationisbeautiful.net
- ▶ dd.dynamicdiagrams.com

If you need just one blog, go ahead and subscribe to Flowing Data (www.flowingdata.com). I guarantee you will not regret it. This blog is amazing; it always finds ways to surprise me.

If you're mostly interested in conceptual data visualization, the people to follow are Dave Gray (www.davegrayinfo.com) and Dan Roam (digitalroam.typepad.com).

Practice

The best thing you can in this field is to allocate more time for slide design. This alone won't make your slides any better, but coupled with good ideas you get from reading blogs and books, it can do the trick.

Emulate slides you like—don't be ashamed to borrow—but always adapt them for your own purposes. Don't just take somebody else's slide and insert your presentation. Try to assimilate it and make it yours. As American film director Jim Jarmusch said:

> Steal from anywhere that resonates with inspiration or fuels your imagination. Devour old films, new films, music, books, paintings, photographs, poems, dreams, random conversations, architecture, bridges, street signs, trees, clouds, bodies of water, light, and shadows. Select only things to steal from that speak directly to your soul. If you do this, your work (and theft) will be authentic. Authenticity is invaluable; originality is non-existent.

Make sure you have the latest version of PowerPoint, Keynote, or any other software you might be using. Slideware programs have made great progress in terms of aesthetics in the last couple of years and having the latest version really makes a visible difference. On a broader scale, your working environment matters a lot: consider the aesthetics of your operating system, your office, and the streets you walk on every day. It is hard to create bad slides if your environment is beautiful. Nothing changed my slides more than switching to a Mac, but that was a time when the difference between Windows XP and OS X was dramatic. You probably won't achieve the same effect now. If you have the option of switching to something more beautiful from something less beautiful, go ahead and do it. It can make a difference.

Finally, if you have a blog and you don't work for a secretive organization, publish some of your slides. I frequently get really good feedback from people reading my blog.

▶ The downside is that I also get plenty of worthless advice, but that also teaches me to distinguish between the two.

DELIVERY RESOURCES

Delivery is the best-researched subject of the three. There are countless books, blogs and workshops. However, you have to really distinguish between 20th century public speaking and 21st century public speaking here. Most of the resources still focus on making you look confident when you don't quite feel confident. I am much more interested in playing with one's nervousness the way Woody Allen does it. To me, nervousness is not the problem—lying is.

The Book

I have read dozens of books on public speaking. *Confessions of a Public Speaker* by Scott Berkun is at the top of my list. It has a five-star rating on Amazon and deservedly so. It is written in an extremely accessible conversational style. It is full of industry insights and great stories. What's even more important, this book is very true to its title; it is in fact a confessional book. If you want to read a book on public speaking, this is the one.

Here's a relatively random quote from it:

> The easiest way to be interesting is to be honest. . . . If you're honest, even if people disagree, they will find you interesting and keep listening.

And this is what the book is all about. It is about daring to say the truth to the microphone and the many details you need to be aware of in the process. It was a great inspiration for me when I was writing this book. It is so good that it's the only resource I mention here.

Workshops

Among other things, Scott Berkun recommends taking a theater improv class for those willing to be more entertaining onstage, and I am 100 percent behind him in this recommendation. I did that well before I read *Confessions of a Public Speaker* and I can attest that it really, really works.

I studied in New York in a place called the UCB Theater, which is among the best comedy improv groups in the United States, but there are of course many others. Chicago and Los Angeles are famous for their improv scenes, and if you go to other places like The Second City or The Groundlings I am sure you won't be disappointed. The somewhat tricky part is to keep practicing after the class, especially if you don't have a group in your own city. I had it hard because I wasn't able to find a comedy improv group in Moscow, Russia (the largest city of Europe with a population of 15 million). I had to start one. After about a year of weekly practice I quit, but the group still exists and is lead by a professional standup comedian. So it is possible and you need a good book with exercises like *The Improv Handbook: The Ultimate Guide to Improvising in Comedy, Theatre, and Beyond* by Tom Salinsky. You can also get a lot of information from free online resources like www.learnimprov.com.

I took a couple of acting classes in my life, and I hated it. I'm really not the acting type, but you might be. I also took many classes on other performance arts like dancing, physical theatre, mime, and standup. These are immensely useful for public speaking. They teach you to look foolish on stage and be cool with it. They teach you to speak your heart even when you have no idea what to say. A course on standup from the American Comedy Institute also made my presentations much more fun to watch. A five-minute routine I did in Gotham Comedy Club in New York is one of the most thrilling and memorable experiences of my life. So again, borrow other fields. As Jean-Luc Godard said, "It's not where you take things from—it's where you take them to."

Practice

Follow these main points when you practice your delivery approach:

1. If there's a chance to be in front of the audience, jump on it.

2. If it's possible to record your performance without appearing narcissistic, do it.

3. Watch the recording. This might be far more difficult for you than the previous point, but seriously, watch it. Yes, I know you probably think it's horrible. Watch it anyway.

PRESENTATIONS TRANSFORM

So, here's my final message: presentations change. I don't necessarily mean that they change the audience. That may happen, but I am not talking about that. Presentations change you and your own ideas. This is not about becoming rich and famous through public speaking. This is about becoming a better person. You'll become more knowledgeable, more understanding, more authentic, and more passionate.

Presentations transform your thinking. When you say what you think in front of a group of people and see them react, this somehow changes your thinking. I can't explain why or how this happens, but it does happen every time. When I tell my idea to the group, it may or may not sound right. I know this within seconds. It has to do with how I feel and how people look. It's not about positive feedback; they might not approve of the idea, they might even get angry, but I'd still know the idea is excellent. All I need is to listen to myself and watch them while I'm speaking. And if I'm not busy worrying about my public image, I will notice it. Frankly, this is the main reason I love public speaking so much.

Presentations transform your understanding. There is an old joke about a professor complaining to his friend about how stupid his students are: "I explained the topic once, but they didn't get it. So I explained it a second time, and they still didn't get it. Then I got angry and explained it for the third time; now even I got it, and they still didn't have a clue." I guess that's another law: if you keep trying to explain something to somebody, sooner or later you'll understand it yourself. Somehow you'll find better explanations that make dramatically more sense.

Presentations transform you. If you desperately try to sell something and the pitch doesn't come out right, despite your best efforts, you know you need to change the product. Or better yet, invent your own.

In 2003, a *Time* magazine journalist, Joe Klein, was having dinner with several political consultants previously in charge of Al Gore's presidential campaign. Klein asked one of them, Tad Devine, why Gore didn't speak much about the environment during the campaign.

▶ Practice is important but without feedback it is worthless. I've seen people practice the same mistakes for many years. Watch yourself and apply the good advice you get from books, blogs, and seminars the next time you present.

"Because it wasn't going to help him win," was the answer. Klein asked whether the consultants considered if Gore might have been "a warmer, more credible and inspiring candidate" if he would have talked more about the things he really cared about. To which Devine replied, "That's an interesting thought." After *An Inconvenient Truth* this thought is no longer just "interesting." It's obvious.

▶ Public speaking is not the best form for communicating facts or even ideas. Public speaking is most suitable for communicating worldviews.

Presentations transform your worldview. I love the tagline of the TED conference, which is "Ideas worth spreading." But what I find that TED is most successful in spreading is the TED worldview: radical openness, infinite optimism, curiosity with the world's wonders and, above all, passion for your work.

Speakers at TED might speak about technology, entertainment, or design, but they always try to be profound. They always try to talk about the philosophy of life, and this is what makes them so successful as speakers in the end. Not only does this make the audience better people, it makes the speakers better people. The secret is that by asking others to be more optimistic about the future, you become more optimistic yourself. You can't help but practice what you preach to a somewhat bigger extent than you did before. Little by little, optimism, openness, and curiosity win. Your speech can change the world, and it also changes you. So go ahead and be profound in your next presentation. Sure, you might fail. It's not an easy task, but hey, doing anything interesting is dangerous. Re-read Chapter 3 and try again.

In 1994, Stephen Hawking, already a world-renowned physicist, voiced a commercial for British Telecom. I don't know what his motivation was, but he ended up producing one of his most memorable and widely known quotations. Here it is, slightly abridged:

> *For millions of years, mankind lived just like the animals. Then something happened which unleashed the power of our imagination. We learned to talk and we learned to listen. Speech has allowed the communication of ideas, enabling human beings to work together to build the impossible. With the technology at our disposal, the possibilities are unbounded. All we need to do is make sure we keep talking.*

And this is my final word of advice and what I want to end with. Just make sure you keep talking.

Index

A

acts, in story, 76–79
  climax, 77
  development, 77
  exposition, 76–77
  inciting incident, 76
  recapitulation, 77
  rising action, 77
Adams, Scott, 189
advertising, villains in, 67–68
aesthetics, in slides, 164–165
  featurism, 164
  purpose, 165
  usability and, 165
  Wabi-sabi, 195
agenda slides
  "Death by PowerPoint," 94
  exposition, 85
AirPlay, 17
AirPrint, 17
Aliev, Arif, 58
analytical charts, 146–148
The Anatomy of Story: 22 Steps to Becoming a Master Storyteller (Truby), 54, 76, 271
Anderson, Chris, 206
Anderson, Hans Christian, 78
anecdotes, 5
animation, in presentations, 159–161
  complex effects, avoidance of, 159–160
  fonts, 160
  KeyNoteNF, 160
  purpose, 160
  speed, 160

antagonists, 87
antithesis, 15. *See also* contrast, in presentations
Apple, slide templates, 117
arcs. *See* emotional arc
Ariely, Dan, 18
Aristotle, 4–5, 76
The Art of Dramatic Writing (Egri), 78
"The Art of Start" (Kawasaki), 34, 55, 61, 207
Atkinson, Cliff, 8
audiences
  assistance from, 255
    during delivery mistakes, 261
  conflict for, expectations of, 68
  confrontation with, in presentations, 226–232
  delivery to, 208–212
    broadcasting mode, 210
    empathy in, 211
    as focus of presentation, 210–211
    reading audiences, 211–212
    strategies, 210–211
  expectations for, 37–38
  feedback, 13
  goal-setting for, connection in, 28
  likability and, 37
  pandering to, 36
  second-act syndrome for, 51
  viewpoint of, 39
authenticity
  in delivery, 244–245
  improvisation, 248
  in slide photos, 123
  of story, 47

B

Bach, Johann Sebastian, 27
bad conflict, 19
ballroom style slides, 110
bar charts, 152–154
Beautiful Evidence (Tufte), 147
behavior. *See* on-stage behavior
believability, in delivery, 246–247
  from consistency, 246
Belykh, Nikita, 206
Benson, Herbert, 255
Benson's relaxation response, 255
Benyus, Janine, 206
Berkun, Scott, 276
Beyond Bullet Points: Using Microsoft Office PowerPoint 2001 to Create Presentations That Inform, Motivate, and Inspiration (Atkinson), 8
Bishop, Todd, 204
Blink (Gladwell), 80
body awareness, 255
Bohr, Neils, 19
Brain Rules (Medina), 89
Bristol, Scott, 33
British Design Council, 10
British Index FTSE, 11
broadcasting mode, 210
Brookes print, as comparison slide, 137
BRUNO program, 7
bubble charts, 142, 158–159
bullet points, 18, 45
  in lists, in text slides, 121
  photos as, 126

C

call for action, 98–99
Campbell, David, 271
Campbell, Joseph, 78
Cannell, Charles, 205
Carlzon, Jan, 68
Carpenter, Lea, 233
Chalybäus, Heinrich Moritz, 15
change slides, 139–141
chartchooser.com, 161
charts
  analytical, 146–148
  bar, 152–154
  colors, 150
  column, 150–152
    common mistakes, 152
    coxcomb, 151
  contrast in, 19
  KeyNoteNF, 152–153
  legends, 150
  line, 155–156
  pie, 149
  PowerPoint, 152–153
  presentational, 146–148
    affirmations, 146
    contrasts, 147
    editing, 147–148
    by Minard, 146
  sparklines, 148
  3D, 150
Ching, Bruce, 62
chunks of information, in short-term
  memory, 16–17
clarity, in delivery, 202–204
client-centric presentations, 35–37,
  66–68
  client as always right, 35–36
  empathy in, 37
  imprudence, 36–37
  "Meet Henry" method, 66
  pandering in, 36
  vision in, 36
clients. See also audiences
  as always right, 35–36
  empathy and, 37

imprudence, 36–37
  pandering to, 36
  vision for, 36
climax, 77
clip art, 127–128
Coleman, Lerita, 205
Collins, Jim, 2, 15, 32
color, in slide design, 172–177
  color wheel oppositions, 174
  guidelines, 177
  matching techniques, 174
  program sources, 174
  symbolism and meaning with, 176
  Windows Paint, 175
column charts, 150–152
  common mistakes, 152
  coxcomb, 151
communication
  presentations as, 2
  through story, 6
comparison slides, 54–55, 136–144
  Brookes print, 137
  bubble charts, 142
  change, 139–141
  matrix, 141–143
  scale, 138–139
  startup positioning, 142
  Venn diagrams, 141–143
concept mapping editors,
  44–45
conclusions, in story, 98–99
  call for action, 98–99
  case studies, 100–101
  moral, 99
  wrap-ups, 98
conference room style slides, 110
Confessions of a Public Speaker
  (Berkun), 276
confidence, in goal-setting,
  28–29
confidence monitors, 214, 216
conflict
  absence of, 52
  audience expectations, 68
  avoiding the obvious, 62
  bad, 19

comparison slides, 54–55
  definition, 52
  in diagrams, 134
  emotional resonance, 62
  establishment of, 54–55
    problem-solving, 54
  familiarity, 62
  genres, 53
  good, 19
  heroes in, 63–66
    creation, 65
    flaws in, 67
  in iconic presentations, 55
  in personal stories, 69–72
    opposition in, 70
    personal strengths, 71–72
    weaknesses in, 71–72
  problems as, 56–59
    with external forces, 58
    interpersonal, 56–57
    moral, 56
  solutions, 61–62
  in story, 18–19
  tension, 59–61
    in questions, 60
    second-act syndrome, 51
  unintentional associations, 62
  unpredictability, 18–19
  villains, 63–66
    creation, 65
confrontation, in presentations,
  226–232
  discussions, 227–228
  of experts, in audience, 227
  feedback, 231–232
  hostility, 230–231
  humor, 228–229
  offensiveness as strategy,
    229–230
  strong language, 230
conscious bandwidth, human
  senses, 10
consistency, in presentations, 21
  believability from, 246
  slide templates, 117
contact improvisation, 258

contrast, in presentations, 15, 18–19.
    See also conflict
charts, 19, 147
delivery
    confrontation, 226–232
    learning from others, 232–240
    perfection *versus* passion, 223–226
diagrams, 19
Kirov Oblast case study, 169
slides, 19
    design, 167
    templates, 117
control, in delivery, 251–252, 255–256
audience assistance, 255
Benson's relaxation response, 255
body awareness, 255
Copeland, H. Liesel, 218
corporate story, 68–69
Cowan, Nelson, 17
coxcomb chart, 151
creativity, 37
crisis, 79. *See also* conflict

D

data visualization, 144–155
animation, 159–161
    complex effects, avoidance of,
        159–160
    fonts, 160
    KeyNoteNF, 160
    purpose, 160
    speed, 160
charts, 146–154
    analytical, 146–148
    bar, 152–154
    colors, 150
    column, 150–152
    contrast in, 19
    KeyNoteNF, 152–153
    legends, 150
    line, 155–156
    pie, 149
    PowerPoint, 152–153
    presentational, 146–148
    sparklines, 148
    3D, 150

resources, 161
statistics, 155–159
tables, 155
Davis, Philip, 245
de Place, Eric, 225
"Death by PowerPoint," 269
agenda slides, 94
progress tracking, 95
Deceptive Communication (Stiff), 246
decorative fonts, 184–186
delivery, 13–14, 22, 268
audience engagement, 208–212
    assistance as, 255
    broadcasting mode, 210
    empathy in, 211
    as focus of presentation, 210–211
    during mistakes, 261
    reading and audience, 211–212
    strategies, 210–211
believability, 246–247
    from consistency, 246
clarity, 202–204
common questions, 215–218
contrast
    confrontation, 226–232
    learning from others, 232–240
    perfection *versus* passion, 223–226
control, 251–252, 255–256
    audience assistance, 255
    Benson's relaxation response, 255
    body awareness, 255
eye contact, 212–215
    confidence monitors, 214
    field of view, 214
    obstructions, 215
    presentation space layout, 215
fear, 13–14
humor, 218–220
    by Gore, 219
as idiosyncratic, 225
improvisation, 245–251
    audience assistance, 261
    authenticity, 248
    contact, 258
    context, 248–251
    functional shifts, 245

mistakes and, 258–262
    truth-telling, 245, 262–263
listening to, 257
mistakes in, integration of, 258–262
monotony in, 222–223
pace, 205–207
    speed, 205–206
    time limits, 206
physical posture, 256
public speaking elements, 13–14
rehearsal, 253–254
    video recording of, 254
resources, 275–277
    books, 276
    practice, 277
    workshops, 276
scientific presentations, 200–201
    success factors, 201
speech patterns, 251–253
stage fright, 13
voice, 207–208
Demosthenes, 69
design, 10–12. *See also* color, in
        slide design
bar charts, 154
division of labor argument, 11–12
images, 188–191
    formatting, 189–190
    pixilation, 189
    proportions, 191
    sizing, 189
    with text, 191–195
slides, 10–11
    colors, 172–177
    contrast, 167
    editing, 167–168
    focal point, 167
    fonts, 177–186
    hierarchy, 172
    illustrations, 126–131
    Kirov Oblast case study, 166–171
    minimalism, 166
    photos, 122–126
    production, 106–107
    proportions, 171–172
    sweet spot, 167

templates, 113–117
text, 118–122
whitespace, 171
typography, 186–188
    capital letters, 186–187
    contrasting fonts, 188
    fonts, 177–178
    justified type, 187
    letter spacing, 187
Design Index Report, 10–11
Devine, Ted, 277–278
diagrams
    contrast in, 19
    process, 135
    in slides, 134–136
        conflict, 134
        legends, 135
        organigraphs, 135
        organizational chart, 134, 136
    SmartArt, 143
    Venn, 141–143
Diallo, Amadou, 34
Diemand-Yauman, Connor, 178
digit-recall diagram, 17
discussions, in presentations, 227–228
division of labor argument, 11–12
Doherty-Sneddon, Gwyneth, 213
dramatic code, 76
Duarte, Nancy, 71, 270, 271
Dunne, Peter, 26, 47

E

editing
    presentational charts, 147–148
    slide design, 167–168
        Kirov Oblast case
            study, 166–171
Egri, Lajos, 78
Elkman, Paul, 211
Elop, Stephen, 246
emotional arc, 79–80
emotional hook, 87
Emotional Structure (Dunne), 26
empathy
    for clients, 37
    in presentation delivery, 211
ethos, in persuasion, 4

exposition, 82–85
    agenda slides, 85
    case studies, 99
    hero introduction, 84
    introduction, 83–84
    of situation, 85
    in story acts, 76–77
    welcome slides, 84
eye contact, in delivery, 212–215
    confidence monitors, 214, 216
    field of view, 214
    obstructions, 215
    presentation space layout, 215

F

fabula, 76
Faust (von Goethe), 173
fear, 13–14
    stage fright as opposed to, 13
featurism, 164
feedback
    from audiences, 13
    confrontation and, 231–232
Fichte, Johann Gottlieb, 15
Field, Syd, 76
field of view, eye contact and, 214
focus, in presentations, 15–18
    organization, 16
    purpose, 16
    shifts, 27
    short-term memory limits, 16–17
        chunks of information, theories
            for, 16–17
        digit-recall diagram, 17
    in story, 26–27
foils, 108
fonts, 30. *See also specific fonts*
    in animation, 160
    decorative, 184–186
    handwriting, 185
    monospaced, 181
    Sans serif, 183–184
    script, 184–186
    serif, 182–183
slides
    design, 177–186
    emotional responses, 178

italicization, 179
templates, 115–116
types, 179
typography, 177–178, 188
Ford, Henry, 35
Forethought, Inc., 7
Frankl, Viktor, 33
FreeMind, 44
Freytag, Gustav, 78
functional shifts, 245

G

Gallese, Vittorio, 234
Garber, Angela, 7
Gates, Bill, 87, 204
Giffords, Gabrielle, 125
Gilbert, Daniel, 89–90, 233
Gilbert, Elizabeth, 89–90
Gladwell, Malcolm, 21, 34,
    208, 233
    at TED conference, 80–82
    speech timeline, 82
goal-setting, in
    presentations, 27–35
    audience connection, 28
    confidence in, 28–29
    hierarchy, 38
    impact in, 29–31
    information in, 28
    measurability in, 28
    motivation, 27
    multiple goals and, 29
    questions in, 29
    recall in, 29–31
        definition, 30
        educational context, 30
        memory and, 30
    values and, 31–33
        in corporate structure, 32
        definition of, 33
        as emotional state, 33
        in goal-setting, 31–33
        logic and, 33
        promotion of, 32
    vision, 33–36
        clients' needs, 36
        persistence, 34

Godard, Jean-Luc, 76
Godin, Seth, 21, 108
Goldwyn, Samuel, 35
good conflict, 19
Good to Great (Collins), 2, 15, 32
Gore, Al, 12, 21, 58, 72
  use of humor, 219
Grishkovets, Evgeny, 233, 239
Guelman, Marat, 71–72

H

Han Xiang, 247
Handel, George, 36
handwriting fonts, 185
Hardt, Dick, 34, 55, 111, 184
  personalized presentation, 70
Has, Wojciech Jerzy, 48
Hawking, Stephen, 278
Heath, Chip, 26, 94
Heath, Dan, 26, 94
Hegel, Georg, 15
Henry, Patrick, 63
heroes
  in conflict, 63–66
    creation, 65
    flaws in, 67
  in exposition, 84
  monomyth, 78
The Hobbit (Tolkien), 64
hostility, in presentations, 230–231
How to Lie with Statistics, 158
human senses
  conscious bandwidth, 10
  neurophysiological research, 9
  unconscious bandwidth, 10
humor, in delivery, 218–220
  as confrontation, 228–229
  by Gore, 219

I

Iacoboni, Marco, 234
icons, 128–129
IHMC CmapTools, 44
illustrations, in slides, 126–131
  clip art, 127–128
  emotionality, 127

icons, 128–129
infographics, 127, 130
levels of abstraction, 127
pictograms, 128–129
  sources, 131
process maps, 129–130
images, in design, 188–191. *See also*
  illustrations, in slides; photos,
  in slides
  formatting, 189–190
    vector graphics, 190
  pixilation, 189
  proportions, 191
  sizing, 189
  with text, 191–195
    consistency in, 193
    gradients, 194–195
impact, in goal-setting, 29–31
improvisation, 245–251
  authenticity, 248
  contact, 258
  context, 248–251
  functional shifts, 245
  mistakes and, 258–262
    audience assistance for, 261
  truth-telling, 245, 262–263
imprudence, 36–37
inciting incident, 76
An Inconvenient Truth, 12, 58, 86
infographics, 127, 130
interpersonal problems, 56–57
Izzard, Eddie, 249, 259

J

Jobs, Steve, 29, 33–34, 55–57, 69, 204
  on conflict with competition, 56–58
  font use, 184
  LATCH organization, 91, 95
  presentations for
    matrix slides, 141–143
    personalized, 70
    scale slides, 139
    slide choice, 109
    timelines, 89–90
  second-act syndrome, 60–61
Jo-ha-kyū story structure, 78

*Journal of Personality and Social
  Psychology*, 205
Jurassic Park, 18

K

Kant, Immanuel, 15
Kawasaki, Gary, 34, 55, 61, 90, 207, 224
  personalized presentation, 70
KeyNoteNF, 42
  animation effects, 160
  charts, 152–153
  Master Slides, 113
King, Martin Luther, Jr., 34, 55
  personalized presentation, 70
Kirov Oblast case study, in slides,
  166–171
  contrast, 169
  editing, 170–171
  focus, 169
Kitano, Takeshi, 78
Klein, Joe, 277–278
Kouzes, Jim, 247
Kukushkin, Mark, 205

L

Lapin, Andrei, 233, 249
LATCH organizational scheme, 90–97
  alphabet, 94
  category, 95
  hierarchies, 96–97
  for Jobs, 95
  location, 91–93
  metaphors, 91–93
  process diagrams, 96
  time, 95
The Leadership Challenge (Kouzes/
  Posner), 247
learning from others, 232–240
  choice of subject, 235
  passion, 234–235
  transcripts, 238–239
  through video, 236–237
    camera operation, 239–240
legends, in diagram slides, 135
Lessig, Lawrence, 34, 55, 111, 184
Libet, Benjamin, 33

line charts, 155–156
lists, in text slides, 119–122
   bullets, 121
   design rules, 120
   order, 122
   spacing, 121
live presentations, 110
LJMap.com, 33
logic
   story and, 6
   in story problems, 87
   values and, 33
logos, in persuasion, 4–5
The Lord of the Rings (Tolkien), 20
Lustig, Robert, 230

M

Made to Stick (Heath), 26, 94
"The Magical Number Seven, Plus
   or Minus Two: Some Limits on
   our Capacity for Processing
   Information" (Miller), 16
Mandela, Nelson, 5
Mann, Merlin, 208
ManyEyes web site, 161
Martin, Roger, 166
Master Slides, 113
matrix slides, 141–143
Maugham, Somerset, 15
McKee, Robert, 52, 271
Medina, John, 89
"Meet Henry" method, 66
memory
   recall and, 30
   short-term limits, 16–17
Merz, Hans-Rudolf, 219
Microsoft. *See* PowerPoint
Miller, George A., 16–17
   digit-recall diagram, 17
Miller, Norman, 205
Minard, Charles, 95, 139
   presentational charts, 146
   process diagrams, 97
mind mapping applications, 43–44, 46
   concept mapping editors and, 44
   learning curve, 43

MindManager, 44
MindMeister, 44
Minto, Barbara, 5
*The Minto Pyramid Principle: Logic in
   Writing, Thinking, & Problem Solving*
   (Minto), 5
Mintzberg, Henry, 135
mistakes, in delivery, 258–262
   audience assistance for, 261
monomyth, 78
monospaced fonts, 181
monotony, 222–223
morals
   problems with, 56
   in story, 99
motivation, 27
myths
   monomyth, 78
   story and, 26

N

New Oxford American Dictionary, 4
Nightingale, Florence, 150–151
   coxcomb chart, 151
The Non-Designer's Design Book
   (Williams), 166, 273
Norretranders, Tor, 9
Noteliner, 42
Novak, Joseph, 44

O

Obama, Barack
   bubble chart, 142, 158–159
   presentation
      change slides, 139–140
      illustrations in, 129
      infographics, 130
      line charts, 157
      photos in, 125
      text slides, 118–120, 158
Oberauer, Klaus, 17
Oksenberg, Lois, 205
OmniOutliner, 43
OneNote, 43
on-stage behavior, 21
Oppenheimer, Daniel, 178

optical illusions, 158
organigraphs, 135
organization
   in diagrams, 134, 136
   focus and, 16
outliners, 42–43

P

pace, in delivery, 205–207
   speed, 205–206
   time limits, 206
The Paradox of Choice (Schwartz), 111
passion, in delivery, 223–226
   learning from others, 234–235
pathos, in persuasion, 4
percentages, visualization of, in slides,
   148–150
   pie charts, 149
perfectionism, delivery and, 223–226
performance, in presentations, 3
Period Table of Visualization Methods
   web site, 161
persistence, of vision, 34
The Personal Brain, 44
personal stories, in presentations, 69–72
   opposition in, 70
   personal strengths, 71–72
   weaknesses in, 71–72
persuasion, modes of, 4–5
Persuasive Communication (Stiff), 246
Peters, Tom, 118
photos, in slides, 122–126
   authenticity, 123
   as bullet point, 126
   as evidence, 122
   as explanation, 122
   as illustration, 122
   stock, 123–124
      clichés in, 124
      sources, 123, 126
pictograms, 128–129
   sources, 131
pictorial superiority, 8
pie charts, 149
Pink, Dan, 89–90, 99
plateaus, 79

Poetics (Aristotle), 76
poets, 5
Posner, Barry, 247
PowerPoint, 7
  charts, 152–153
  Master Slides, 113
  slide templates, 115
  Vajrayana approach, to slides, 108
Predictably Irrational: The Hidden
    Forces That Shape Our Decisions
    (Ariely), 18
presentations. *See also* animation, in
    presentations; data visualization;
    delivery; design; slides
  aspects, 3
  authenticity, 244–245
  bullet points, 18
  case studies, 99–101
  checklist, 266
  client-centric, 66–68
    as always right, 35–36
    empathy and, 37
    imprudence, 36–37
    pandering to, 36
    vision for, 36
  as communication, 2
  complexity, 2
  confrontation in, 226–232
    discussions, 227–228
    of experts, in audience, 227
    feedback, 231–232
    hostility, 230–231
    humor, 228–229
    offensiveness as strategy, 229–230
    strong language, 230
  consistency in, 21
  contrast, 15, 18–19
    charts, 19
    diagrams, 19
    slides, 19
  definitions, 2–4
  delivery, 22
  discussions, 227–228
  focus, 15–18
    organization, 16
    purpose, 16
    shifts, 27

short-term memory limits, 16–17
  in story, 26–27
fonts, 30
goal-setting, 27–35
  audience connection, 28
  confidence in, 28–29
  impact in, 29–31
  information in, 28
  measurability in, 28
  motivation, 27
  multiple goals and, 29
  questions in, 29
  recall in, 29–31
  values and, 31–33
  vision, 33–36
hostility in, 230–231
live, 110
on-stage behavior, 21
performance, 3
personal stories in, 69–72
  opposition in, 70
  personal strengths, 71–72
  weaknesses in, 71–72
practice for, 272–273
without presenters, 110
principles, 14–22
  contrast, 15, 18–19
  focus, 15–18
  unity, 15, 19–22
resources, 269–270
  practice, 272–273
scientific, 200–201
  success factors, 201
slides, 3, 7–13, 22
  BRUNO program, 7
  design aspects, 10–11, 106–107
  Hewlett-Packard development, 7
  PowerPoint, 7
  projectors, 7–8
  purpose, 9
  as selling point, 12
  teleprompters, 8
story, 4–7
  anecdotes, 5
  causal evidence and, 6
  communication through, 6

emotional component, 5
facts in, 6–7
focus in, 26–27
ideas, 26–27
logic and, 6
myth and, 26
rhetoric, 4–5
storytelling as opposed
  to, 5
urban legends, 26
as transformative, 277–278
unity, 15, 19–22
  consistency, 21
  constraints, 22
  definition, 76
  information compression, 20
  lists, 20
  S-curve, 19
  viewpoints, 39
Presentation Zen: Simple Ideas on
    Presentation Design and Delivery
    (Reynolds), 8
presentational charts,
    146–148
  affirmations, 146
  contrasts, 147
  editing, 147–148
  by Minard, 146
presenters
  presentations without, 110
  second-act syndrome, 51
  viewpoint of, 39
process diagrams, 96, 135
  for Minard, 97
projectors, 7–8
public speaking
  elements, 13–14
  as entertainment, 5
  passion in, 223–226
  voice, 207–208

Q

questions
  delivery and, 215–218
  in goal-setting, 29
  tension in, 60

R

Raikher, Yuri, 223
Really Bad PowerPoint (Godin), 108
recall
definition, 30
educational context, 30
in goal-setting, 29–31
impact and, 31
memory and, 30
recapitulation, 77
rehearsal, for delivery, 253–254
video recording of, 254
Resonate: Present Visual Stories that Transform Audiences (Duarte), 71, 271
Reynolds, Garr, 8, 108, 110, 269
rhetoric, 4–5
Rhetoric (Aristotle), 4
rising action, 77
Rizzolatti, Giacomo, 234
Robbins, Tony, 206
Robinson, Ken, 21, 37, 239
Roche, Frank, 33
Rothafel, Samuel, 35

S

Sagarin, Brad, 229
St. John, Richard, 89–90
Sans serif fonts, 183–184
The Saragossa Manuscript, 48
Savander, Niklas, 56
Say It with Charts: The Executive's Guide to Visual Communication (Zelazny), 108, 146, 273
Say It with Presentations (Zelazny), 108
scale slides, 138–139
Schell, Jesse, 47
Scherer, Cory, 229
Schiller, Phil, 62
Schwartz, Barry, 21, 111
Schwarz, Norbert, 178
Schwertly, Scott, 66, 110
scientific presentations, 200–201
The Screen Writer's Workbook (Field), 76
Screenplay (Field), 76
script fonts, 184–186

S-curve
emotional arc, 79
for presentation unity, 19
second-act syndrome, 59–61
serif fonts, 182–183
short-term memory, 16–17
chunks of information, limits of, 16–17
theory of four, 17
theory of seven, 16
digit-recall diagram, 17
Sinek, Simon, 31
slides, 3, 7–13, 22, 267–268. *See also* design; illustrations, in slides; photos, in slides; text slides
aesthetics, 164–165
featurism, 164
purpose, 165
agenda
"Death by PowerPoint," 94
exposition, 85
ballroom style, 110
choices, 110–113
client thinking, 113
form, 111
process, 111
for scientific community, 113
substance, 111–112
comparison, 54–55, 136–144
Brookes print, 137
bubble charts, 142
change, 139–141
matrix, 141–143
scale, 138–139
startup positioning, 142
Venn diagrams, 141–143
conference room style, 110
design aspects, 10–11
color, 172–177
contrast, 167
editing, 167–168
focal point, 167
fonts, 177–186
hierarchy, 172
illustrations, 126–131
Kirov Oblast case study, 166–171
minimalism, 166

photos, 122–126
production, 106–107
proportion, 171–172
sweet spot, 167
templates, 113–117
text, 118–122
whitespace, 171
diagrams, 134–136
conflict, 134
legends, 135
organigraphs, 135
organizational chart, 134, 136
SmartArt, 143
functions, 106
Hewlett-Packard development, 7
BRUNO program, 7
images with text, 191–195
consistency in, 193
gradients, 194–195
percentages, 148–150
PowerPoint, 7
presentational, 146–148
production, 106–107
design, 106–107
finalization, 106
projectors, 7–8
pictorial superiority, 8
purpose, 9
resources, 273–275
books, 273–274
practice, 275
web site feeds, 274
scale, 138–139
as selling point, 12
strategy, 41
tables, 143–144
teleprompters, 8
templates, 113–117
Apple, 117
clarity, 116–117
consistency, 117
contrast, 117
corporate style guidelines, 114
fonts, 115–116
PowerPoint, 115

transitions, 160
Vajrayana approach, 107–111
  foils, 108
  PowerPoint, 108
  problems, 112
  welcome, 84
Zen approach, 110–111
  live presentations, 110
slide presentation programs, 7
slide templates. *See* templates, for slides
slide transitions, 160
Small Business Computing, 7
SmartArt diagrams, 143
solutions, in story, 88–97
  case studies, 100
  LATCH organizational scheme, 90–97
    alphabet, 94
    category, 95
    hierarchies, 96–97
    for Jobs, 95
    location, 91–93
    metaphors, 91–93
    process diagrams, 96
    time, 95
  timing, 89–90
Song, Hyunjin, 178
spacing, in text slides, 121
Speak to Win: How to Present with Power in Any Situation (Tracy), 14
speech patterns, in delivery, 251–253
stage fright, 13
Start with Why (Sinek), 31
statistics, 155–159
sticky notes, 40–41
Stiff, James, 246
stock photos, for slides, 123–124
  clichés in, 124
  sources, 123, 126
story, 4–7, 266–267. *See also* conflict; unity, in presentations
  acts, 76–79
    climax, 77
    development, 77
    exposition, 76–77
    inciting incident, 76
    recapitulation, 77
    rising action, 77

anecdotes, 5
authenticity, 47
causal evidence and, 6
communication through, 6
conclusions, 98–99
  call for action, 98–99
  case studies, 100–101
  moral, 99
  wrap-ups, 98
conflict in, 18–19
corporate, 68–69
emotional arc, 79–80
  crisis, 79
  plateaus, 79
  S-curve, 79
emotional component, 5
exposition, 82–85
  agenda slides, 85
  hero introduction, 84
  introduction, 83–84
  of situation, 85
  in story acts, 76–77
  welcome slides, 84
facts in, 6–7
  cherry-picking, 47
focus in, 26–27
heroes in, 63–66
  creation, 65
  flaws in, 67
  monomyth, 78
ideas, 26–27
linearity, 39
logic and, 6
material collection, 39–46
  brain dumps, 44–45
  brainstorming, 45
  hierarchies, 46
  visual thinking tools, 42–46
myth and, 26
personal, 69–70
problems, 86–87
  antagonists, 87
  case studies, 99
  emotional hook, 87
  logic, 87
rhetoric, 4–5

selling of, 47–48
sequences, 41
solutions, 88–97
  case studies, 100
  LATCH organizational scheme, 90–97
  timing, 89–90
storytelling as opposed to, 5
strategy slides, 41
structure, 76–79
  classical, 77
  types, 78
unity in
  definition, 76
  dramatic code, 76
urban legends, 26
villains, 63–66
  creation, 65
visual thinking tools, 42–46
  concept mapping editors, 44
  mind mapping applications, 43–44
  outliners, 42–43
Story: Substance, Structure, Style and The Principles of Screenwriting (McKee), 52, 271
story arcs. *See* emotional arc
story sequences, 41
storytelling, 22
  resources, 270–273
    books, 271
    workshops, 271–272
  story as opposed to, 5
strategy slides, 41
synthesis, 15. *See also* unity, in presentations
syzuzhet, 76

T

tables, 143–144
  data visualization, 155
Taylor, Jill Bolte, 21
TED conference, 21, 72
  Gladwell at, 80–82
    speech timeline, 82
  speech timelines, 89–90
  time limits, of presentations, 206
TEDx conference, 71–72
teleprompters, 8

templates, for slides, 113–117
  Apple, 117
  clarity, 116–117
  consistency, 117
  contrast, 117
  corporate style guidelines, 114
  fonts, 115–116
  PowerPoint, 115
tension, 59–61
  in questions, 60
  second-act syndrome, 59–61
text slides, 118–122. *See also* typography
  lists, 119–122
    bullets, 121
    design rules, 120
    order, 122
    spacing, 121
  for Obama, 158
  problems, 118
Theory of Colours (von Goethe), 173
thesis, 15. *See also* focus, in presentations
Thinklinkr.com, 43
3D charts, 150
Tolkien, J.R.R., 20, 64
Tracy, Brian, 14
transcripts, 238–239
Truby, John, 54, 76, 271
truth-telling. *See* authenticity
Tufte, Edward, 108, 139, 147–148
Twain, Mark, 253
typography, 186–188
  capital letters, 186–187
  contrasting fonts, 188
  fonts, 177–178
  justified type, 187
  letter spacing, 187

U

unconscious bandwidth, human senses, 10
unity
  in presentations, 15, 19–22
    consistency, 21
    constraints, 22
    definition, 76
    information compression, 20
    lists, 20
    S-curve, 19
  in story
    definition, 76
    dramatic code, 76
urban legends, 26
The User Illusion: Cutting Consciousness Down to Size (Norretranders), 9

V

Vajrayana approach, to slides, 107–111
  foils, 108
  PowerPoint, 108
  problems, 112
values
  in corporate structure, 32
  definition of, 33
  as emotional state, 33
  in goal-setting, 31–33
  logic and, 33
  promotion of, 32
Van der Heyden, Ludo, 135
Vanjoki, Anssi, 56, 246
Vaughn, Erikka, 178
Venn diagrams, 141–143
video recording, 236–237
  camera operation, 239–240
  of rehearsal, 254

villains, 63–66
  in advertising, 67–68
  creation, 65
vision, 33–36
  clients' needs, 36
  goal-setting, 33–35
  persistence, 34
The Visual Display of Quantitative Information (Tufte), 147
visual thinking tools, 42–46
  concept mapping editors, 44–45
  mind mapping applications, 43–44, 46
  outliners, 42–43
    multiple level creations, 42
Vogler, Chris, 271
von Goethe, Johann Wolfgang, 173

W

Wabi-sabi, as aesthetic concept, 195
Warde, Beatrice, 12
Watzlawick, Paul, 116
welcome slides, 84
whitespace, in slide design, 171
Williams, Robin, 166, 273
Windows Paint, 175
Wurman, Richard Saul, 90

X - Y

yEd, 44
Yeltsin, Boris, 209

Z

Zelazny, Gene, 108, 146, 273
Zen approach, to slides, 110–111